RESURRECTING EMPIRE

Western Footprints and America's Perilous Path
in the Middle East

RASHID KHALIDI

Beacon Press
Boston

D0037431

BEACON PRESS
25 Beacon Street
Boston, Massachusetts 02108-2892
www.beacon.org

Beacon Press books
are published under the auspices of
the Unitarian Universalist Association of Congregations.

09 08 07 06   8 7 6

This book is printed on acid-free paper that meets the
uncoated paper ANSI/NISO specifications for permanence as revised in 1992.

Text design by Sara Eisenman and Isaac Tobin
Composition by Wilsted & Taylor Publishing Services

LIBRARY OF CONGRESS CATALOGING-IN-PUBLICATION DATA

Khalidi, Rashid.
Resurrecting Empire : Western footprints and
America's perilous path in the Middle East / Rashid Khalidi.
p. cm.
Includes index.
ISBN 0-8070-0234-8 (cloth)
ISBN 0-8070-0235-6 (pbk.)
1. Middle East – Relations – United States. 2. United
States – Relations – Middle East. 3. Democracy – Middle East.
4. Arab-Israeli conflict. I. Title: America and the western
adventure in the Middle East. II. Title.
DS63.2.U5K49 2004
303.48'273056 – dc22

CONTENTS

THE PERILS OF
IGNORING HISTORY

I wrote this book before, during, and immediately after the March 2003 invasion of Iraq, out of a desire to warn against what I believed was a looming disaster. It was first published in April 2004. I write today against the background of twenty months of a chaotic, mismanaged American occupation of Iraq. Before and after the book appeared, I spoke publicly about mistakes I perceived the United States was making in the Middle East.[1] Everywhere I spoke, I found deep misgivings about the war, and a strong undercurrent of unease about the Bush administration's approach to the Middle East. This book is an attempt to explain why there are solid, historical grounds for such misgivings and such unease.

As the United States has marched into the Middle East as an occupying power responsible for creating a new political order in a major Arab country, seemingly stepping into the boots of former colonial rulers, it is difficult for someone familiar with the history of this region to avoid a sense of déjà vu. Nothing so ambitious, or so fraught with peril, has been tried there since just after World War I, when Britain and France engaged in their last burst of colonial expansion under the guise of League of Nations mandates. Their effort was strongly resisted by Middle Easterners, but it also resulted in the creation of many of the states, and produced many of the problems, in that region today. This historical context was largely ignored in the lead-up to war. Even less attention was paid to how Middle Easterners perceived American actions in terms of that recent history.

Moreover, as an American who grew up during the Vietnam War era, it is hard to avoid a fear that the ghosts most of us thought had been permanently laid to rest then—the ghosts of American military overreach and imperial arrogance—are back to haunt us. And for an American academic of Arab ancestry with family in many parts of the Middle East, who travels to the region regularly, and with students and colleagues teaching and studying all over it, it is hard to remain silent when it is crystal clear that what is happening there bears no resemblance whatsoever to the optimistic picture painted by the Bush administration.

This is particularly painful for me as a historian, because most of the extensive public debate about the relationship between the United States and the Middle East since September 11, 2001, has been taking place in a historical vacuum. The debate has been largely driven by denigrating stereotypes about Arabs, Islam, and the Middle East. It has rarely been grounded in a careful reading of how the history of the region's stormy recent encounters with the West may affect a new phase of American involvement in the vast area between Morocco and central Asia, and between the Mediterranean and the Indian Ocean.

A word on differing attitudes to history is in order here. One of the aims of this book is to give readers some of the basic history of the modern Middle East. This includes in particular the history of Western occupation and indigenous resistance, of attempts to establish constitutional systems in Middle Eastern states, of Western control of Middle Eastern oil, and of Western, and especially American, involvement in the Palestine question. Such knowledge is sorely lacking in the United States. But many Americans consider history, any history, as irrelevant to the present and the future. Perhaps this peculiarly American lack of interest in history—especially the history of others—is rooted in the fact that the United States is a vast continental island that never in its own history suffered foreign occupation, and that for the last two centuries had little reason to fear attack on its homeland by others—at least not until 9/11. In this providential isolation, the United States has been nearly unique among the countries of the world. For most other peoples, ignoring others' history is an impossible luxury.

Not surprisingly, most Americans do not realize that many influential Middle Eastern intellectuals had a liberal orientation for more than a century. They are unaware of the early constitutional experiments that took place in the Middle East, and of efforts to establish parliamentary systems there in the twentieth century. They are unlikely to know how Western powers undermined these systems by their repeated interventions, and how much resentment this caused among Middle Easterners. There has nevertheless been much airy pontification about the absence of democratic traditions in the Islamic world, how "Islam" is antithetical to democracy, and why "they" resent "us" because of our way of life. This contemptuous dismissal of real history, real experience, and real traditions in favor of crude stereotypes has received little response from the only people qualified to counter it: experts on the Middle East.

Silence on the part of the experts is part of a larger problem, of why public discourse in the United States about foreign affairs is so often driven by the lowest common denominator, by ill-informed pundits rather than by people who are actually knowledgeable about the rest of the world. Perhaps it is because many prefer to hear what is familiar and reassuring, rather than what is strange and discomforting. Another of the objectives of this book is to reflect the history lying behind Middle Eastern perceptions of the American role there, perceptions that may not match what Americans think of their country's role in the world. Some would cavalierly dismiss others' views of the

United States, or would address them solely via "strategic information" campaigns. This is to underestimate dangerously what is at work here: these perceptions and the history behind them are extremely important, for how others perceive us, and how they perceive their own history, rather than how we perceive ourselves, will determine how others act. We should be able to consider whether these perceptions may in fact be accurate, even if they are unflattering, without being told that we are anti-American or "blame-America-firsters." This is an essential element of the respect for the views of others that we would expect to receive for our own views, but which is often missing when the views of Middle Easterners are concerned.

But the inaccuracies and distortions in discussions of the Middle East cannot be blamed solely on the media, the Beltway think tanks, and policy makers. As stated above, blame for this situation also lies with Middle East experts, many of whom have not tried hard enough to speak to broader audiences, who disdain the process of clarification that is necessary for communicating with the general public about complex subjects, and who are rarely institutionally rewarded for doing so. Like other academics, I struggle with a tendency to overelaborate when writing for a nonspecialist audience such as the one at which this book is directed. I hope I have overcome that tendency. Given how little Americans know of the rest of the world, and the importance of historical knowledge with respect to the Middle East, it is the duty of experts to do everything possible to inform the general public in a way that has not been done in the past. This book is an effort to do just that.

That the American public knows too little about a region their country is getting more and more deeply involved in is also partly a function of the pervasive atmosphere of intimidation that makes many Middle East experts reluctant to express themselves frankly. This is true generally about Middle East issues, and particularly true about the sensitive issues touching on Israel and Palestine. It is in some measure a function of the fact that many Americans have intense feelings about this subject combined with limited knowledge, a combination not conducive to the shedding of light on a complex issue. It is also a function of the gross oversimplification that is operative in both the political and media arenas, oversimplification that reaches near toxic levels where the Middle East is concerned. Such an atmosphere is extremely harmful to American public discourse, especially to the necessary process of infusing the debate on U.S. actions in the Middle East with the context and background without which it is impossible to understand what is happening there or why.

If this book can transcend these barriers and help to initiate an informed debate about what the United States faces as it intervenes ever more deeply in the Middle East, it will serve a useful purpose. For the Middle East is a region where history matters a great deal, and whose peoples have a very long history, with which they are quite familiar. The United States is deeply entangled in the affairs of this region today, and as Americans concerned for our country, we should pay careful attention to that history. We ignore it at our common peril.

What has happened since this book was first published? In spite of a mock "transfer of sovereignty" at the end of June 2004, most elements of real sovereignty in Iraq are in American hands, a stubborn antioccupation insurgency is still untamed, while bloody terrorism continues unabated. Far from being a beacon to the rest of the region, Iraq looks to its neighbors like nothing so much as an endless, slow-motion train wreck. Twenty months after the invasion, nothing in Iraq looks as those who advocated the war had predicted. And yet the grim litany of disaster that we have witnessed since March 2003 should have been expected, indeed some of it was virtually inevitable, given the ambitious aims of those who decided on waging the Iraq War, and given their hubris and their ignorance of Middle Eastern realities. Leaving aside the stated pretexts for the war, which now stand revealed as spurious, from nonexistent "weapons of mass destruction," to nonexistent links between the Iraqi Ba'thist regime and al-Qa'ida, it is clear that the Bush administration had several, largely unacknowledged, war aims.

This was a war fought firstly to demonstrate that it was possible to free the United States from subordination to international law or the U.N. Charter, from the need to obtain the approval of the United Nations for American actions, and from the constraints of operating within alliances. In other words, it was a war fought because its planners wanted to free the greatest power in world history from these Lilliputian bonds, and saw the tragedy of 9/11 as a golden opportunity to achieve this long-cherished goal. For them, this was a war of choice, and Iraq was a suitable guinea pig for a new hyperunilateral American approach that would "shock and awe" the rest of the world.

The Iraq War was fought secondly with the aim of establishing long-term American military bases in a key country in the heart of the Middle East: Pentagon officials still talk of retaining "fourteen enduring bases" in Iraq. American planners saw these as replacements for the increasingly contested bases established in Saudi Arabia in the wake of the 1991 Gulf War. It was a war fought thirdly to destroy one of the last of the third world dictatorships that had at times defied the United States and its allies (notably Israel). The administration clearly envisioned, and still seems to envisage, creating in its place a pliable client regime. It was a war fought finally to reshape, along the radical free-market lines so dear to Bush administration ideologues, the economy of a country with the world's second-largest proven reserves of oil. This made Iraq a particularly attractive target for leading members of the administration, from President George W. Bush and Vice President Dick Cheney to then–National Security Advisor Condoleezza Rice, who had all been intimately involved with the oil business. All these things—the demonstration effect of a unilateral, "preemptive" war, military bases, a client regime, and access to oil—were seen as vital to fending off potential twenty-first-century great-power rivals.

Mesmerized by these ambitious goals, key figures in the Bush administration exhibited a scorn for the lessons of history, and a contempt for international law, that determined the painful outcomes that have transpired since the End of Major Combat Operations in Iraq was celebrated on May 1, 2003, with President Bush's theatrical landing of a fighter jet aboard an aircraft carrier, where a now infamous banner announced "Mission Accomplished."

In fact, major combat operations were just beginning. By the fall of 2003 a stubborn insurgency had developed in several regions of the country, and in April 2004 an uprising across much of Iraq caused the understrength American occupation forces briefly to lose control of many crucial strategic points. American deaths in Iraq stood at over 1,300 and other U.S. casualties at about 10,000 at the end of 2004. From 20,000 to 100,000 Iraqis had died, though we have no way of knowing the real figure. Clearly, things in Iraq have not been getting better since the occupation began, and clearly, the core assumptions on which the occupation was organized have proven to be profoundly flawed.

The hubris that allowed Pentagon planners to think that they were somehow immune to the lessons of history produced a grossly mismanaged occupation that has become hated by most Iraqis and has engendered fierce resistance. This all came to a head in a small city on the Euphrates River called Falluja. Clashes there between U.S. troops and Iraqi demonstrators in the spring of 2003 led to the deaths of many demonstrators. In the year that followed, Falluja became one of the main flash points of an insurgency that spread to much of Iraq. An American siege of the city in April 2004 was broken off after the ferocity of the resistance showed that the levels of force required to bring it back under U.S. control would be politically counter-productive. Then, in a weeklong assault by several thousand Marines and soldiers in November 2004, 71 U.S. troops were killed and over 400 wounded, and an unknown number of Iraqi insurgents and civilians died. Much of the city was reduced to rubble after most of its 300,000 people became refugees, an-other case of "having to destroy the town in order to save it." This offensive brought what was left of Falluja back under U.S. control, but at a great political cost.

Those who knew the history of Iraq recalled that for genera-tions, radical Salafi and Wahhabi doctrines had influenced the Sunnis of Falluja, known as the city of mosques. Falluja was ex-posed to these doctrines because, as one of a string of towns along the Euphrates, it was close to the great desert highway that since time immemorial had linked the Nejd region (where Wahhabism began) and Jabal Shammar, in what is now eastern Saudi Arabia, with the great merchant towns of Aleppo and Mosul to the north. It was located as well along the desert road to Amman. In consequence, people in this crossroads town had family connections to tribesmen and town dwellers around the fringes of the Saudi, Jordanian, Syrian, and Iraqi deserts. But be-yond Falluja being a nodal point for extensive, long-standing religious and tribal networks, it was there that the killing of a

British colonial official, Lieutenant Colonel Gerald Leachman, by a local leader, Sheikh Dhari, in 1920 sparked a great Iraqi revolt that produced thousands of casualties and led to British forces temporarily losing control of much of Iraq. Dhari's grandson, Sheikh Harith al-Dhari, is the spokesman for the Council of Muslim Ulema, and an outspoken critic of the U.S. occupation. The small city of Falluja, historically a symbol of resistance to foreign control, thus combined key religious, tribal, and nationalist aspects of Iraq's history.

Also crucial in producing the Iraqi quagmire was the undisguised hostility to international law and other global restraints on the freedom of action of the United States of the "muscular nationalists" who dominate the Bush administration, notably Cheney and Secretary of Defense Donald Rumsfeld. Since beginning their careers in the executive branch in the mid-1970s, Cheney and Rumsfeld had always chafed at congressional limits on the president's unfettered power to make foreign policy. In the past, they had repeatedly shown their contempt for these domestic, as well as other international and legal, constraints on the freedom of action, and freedom from public scrutiny, of the executive branch. Symptomatic of this contempt was Cheney's stubborn refusal to make public the proceedings of the Bush administration's National Energy Policy Development Group, headed by Cheney and composed largely of his old cronies from the oil business. For Cheney and Rumsfeld, the Iraq War was a golden opportunity to unfetter the imperial presidency, cut Congress down to size, muzzle the press, profit the private interests with which they were connected, and conclusively show the world that it could have no influence over the actions of the United States.

However, their determined attempts to free the United States from the restraints of one specific aspect of international law—the 1949 Geneva Convention on the treatment of prisoners of war—in Afghanistan, at Guantánamo Bay, and in the detention camps in Iraq, ran counter to the concerns of a pair of powerful institutions: the uniformed military and the press. The American military is committed to the idea that respect for the Geneva Convention on the treatment of prisoners of war is in the United States' interest because it protects U.S. military personnel should they be captured in wartime. Officers of the Judge Advocate General's Corps vigorously opposed the efforts of Rumsfeld and his subordinates, backed by White House counsel Alberto Gonzales and officials of the Justice Department, to undermine and subvert the limitations imposed by the Geneva Convention. By revealing the ways in which the Bush administration had eroded legal protections for Iraqi and other prisoners, these officers began the process of tearing down the edifice of contempt for law that administration policy had sought to erect. This process began with the uncovering of the Abu Ghraib prison torture scandal. Later revelations of the death under torture of as many as three dozen detainees in Afghanistan and Iraq and elsewhere in secret prison camps came from military sources disgusted with the actions of their civilian superiors. Worse was yet to come when film emerged that seemed to show the killing of a wounded, unarmed Iraqi insurgent prisoner by a Marine in Falluja.

As in Vietnam, the press then did the rest. The American media, much of which had shown pathetic servility toward the Bush administration over Iraq, suddenly found itself handed a story that had all the elements of an explosive political scandal. As in Vietnam, a single journalist, Seymour Hersh, played a key role in setting the avalanche in motion. The Bush administration, with its high-handed past treatment of the press and of the uniformed military, soon saw the tables turned. Journalists who had been routinely intimidated at press conferences by Donald Rumsfeld and his subordinates now demanded answers. Meanwhile, senior military officers whose advice had been ignored by the secretary of defense began to speak out frankly about the abuse going on in the gulag archipelago of military detention camps erected by Rumsfeld and his underlings from Afghanistan to Cuba to Iraq. As the scandal unfolded, it became clear that directives and legal opinions from the White House, the Justice Department, and the top civilian levels of the Pentagon were responsible for these systematic abuses. This revelation was no surprise in view of the expressed opinions of Gonzales that the Geneva Conventions were "quaint" and "outmoded," and of Rumsfeld's undersecretary for policy, Douglas Feith, the man in the Pentagon responsible for managing the occupation of Iraq, that the first Geneva Convention was "law in the service of terrorism," according to an April 29, 2004, report coauthored by the Committees on Military Affairs and Justice and International Law of the Association of the Bar of the City of New York. A war launched with ambitious but unacknowledged aims, on false pretexts that failed to win U.S. public support, and which was then rebaptized as a war to bring democracy and human rights to Iraq, was shown to have produced the systematic abuse of the human rights of Iraqis and others by American military personnel with the sanction of the highest levels of the executive branch.

No one can say how much further harm will be inflicted on the Middle East by continued attempts to achieve these aims, or how much deeper the United States will consequently sink into a moral, political, and military quagmire largely of our government's making, whether in Iraq or as a result of further interventions in Iran, Syria, or elsewhere. Nor can one say whether atrocities like Abu Ghraib, growing U.S. and Iraqi casualties, the destruction of cities like Falluja, and revulsion against imperial overreach will ultimately bring the American people to recoil from this war as they did from Vietnam. But there can be no question that by trying to achieve these aims, the United States has embarked on a perilous adventure in a region whose modern history has been unkind to such ambitious imperial projects.

CHAPTER ONE

THE LEGACY OF THE WESTERN ENCOUNTER WITH THE MIDDLE EAST

The people of England have been led in Mesopotamia into a trap from which it will be hard to escape with dignity and honour. They have been tricked into it by a steady withholding of information. The Baghdad communiqués are belated, insincere, incomplete. Things have been far worse than we have been told, our adminis-tration more bloody and inefficient than the public knows. It is a disgrace to our imperial record, and may soon be too inflamed for any ordinary cure. We are to-day not far from a disaster. . . . Our unfortunate troops, Indian and British, under hard conditions of climate and supply, are policing an immense area, paying dearly every day in lives for the willfully wrong policy of the civil admin-istration in Baghdad. —T. E. LAWRENCE, "A REPORT ON MESOPOTAMIA," SUNDAY TIMES (LONDON), AUGUST 22, 1920

In the seemingly interminable political buildup to the United States' second war on Iraq in twelve years, many reasons, some of them contradictory, were advanced for an enterprise that even its proponents admitted was a novel departure for the United States. Perhaps this was because this was explicitly intended to be a war of choice, an optional war, or in the terms preferred by the Pentagon and President George W. Bush, a preemptive or preventive war.[1]

The 2003 war on Iraq was indeed a momentous departure from what most Americans fancied had always been the posture of their country in the twentieth century with respect to military conflict: that the nation would go to war only after being attacked. Notwithstanding invasions of Mexico, Cuba, the Dominican Republic, Panama, Grenada, and numerous other smaller countries beginning in the mid-nineteenth century, and even given the different valences and meanings attached to what happened (and irrespective of what actually happened) to the *Lusitania* in 1915, and at Pearl Harbor in 1941, the 38th parallel in 1950, and the Gulf of Tonkin in 1964, Americans deeply cherished the notion that they went to war only when forced to do so.

The 2003 war in Iraq clearly does not fit into this pattern, for evil and aggressive though the Iraqi Ba'thist regime of Saddam Hussein certainly was, it had never directly attacked the United States. Far from being able to threaten the greatest superpower in world history, Iraq was apparently considered to be so little of a threat by its immediate neighbors that most of them were reluctant to support an unprovoked war on it, in spite of intense American pressure to do so. (Most of the same countries had willingly participated in the 1991 war, which Iraq, when it was much stronger, had clearly provoked.) In consequence, as an acute observer noted, President Bush's much touted "coalition of the willing" was more like "a coalition of the coerced, the cowed and the co-opted."[2] This was thus neither a war to protect the United States nor one to defend its regional allies. In fact, as some of the proponents of waging war on Iraq have openly stated, the 2003 campaign was meant to be the first in a new category of wars they advocated the United States should launch on its own in the twenty-first century. These were to be wars waged to assure that American values prevailed—as President Bush stated in September 2002, "these values . . . are right and true for every person, in every society"—or as others perceived it, to guarantee the United States' continued hegemony. The president added that "as a matter of common sense, America will act against . . . emerging threats before they are fully formed," since "in the new world we have entered, the only path to peace and security is the path of action."[3] This approach was dubbed "a distinctly American internationalism" by the Bush administration.[4]

THE RUSH TO WAR IN IRAQ

The administration's revolutionary departure from previous practice with respect to military engagement was enshrined in the National Security Strategy of the United States of America, released in September 2002. This new doctrine asserted that "the best defense is a good offense." It went well beyond the traditional understandings of what constitutes a preemptive or a preventive war, and beyond most accepted notions of the limits imposed by international law and the sovereignty of independent states, in ominously referring to the United States hereafter "convincing or compelling states to accept their sovereign responsibilities." It went on: "We will not hesitate to act alone, if necessary, to exercise our right of self-defense by acting preemptively" (p. 6). Referring to possible attacks by terrorists or rogue states, it declared: "To forestall or prevent such hostile acts by our adversaries, the United States will, if necessary, act preemptively" (p. 15).[5] In the measured words of the eminent historian Sir Michael Howard, this new doctrine constituted "one of the most important documents in the history of America, and its full implications are just beginning to sink in," for, he added, Bush "seemed to be demolishing the whole structure of international law as it had developed since the 17th century."[6] In light of what has since followed, it is clear that this major doctrinal shift has still not received anything like the attention it deserves.

In their attempts to garner support for the first venture based on this new doctrine, what has been called the "War Party,"[7] the group of advisors that closely surrounds President Bush, adduced several main reasons for the unprecedented step of an unprovoked invasion of Iraq. Among them were the dangers supposedly posed to the United States and its allies by Iraq's possible (certain, according to these proponents of war) possession of a range of nonconventional weapons— "weapons of mass destruction," in the lurid and not particularly accurate term employed by the administration and parroted by the media (often then boiled down to the acronym WMD, thereby conflating banned battlefield armaments like gas with nuclear weapons, designed originally for use against civilian population centers, and so used in 1945). These dangers took on added menace in view of Iraq's aggression against two of its neighbors, Iran in 1980 and Kuwait in 1990, and its intensive use of poison gas against Iranian forces during the Iran-Iraq War.[8]

The threat posed by Iraq was at times amplified by the repeated suggestions that it might offer nuclear, chemical, or biological weapons to clandestine terrorists like those of al-Qaʻida, who less than two years earlier had attacked New York and Washington with devastating effect. Likely or not, this chilling scenario tapped into the deep well of anxiety these attacks had left behind among many Americans. And the administration was working fertile ground: polls for as long as two years after the event showed that the existence of an Iraqi connection with 9/11 was accepted by a large majority of Americans, despite the fact that there was no evidence whatsoever for such a connection.[9] The completely new element constituted by the profound popular concern about the possibility of new terrorist attacks on the U.S. homeland was recognized and regularly exploited to drum up support for the war in Iraq by supporters of the administration. It was prominently featured in President Bush's second State of the Union message on January 28, 2003, in his speech of March 17, 2003, presenting a forty-eight-hour ultimatum to the Iraqi regime, and in numerous other administration policy statements.

But the threats posed by the Iraqi regime to the United States, its allies, and its interests, whether they were in fact as serious as was affirmed or not, were apparently not enough to convince Americans to support the war unreservedly and in massive numbers, forcing the president and his supporters to marshal other justifications. Some argued that these were in fact the truest, deepest moral justifications for such a war of choice, and were the ones that made war necessary. The most important of them was the argument that inaction was morally unacceptable in the face of what was described as the absolute, indeed Hitlerian, evil represented by the Iraqi regime and its demonic dictator, whose cruelties were detailed by supporters of war inside and outside the government. The American people were told by the Bush administration, echoed by a chorus of voices in the pliant punditocracy and the many right-wing Washington think tanks, that it was imperative that the United States intervene militarily to overthrow the Iraqi government and impose a new one—to engage in "regime change," to use the sanitized term initially favored by the influential proponents of this approach. This blunt (but honest) terminology was later discarded, perhaps because it was seen as insufficiently idealistic to galvanize Americans to support an unprovoked war of choice, in favor of a call to "liberate" and "democratize" Iraq.[10]

The day after the war began, however, the euphoria of their success in helping to launch the United States on the path of

military adventure in Iraq may have slightly intoxicated some
of the leading neoconservative luminaries. At an American
Enterprise Institute (AEI) "black coffee briefing on the war in
Iraq" on Friday, March 21, 2003, described as "a victory cele-
bration" by British journalist Guy Dinmore, three of the most
influential non-office-holding members of this group, William
Kristol, editor of the *Weekly Standard*, Richard Perle, then-
chairman of the Pentagon's Defense Policy Board, and Michael
Ledeen, a former Reagan administration official, reverted
to the unvarnished language of regime change.[11] Specifically,
regime change in Syria and Iran was a central part of the postwar agenda they laid out for what Ledeen said was part of a
"longer war." The agenda they described was global in nature:
it included as well radical reform of the U.N. and "contain-
ment" of France and Germany.[12] This should not come as a
surprise, for Perle has elsewhere written scornfully of "the fantasy of the U.N. as the foundation of the new world order."[13] As
Kristol said to those assembled over coffee at the AEI, there
was "a lack of awe for the U.S." in the Middle East, "an absence
of respect that fostered contempt" for the superpower.[14] It was
this failure of previous U.S. disciplinary actions in the region
that the war on Iraq was presumably designed to correct. For
those with any historical memory, the words of Kristol and
other neocons echoed eerily the doctrine central to the ethos
of earlier Western imperial ventures in the Middle East, that
the locals understand and respect only force.

Regime change, in the thinking of these individuals and
the many others of their ideological persuasion within the
administration, in turn was supposed to be the first step in a
long-overdue process of bringing democracy to the Arab
world. This region was hyperbolically described by a wide
range of those advocating muscular U.S. intervention as mired
in autocracy, dictatorship, and benighted reaction, and beset

by unrepresentative and repressive regimes—and it does indeed present a bleak prospect even to the unbiased eye. Iraq was thus projected as the first in a series of undemocratic Middle Eastern dominos that would fall one after another, from Syria to Iran to Saudi Arabia and beyond, if the United States could simply show the will and resolve to use its unlimited power to act selflessly on behalf of the peoples of this region, groaning under a variety of cruel despots.[15]

Although it was supported by an intensive bombardment of such high-flown rhetoric, the inexorable advance to a war on Iraq waged virtually unilaterally by the United States occasioned persistent dissent in the United States,[16] and far more widespread opposition representing large majorities of the population in Europe, Russia, India, the Middle East, and the Islamic world and most other regions of the globe.[17] The dissenters questioned whether the United States had the right to intervene unilaterally in the affairs of other peoples and countries, whether or not democracy can in fact be "transplanted" as a result of such an intervention, and whether implanting democracy in Iraq or anywhere else in the Middle East was in fact the true objective of U.S. policy. Doubts were raised in particular about the sincerity of the Bush administration on the latter score, because several of its leading figures, including the president and his father, former president George H. W. Bush, Vice President Dick Cheney, and the secretaries of defense and state, Donald Rumsfeld and General Colin Powell, as well as a host of lesser officials, had been on the best of terms for several decades with a variety of Middle Eastern despots, Saddam Hussein himself included.[18]

Beyond this, commentators on the right and left noted that neither muscular nationalists like Bush, Cheney, and Rumsfeld, nor the neoconservative members of the War Party who surrounded them and held key posts throughout the bureaucracy, in right-wing Washington think tanks, and in the media, had ever been noted as advocates of democratization of the Arab world. This is not surprising, since real democracy in the region would mean the free expression of the popular will, including, in all likelihood, calls for the removal of U.S. bases in the Middle East, support of the Palestinians, and opposition to the Israeli occupation and settlement of Palestinian lands, all of which are abhorrent to the neocons. Indeed, several neocon leading lights had served as advisors to extremist Israeli leaders including Benyamin Netanyahu.[19] It was pointed out further that installing a one-man-one-woman-one-vote democracy in a country like Iraq (whose population includes a 60 percent Shi'ite majority that might be expected to sympathize with the predominantly Shi'ite neighboring Islamic republic of Iran) seemed unlikely to be the real intention of the War Party in Washington.[20] For many of them, their hostility to Iran was second only to their obsession with Iraq, although even among these superhawks there were differences of approach and degree in dealing with Middle Eastern regimes they uniformly abhorred. It is now clear that these troubling questions about regime change and democratization, not to speak of how to deal with the aftermath of war and military occupation, legitimate and important though they all were, were cavalierly swept under the carpet by the Bush administration in the lead-up to the war.

But another crucial question, informed by the entire modern history of the Middle East, was also insufficiently considered. This is whether by invading, occupying, and imposing a new regime in Iraq, the United States may be stepping, intentionally or not, into the boots of the old Western colonial powers, and even worse, may be doing so in a region that within living memory concluded a lengthy struggle to expel those hated occupations. This question suggests other related ones:

What are the peoples of the Middle East likely to think of when they see foreign troops on their soil without their consent?[21] What memories are triggered for them by foreign invasion, and what are their reactions to it likely to be?[22] How have they reacted to foreign occupation and control, direct and indirect, in the recent past? How have outside powers helped or hindered the countries of this region in their evolution toward democracy and constitutionalism? What has been their experience over the past century as far as control of their valuable oil resources is concerned, and what historical sensitivities do they have on this score?

This raises a final set of questions about whether anyone in the top ranks of the Bush administration in Washington, where the decision for war meant fateful long-term decisions about the future of the United States' relations with the Middle East, ever took into account these and other aspects of the heavy legacy of the painful Western colonial encounter in this region. Is there any realization in these circles that this encounter ended very recently in terms of the extremely long and tumultuous history of the countries of the Middle East, perhaps humankind's longest history, and that memories of it are still vivid?

A CENTURY OF TRANSFORMATION IN THE MIDDLE EAST

Before discussing American relations with the Middle East, it is necessary to explain how Middle Easterners came to view the West generally in the decades preceding the mid-twentieth century, how the European powers eventually dominated and occupied virtually the entire region, and how constant resistance to this process ultimately led to their expulsion. For it is against this background that we must understand the changes in perceptions of the United States over the past few decades, and how America has shifted from being seen almost entirely positively to being the focus of the dissatisfaction of many and the hostility of many others.

Long before the United States suddenly became a power in the Middle East during World War I, only to virtually disappear and then return during World War II, the peoples of that region had already had lengthy experiences with the West. These experiences had both positive and negative aspects, and the resulting associations would later on attach to the American newcomers to the region. The positive aspects were associated with Western scientific, technical, educational, and cultural advances, military and governmental efficiency, and liberal values, all of which came to be appreciated by increasing numbers of people in the Middle East, particularly intellectuals, the educated, and the growing middle and urban working classes. The desire to emulate and reproduce these values gradually spread in these sectors of Middle Eastern society. On the other hand, the negative aspects affected nearly the entirety of society. They related primarily to the gradual domination and subjugation of the region, and ultimately the occupation of most of the countries of the Middle East, by the European powers. This lengthy and painful process left deep and lasting scars, and naturally affected the reception of Western values among Arabs, Turks, Iranians, and other Middle Easterners.

The modern history of Western intervention in the Middle East is long and complex. It is conventionally dated to the French invasion of Egypt in 1798, but in fact this date is both too early and too late. It is too early in the sense that there was a long hiatus between Napoleon's brief occupation of Egypt and Palestine and the much longer-lasting European subjugation and occupation of most Arab countries from the 1830s until the mid-twentieth century. It is too late in the sense that well before Napoleon's invasion, both the Ottoman Empire (which then comprised Turkey, the Balkans, much of North Africa, Egypt, and most of the rest of the Arab world) and Iran had for well over a century been experiencing a debilitating series of military defeats at the hands of the European powers that led to repeated cessions of territory, initially mainly on their northern frontiers. This process of consecutive defeats and losses of territory continued with little interruption throughout the nineteenth century, and indeed accelerated as time went on. These painful reverses, experienced over many generations, helped shape a growing sense in the countries of the Middle East that they were inexorably losing ground to external powers far stronger than they were, and spurred a search for the means to resist these unceasing encroachments.

While many remedies were suggested for reversal of this process of defeat and contraction, the one most generally accepted by regional elites was the adoption of Western forms of government and military organization, and reform of education and the legal system. By contrast, others in society rejected some or all Western values. They saw the only hope for improving the situation in a return to what they believed were Islam's original values, which they argued had once made their ancestors powerful and feared. There were many examples of such a reaction taking place in different regions and eras, from the Wahhabi movement in the Arabian Peninsula starting in the eighteenth century, to that of the Mahdi in the Sudan in the late nineteenth century, to more recent groups like the Muslim Brotherhood, founded in Egypt in 1928.

However, the process of institutional reform and governmental transformation was inescapable. Most of the growing numbers of those educated in modern schools and who were incorporated into the reformed bureaucracy and advanced sectors of the economy soon came to admire and seek to have their societies implement Western political doctrines, notably the equality of citizens before the law, constitutionalism, and parliamentary democracy. Those engaged in governmental reforms most frequently aspired to make the necessary changes in their system of governance while retaining the Islamic basis that underpinned it,[23] and at the same time sought to modernize and energize the religious establishment. There were thus persistent efforts in Tunisia, Egypt, the Ottoman Empire, Iran, and several other parts of the Middle East to carry out reforms that would help preserve these countries' autonomy and independence in the face of continuous Western encroachments, while at the same time respecting their cultural, religious, and social specificities.

It proved to be a daunting task to reform governmental systems that in many cases had been deeply rooted for centuries. Moreover, some of these systems had proven extremely successful and resilient for most of that period, as is demonstrated by the fact that the Ottoman Empire remained the dominant power in the Mediterranean and the southeastern regions of Europe for hundreds of years. In consequence of these difficulties, this effort was inevitably a failure in some respects. But the setbacks suffered by these reformers should not obscure their successes: by World War I, both the Ottoman Empire and Iran had succeeded in adopting weak but functional constitutional systems at about the same time as, and in some cases before, many countries of Eastern and southern Europe. They had also managed to modernize their legal and educational systems and their military forces in many key respects. Indeed, for the first three years of World War I, the revamped and strengthened Ottoman army utilized an expanded railway network and succeeded in holding the armies and fleets of the Western allies at bay on three widely separated fronts: in Iraq, Palestine, and the Dardanelles. They even administered resounding defeats to Allied forces, at Kut in Iraq and at Gallipoli. Few in the West realized or appreciated how great a transformation had been wrought in the formerly ramshackle Ottoman military establishment: four years before being decisively defeated by Ottoman forces at Gallipoli, the British commander there, Sir Ian Hamilton, had contemptuously talked of how easy it would be to defend Egypt against the Ottomans because of what he described as the "Oriental mentalities" of their officer corps.[24]

These transformations in the governmental and military apparatuses of state were profound. The concomitant changes in the lives and mentalities of many people in the Middle East, including strata well beyond a narrow elite, were equally vital. Such changes resulted from the spread of modern means of transportation and communications (with railway networks in the region expanding from 6,700 to 18,600 kilometers between 1890 and 1914[25]), and the extensive reach of modern education. The number of modern schools in the Ottoman Empire increased particularly rapidly: thus the number of state secondary schools grew from 1 in 1883 to 51 in 1894;[26] while there were no state primary schools in 1872, by 1885 there were 158 in the Jerusalem district alone.[27] In addition to these state schools, there were growing networks of European Christian missionary schools sponsored by various denominations, schools of the Alliance Israélite Universelle, and private secular and Muslim schools, such as those of Jam'iyat al-Maqasid al-Khayriyya al-Islamiyya in Beirut. Although the statistical indicators of change are not comprehensive or finely tuned, it is clear that literacy increased greatly, as did social mobility and commercial activity, albeit with great variations from region to region and between classes and ethnic and religious groups.

These profound changes reached broad segments of the population, although the transformations that ensued were frequently dismissed as superficial by outside observers. There are countless accounts by Western travelers, merchants, and diplomats emphasizing how primitive and xenophobic were the populations of this region even after the transformations of the nineteenth century began.[28] Over the past two centuries, many of these Western observers were unsparing in their depictions of Middle Eastern societies sunken in unchanging barbarism and ignorance. However, the ability of many of these foreigners to understand what they saw and were told was frequently limited, since they did not speak the local languages,[29] and their own ignorance and biases were often so debilitating as to blind them to the realities before their eyes. This is not particularly surprising, given that they were the products of Western societies whose narrow-mindedness and bigotry were minutely depicted by acute observers like Dickens and Flaubert. It is also worth noting that classifying Eastern societies as barbaric and backward was part of a process that justified colonial domination of them by "superior" Western countries.[30]

What Western observers often failed to notice in their fixation on Middle Eastern conservatism and reaction were the assets that these societies already possessed in terms of a deep respect for learning that was integral to Islam, and a willingness to experiment and to change. In consequence, they missed many of the profound and lasting modifications brought about by the processes of reform and modernization. Thus the major legal and political transformations of the Ottoman Empire from 1839 onward, which were ultimately to lead to the promulgation of a constitution in 1876 (and were to lay the groundwork for the secular Turkish republic of the twentieth century), were often disparaged by contemporary

Western observers as nothing more than the grudging acquiescence of reluctant Ottoman officials to the principled urgings
of liberal British and other European diplomats.[31] Indigenous
views present quite a different picture from those of outsiders:
not surprisingly, they give the latter much less credit for these
reforms.[32] Similarly, although the bigoted attitudes of many
Europeans of this era are apparent, one has to read the memoirs of Middle Easterners of the period to see how deep was
their resentment of these attitudes.[33]

By the early twentieth century, benefiting from the spread
of education and the increased mobility of people, goods, and
ideas, many among the elites and the growing professional,
middle, and working classes in countries like Turkey, Egypt,
and Iran had become imbued with the desire to establish
constitutional democracy, the rule of law, and modern governmental arrangements. They often looked to the liberal constitutional systems of Great Britain, France, and the United
States as models. They also hoped that these democracies
would help them to overcome both the powerful and enduring
autocratic tendencies within their own governments and societies, and the unrelenting pressure of the monarchical empires
of central and eastern Europe. These great empires were intent
on continued expansion southward into areas controlled by
the Islamic powers of the Middle East. While stubbornly
resistant to constitutional reform at home and anywhere else,
they also feared that reform in the Middle East would
strengthen the capability of the Muslim states to their south to
block their imperial expansion in that direction.

The fragile constitutional regimes established in Iran and
the Ottoman Empire by the revolutions of 1906 and 1908 (the
latter involved a restoration of the 1876 constitution) were
among the first fruits of this strong desire among major
segments of the population for limitations on the strong,

millennia-old tradition in Egypt, Mesopotamia, Turkey, and Iran of the absolute power of the state. While far from perfect in many respects, these new parliamentary regimes represented a remarkable transformation in their societies in a relatively brief time, with all the flaws and gaps that were implied by the speed of such a transition taking place in large, poorly integrated, and traditional societies. The proponents of liberal reform in the Middle East, however, were to be sadly disappointed not only by the central and eastern European absolutist monarchies, but also by the liberal Western powers, which they perhaps naively presumed were their natural allies in the struggle against despotism at home and the imperialism of the Hapsburg and Romanov Empires abroad.

THE ERA OF EUROPEAN COLONIALISM

The hopes of Middle Eastern liberals in the western European democracies, notably Britain and France, were ultimately betrayed because the lure of imperial expansion in the vast lands south and southeast of the Mediterranean proved far greater for these European great powers than their commitment to spreading their own democratic and constitutional ideals. This is one of the enduring ironies of the colonial legacy of the democratic West European powers—Great Britain, France, Belgium, and Holland—that dominated the lion's share of the globe by the first half of the twentieth century. Beacons of freedom and constitutional democracy, and constantly removing barriers to suffrage and expanding the rights of the individual at home, these same states conquered and ruled over the peoples of much of the earth without the slightest reference to the liberal principles that animated their own systems of government.

In order to justify this paradoxical deviation from their

principles, a variety of strategies were employed. These ranged from the overt racism that argued that some peoples were too primitive to be allowed to rule themselves, to the more sophisticated arguments of Orientalism about the regions where great civilizations had existed for millennia in East Asia, South Asia, and the Middle East. Clearly, these had once been highly advanced cultures, and thus elicited harder-case arguments about "stagnation" and the stifling embrace of tradition or religion. In all cases, arguments for colonial rule and the denial of self-determination to the subjugated peoples were clothed in the self-serving and patronizing rhetoric of cultural improvement, whether this was described in terms of the white man's burden or the *mission civilisatrice*.[34]

It was thus the lot of most of the peoples of the Middle East to be subjugated over the period of more than a century by states that were increasingly democratic at home and unrelentingly imperialist abroad. France began the occupation and colonization of Algeria in 1830, a process that produced 132 years of conflict with the local population, which fiercely resisted its subjugation. This long war of conquest against stubborn Algerian resistance was accompanied by the sequestration of the land of much of the Algerian population for the benefit of European colonists, and led to great suffering.[35] The long and cruel ordeal of colonization ultimately resulted in the horrors and counterhorrors of the Algerian War of Independence of 1954–1962, a sequence of events over many generations that most observers agree profoundly scarred Algerian society.

Soon after France's invasion of Algeria, Britain seized Aden on the southwestern corner of the Arabian Peninsula, while continuing its slow penetration of the Arabian and Iranian shores of the Persian Gulf. There it developed relations with local potentates, turning them into dependent clients, all the while expanding its influence in southern Iran in competition with that of Russia in the northern parts of the country. Thereafter, France in 1881 occupied Tunis and Britain in 1882 occupied Egypt, inaugurating a European military presence in the heart of two of the greatest historic centers of Arab and Islamic civilization that lasted into the second half of the twentieth century.

In each of these Arab countries, a slightly different form of control was imposed. These ranged from the direct rule of the French in Algeria, which was eventually annexed to France and whose indigenous population lost its rights and lands in favor of newly arrived European colonists (with the exception of the Algerian Jews, who in 1871 were granted French nationality), to various forms of indirect rule preferred by the British, and also adopted by the French in Tunis. In these cases of indirect rule, local potentates were maintained in place—emirs and sheikhs in the Gulf, a khedive in Egypt, and a dey in Tunis—but their power was more apparent than real. In every case, control was firmly in the hands of European "advisors," backed by European and mercenary troops, who ensured that every important aspect of governance developed in accord with the desires of the dominant Western power.

Thus in Egypt, for example, the educational budget was reduced (Lord Cromer, the first and longest-lasting British pro-consul, believed that Western education would "create a group of intellectuals imbued with nationalist ideals and a sense of frustration over their inferior status"[36]), while European bondholders were scrupulously compensated. The Egyptians paid the cost of the British army of occupation (a humiliation visited on most colonized peoples: they paid for their own subjugation), while Britain used Egyptian troops to help it conquer a rebellious Egyptian province, the Sudan, which then became a colony of Britain in all but name. Perhaps most importantly, the evolution of Egypt, Tunisia, and other Middle Eastern countries toward constitutional rule and democracy was stifled, a disappointment felt particularly keenly in Egypt, where moves had been under way to limit the autocratic power of the khedive before the British occupation in 1882.[37]

The expansion of the European powers into the Arab world was completed with Italy's invasion of Libya in 1911 and France's establishment of a protectorate over Morocco in 1912, and with the World War I Anglo-French partitions of the Ottoman Empire. These partitions led directly to European occupation of the remainder of the former Arab provinces of the Ottoman Empire, except for Yemen and what was to become Saudi Arabia. Both of these countries had previously been under Ottoman control, control that was tenuous at best, and they alone remained unoccupied. Libya witnessed an occupation by stages of exceptional brutality, eventually involving the progressive destruction of the country's social structure and expulsion of its population from the fertile coastal regions in favor of Italian colonists. This process left Libya, which had scores of schools in 1911, with only a handful of people who had any modern education by 1945,[38] and had destructive effects that were deep and lasting. In Morocco, in spite of maintaining the sultan in nominal control and ruling indirectly, the French faced repeated revolts that could only be mastered with massive forces and the extensive use of air power. For all the variations in their situations, similar patterns were repeated in most of the Middle East, even in countries that were nominally League of Nations mandates, supposedly under temporary European tutelage until they could become independent.

In the wake of World War I, the only countries in the entire Middle East that were able to resist these external encroachments (besides Yemen and Saudi Arabia) were Iran and the new republic of Turkey. The latter succeeded in doing so largely because of its ferocious and successful military resistance to British, French, and Greek occupation forces in the years after World War I. Both benefited as well from the wartime collapse of the expansionist Romanov Empire in Russia to their north and the rise in its place of a relatively weak Soviet Union, which for a time at least renounced czarist privileges and aspirations and welcomed the existence of these independent states as buffers against the hostile Western powers.

Elsewhere, during the interwar period and until the end of World War II, the Western colonial powers, Britain and France (together with Italy in Libya and Spain in the Western Sahara) maintained a political, economic, and strategic stranglehold over the Middle East. They retained military bases throughout the region and made most of the important decisions, although they were obliged in some cases to allow a few of the trappings of independence. After a massive nationwide uprising against the British in 1919 that enveloped all social classes and regions and was marked by strikes, demonstrations, and attacks on British forces, Britain was forced to acquiesce in Egypt's nominal independence in 1922. It nevertheless retained its military bases, its control over Egypt's foreign relations and the Canal Zone, and other privileges. These restrictive limitations imposed on Egypt's independence, which meant continued British domination of the country and ceaseless interference in its politics, created a situation that even in the view of a historian highly sympathetic to the British "inaugurated a period of uninterrupted crisis in domestic Egyptian politics, which in part prevented parliamentary government and its institutions from taking root in the political life of the country."[39] In practice this meant that for eighteen of the thirty years from 1922 until the military revolution of 1952, the overwhelmingly popular Wafd Party was kept out of power. The impact of this constant external interference with the democratic process in Egypt and elsewhere in the Middle East was profound and wide-ranging.[40]

In the case of the new League of Nations mandates over what had formerly been the Arab provinces of the Ottoman Empire, the British and French had to tread somewhat more warily. According to Article 22 of the Covenant of the League, these countries' "existence as independent nations can be provisionally recognized subject to the rendering of administrative advice and assistance by a Mandatory until such time as they are able to stand alone." Such unequivocal language should have precluded the imposition of a neocolonial system, but it did not prevent the British officials responsible for administering occupied Iraq after World War I from instituting a system of direct military control modeled on the Indian colonial regime of direct rule. This caused so much popular resentment that the country erupted in a nationwide revolt resulting in thousands of Iraqi deaths and two thousand casualties among the ninety thousand British and Indian troops brought in to suppress it.[41] In the end, the revolt could only be mastered by the unrestricted use of overwhelming force, including air power, against the civilian population—a pattern that was to recur repeatedly in the sad history of Western control over this region in the first half of the twentieth century.

While it would surely be a mistake to compare mechanically the situation of the United States in Iraq in 2003 with that of Britain over eighty years earlier, perhaps it would have been useful if more people in Washington had read Iraqi history more carefully before the occupation of Iraq took place. The parsimonious British, their forces stretched thin and their exchequer under strain in the wake of World War I, struggled both with a situation that seemed to be escaping their control and with competing visions of how to govern Iraq.[42] They eventually decided that direct rule was too costly, and brought in a ruler whom the French had just expelled from Syria, the Hashemite king Faisal. He had served their interests well elsewhere, and they correctly surmised that he might act as a buffer against nationalist pressures. The regime King Faisal presided over, dominated by Iraqi officers who had formerly served in the Ottoman army, eventually succeeded in doing this, allowing Britain in 1932 to extend to Iraq the same nominal independence granted Egypt a decade earlier, while retaining the same stifling influence on Iraqi domestic politics. Britain adopted a similar stratagem in the emirate of Transjordan (which in 1946 became the Hashemite Kingdom of Jordan), where Faisal's older brother Abdullah was installed as ruler.

Meanwhile in Syria, after they had driven out the independent Arab government headed by King Faisal in 1920, the French clung to direct rule for longer than had the British in Iraq. Yet they, too, eventually faced a massive revolt in 1925–26, one that was also put down by the liberal use of aerial bombardment against villages, cities, and other defenseless targets.[43] Thus, after having had to fight their way into Damascus at the outset of their rule in 1920, the French lost control of much of the city, together with the adjoining countryside, to nationalist rebels in 1925, and were repeatedly obliged to bombard parts of the Syrian capital using artillery and planes. Even after France finally put an end to the 1925–26 revolt through such indiscriminate brutality, and realized the wisdom of allowing the Syrians some of the trappings of self-government, the sufferings of the people of Damascus at the hands of the colonial power were not over: facing a new revolt in May 1945, French forces bombarded Damascus yet again.

The French in Syria and Lebanon played another card in

the hand of imperial powers, beyond the classic ploy of indirect rule as practiced by the British in the Gulf, Egypt, Iraq, and Transjordan, and which France had successfully utilized in Tunisia and Morocco. This was the manipulation of ethnic and religious rivalries, a time-tested means of divide and rule that the British had perfected in India and then assiduously applied in Egypt, Iraq, and Palestine. The French employed it extensively in Syria and Lebanon, where at one point the policy of divide and rule in order to exploit internal cleavages reached the ridiculous stage of the division of the mandate for Syria into over half a dozen supposedly separate entities—one for the Druzes, one for the Alawis, Lebanon dominated by the Maronites, and so forth. In the end, none of these divisions, except that between Lebanon and Syria, proved to be lasting, although French meddling seriously exacerbated some of the existing sectarian differences.

In North Africa, divisions between Arabs and Berbers, as well as between Muslims and Jews, were exploited by the French authorities, and sometimes by the settler populations themselves, to help the occupying power to maintain its control. Here too, revolts nevertheless erupted, the most notable of them being the massive Rif revolt led by Abd el-Krim that lasted several years, culminating in 1925. It required a French force of 325,000 troops, backed by tanks and planes, and supported by 100,000 Spanish soldiers, to defeat this dangerous challenge.[44]

In Palestine, where the British had endeavored to impose a Jewish national home on a country that in 1917 was over 90 percent Arab, and where the indigenous Arab population came to understand that the full implementation of such a goal necessarily meant their subjugation or expulsion, there were several serious disturbances over the years. A major revolt directed against British rule finally erupted in 1936 and lasted until 1939. It required tens of thousands of British troops to suppress it, the largest such British deployment at the time, all of this to master less than a million Arabs. The tragic events in Palestine involved much more than this, of course, but during the three decades of British rule over the country, this dynamic of colonial repression and indigenous resistance was clearly at work, as elsewhere in the Middle East.[45]

It remains to mention one last incident of colonial repression, in nominally independent Iraq, which in 1941 invoked its treaty with Britain to deny permission for British troops to be landed at Basra. Notwithstanding the absence of such permission, the British ignored the provisions of the treaty that they had imposed on the Iraqis, and with it the fiction of Iraqi independence, and proceeded to invade the country. They defeated the fledgling Iraqi army and reoccupied the country, removing in the process the popular, elected government and reinstalling the hated Hashemite regent and a government that would do their bidding. The final indignity in all of this was that members of the nationalist Iraqi government, who had tried to defend the state's rights under a treaty with Britain, were branded as rebels and stooges of the Axis powers (to which they had indeed appealed for help against the British). The entire episode was labeled a "revolt" in the colonial historiography that still holds sway in the West, although in Iraqi and Arab histories it is understood quite differently as the attempt of a precariously independent state to defend its treaty rights and thereby assert its independence.

These differences in perspective are important: what the conventional view in Britain at the time held to be perfectly understandable—Britain was fighting a war in 1941 and "needed" to land troops in Basra—was regarded quite differently by the Arab populace, and for perfectly good reasons. A similar and even more sweeping difference in perspective can be discerned today: while many in the United States feel that the "necessary" occupation of Iraq followed naturally from the fact that their country was fighting a war on terrorism, this is not how things are perceived in most Arab countries and indeed in much of the rest of the world. This brings us to consideration of the other side of European occupation in the Middle East: the opposition to European rule demonstrated by the peoples of the region, and what this may presage as another Western power embarks on the occupation of a major Middle Eastern country.

RESISTANCE TO FOREIGN CONTROL
IN THE MIDDLE EAST

Histories of the Western subjugation of the Middle East have tended to focus mainly on how this region fit into the overall process of European global expansion, the crucial decisions about intervention that were taken in the various imperial capitals, the rivalries between the great powers, and the nature of the colonial systems they set up. Considerably less attention has been paid to the degree of resistance that this process engendered, and to the stubborn perseverance and changing forms of this resistance.

To recapitulate the high points of more than 170 years of Middle Eastern resistance to foreign military occupation, there were continuous revolts and other forms of lasting nationalist resistance in Algeria, Morocco, and Tunisia from the moment French troops set foot in North Africa in 1830 until the moment they unwillingly withdrew in the mid-twentieth century. In Egypt, the khedive's army resisted the British military in 1882, which thereafter had to conquer and then reconquer the Sudan, and faced a nationwide revolt in Egypt in 1919. Britain found its forces under guerilla attack in the Canal Zone after World War II, until its seventy-four-year "temporary" occupation of Egypt ended with a final, humiliating withdrawal following the fiasco of the 1956 Suez War. Following World War I, Iran and especially Turkey had to struggle tenaciously to force foreign troops to leave their soil.

There was strong resistance to the British advances in Iraq and Palestine during World War I by Ottoman armies made up in large part of Arab conscripts from these countries. In Iraq, these forces won one of the most resounding victories of the war, leading to the surrender of over ten thousand British and Indian troops at Kut al-'Amara in April 1916 at the end of a disastrous campaign that resulted in more than thirty-three thousand British casualties.[46] Only two years after the occupation of Baghdad, an Iraqi national revolt enabled the Iraqis to take control of large parts of the country in 1920, while as already noted, Britain was obliged to conquer the country all over again from its semi-independent government in 1941.

Palestine was almost as hard for Great Britain to conquer in World War I as Iraq, obliging it to wage a hard campaign that took even longer than that in Iraq. After a series of disturbances and riots, the country erupted into a lengthy and bloody nationwide popular revolt against the British from 1936 until 1939. This revolt eventually succeeded in the rebels' taking over several urban centers, and could only be mastered by means of the largest single pre–World War II colonial deployment of British forces. The Syrians resisted the French in similarly stubborn fashion, obliging them to bombard and subjugate Damascus three times in the course of major military efforts, in 1920, during the nationwide Syrian revolt of 1925–26, and again in 1945.

The numbers of people killed by colonial forces as they suppressed this resistance were high. In the most lethal of the French bombardments of Damascus in 1925, in revenge for having been driven out of much of the city, French forces killed over 1,400 people, almost all of them civilians.[47] Earlier in 1925, after a similar humiliation in Hama, the French had killed 344 people, again mainly civilians, during a punitive aerial bombardment of the town. French forces were later to kill as many as 1,000 in a similar attack in May 1926 after they once again lost control of the Damascus neighborhood of the Maydan.[48] The numbers of those killed in the Syrian countryside, especially in the Jabal Druze region where the revolt began, are much harder to determine, but were also undoubtedly very high.

Iraq, Morocco, Libya, and Syria were the laboratory where the military high-technology of the post–World War I era was first tried out, and where the textbook on the aerial bombardment of civilians was written. One Royal Air Force officer wrote of the 1920 Iraq campaign that after "the most prominent tribe which it is desired to punish" had been chosen, "the attack with bombs and machine guns must be unrelenting and unremitting and carried out continuously by day and night, on houses, inhabitants, crops and cattle."[49] The RAF's "Notes on the Method of Employment of the Air Arm in Iraq" stated of this air campaign that "within 45 minutes a full-sized village ... can be practically wiped out and a third of its inhabitants killed and injured by four or five planes which offer them no real target and no opportunity for glory or avarice."[50] Not surprisingly, at least six thousand and perhaps as many as eighty-five hundred or even ten thousand Iraqis were killed during the suppression of the 1920 revolt, many of them civilians.[51] The casualties in Morocco and Syria among civilians during the French military campaigns were similarly high.

In Palestine, although the RAF was used much more sparingly than it had been in Iraq (international and Arab public opinion by this time had become a consideration; there were more eyes watching what happened—this was the Holy Land, after all), Palestinian casualties were nevertheless exceedingly heavy. With over five thousand people killed and nearly fifteen thousand wounded and another fifty-six hundred detained in 1939, by the time the revolt was over, about 5 percent of the Palestinian adult male population had been killed, wounded, or imprisoned.[52]

It is worth considering carefully the full meaning of these formidable European powers' being obliged to conquer, and reconquer, and often conquer once again, their Middle Eastern colonial possessions. It is also worthwhile to ask what motivated poorly armed colonial subjects to rebel repeatedly against the power of the colonial state, with its artillery, its airplanes, its motorized columns, and its unlimited resources, particularly since these subjects were aware of the occupier's readiness to employ this force until it had restored "order." Although the motivation of these Middle Eastern men and women was denigrated and demeaned in colonial accounts as "fanaticism," rather than being seen as patriotism and a desire for freedom, it should not be hard to understand this region-wide resistance in different form over more than a century and a half in terms of a natural opposition to the imposition of alien rule.

In assessing how daunting it was for colonial subjects to revolt against the Western imperial powers at this time, it is easy to forget that all of this took place during the interwar period, an era when none of these powers withdrew from a single colonial possession. The failure of these revolts and other forms of resistance to produce the full independence of any of the colonized countries of the Middle East before the end of World War II was no exception to the overarching pattern of the period. Before the wave of decolonization that followed World War II, driven in part by the emergence of the United States and Soviet Union as superpowers far greater than the old colonial powers that had dominated most of the world until that point, not one colonized country managed to achieve real independence, whether in the Middle East or elsewhere. This lack of success should not invalidate the degree of opposition to external rule, direct and indirect, armed and unarmed, that continuous Middle Eastern (and other colonial) resistance to differing forms of Western control demonstrated.

For even as some of the region's elites came to align themselves with the British and French colonizers, serving as intermediaries and sharing a few of the benefits of the colonial regime, strong popular mass movements arose in all the countries of the Middle East, dedicated to ending colonial control and occupation and committed to achieving national independence. The modern political culture of many countries of this region is still rooted in these movements, often in the form of parties and groups founded in the colonial era that continue to play a role in politics today, like Istiqlal in Morocco, the Republican People's Party in Turkey, the Front de Libération Nationale (FLN) in Algeria, the Néo-Destour in Tunisia, the Wafd in Egypt, and the Ba'th in Syria and Iraq. Today the conservative, ossified, and often decadent descendants of radical movements that long ago struggled for their countries' independence may be unrecognizable in terms of anything other than their names. However, their survival indicates a degree of continuity with the anticolonial past, and an enduring commitment to independence and resistance to foreign control.

Westerners make a serious mistake in thinking that these events are buried in the distant past and thus are long forgotten by the younger generations that now dominate Middle Eastern societies. Leaving aside the fact that any citizen over fifty years old, including the majority of Middle Eastern elites, can recall vividly the waning days of the colonial era, the history of the struggle for liberation from foreign rule has for decades been amply conveyed to several generations of children by the national educational systems in Middle Eastern countries. National holidays, statues, postage stamps, museums, street names, and memorial commemorations reinforce these lessons, cultural markers of societies that are extremely attentive to history, highly politicized, and in large measure literate. Thus while Americans may have short memories (who, in Washington, D.C., recalled Lafayette and Rochambeau, French heroes of the American Revolution, during the frenzied denouncements of French "ingratitude" in early 2003 provoked by France's opposition to war in Iraq?), Iraqis, Turks, Egyptians, Iranians, and other Middle Easterners have extremely long ones. In consequence, the memory of resistance to foreign intervention and occupation is still very much alive among them.[53] Many of the older ones among them also retain memories of the day when most Middle Eastern countries lived under constitutional, parliamentary, and democratic systems, albeit flawed systems, fatally crippled by foreign intervention and occupation, that existed all too briefly. And along with these memories are recollections of what happened to most of these hopeful experiments in democracy, and of the role played by the Western powers in their demise.

THE UNITED STATES IN
MIDDLE EASTERN EYES

Notwithstanding the friction and conflict that are generally associated with interactions between Americans and Middle Easterners, until relatively recently the relationship between the United States and the Middle East was pacific and mutually satisfactory. From the nineteenth century until at least the middle of the twentieth, the United States was in fact viewed quite positively in the Middle East as a non- or anti-colonial power, as having no imperialistic designs on the region, and as engaged primarily in benevolent activities there such as education and health care. Beyond this, the United States was often seen as a beacon of hope for those aspiring to democracy and freedom from foreign control.

Unlike Britain and France, liberal, democratic powers at home that were hated, illiberal colonizers in the Middle East, and unlike the autocratic, imperialist, expansionist empires of Austria-Hungary and Russia, the United States had never tried to impose its will on the peoples of the region, or to occupy or colonize them. In keeping with the admonitions of the founding fathers to avoid "entangling alliances" and to beware the dangers to the republic at home of adventures with empire abroad,[54] American leaders long eschewed involvement in the imperialistic machinations of the European powers in this and other parts of the globe. The main exception was Latin America, where the Monroe Doctrine (the force of which came largely from the power of Great Britain, vigorously wielded by the liberal foreign secretary George Canning[55]) kept the monarchical European powers out, but also gave the United States a privileged position in the western hemisphere that it exploited to its great benefit.

Where the United States was involved in the Middle East, it was via the work of Protestant missionaries, who established churches, schools, and hospitals. This effort aroused surprisingly little local antagonism, since the missionaries quickly learned to confine their proselytizing to local Orthodox and Catholic Christians and to Jews, rather than targeting members of the Muslim majority, who were generally unresponsive to conversion. Such an effort, moreover, would have been strongly opposed by local governments, while apostasy from

Islam was strictly forbidden by Islamic law, on pain of death. Within decades of the start of this work, focused primarily on the countries that today comprise Turkey, Egypt, Lebanon, Syria, and Palestine/Israel, there was an extensive network of American missionary schools and other institutions. These came to be the nuclei of three of the region's best universities today, the American University of Beirut, the American University in Cairo, and Bogaziçi University in Istanbul. By early in the twentieth century, many members of the region's elite, Muslims and Jews as well as Christians, were eagerly sending their children to these and other American-run institutions.

During World War I, President Wilson's enunciation of his Fourteen Points in January 1918 briefly signaled a more activist American global policy, and inspired hope in peoples the world over seeking to escape from oppressive European colonial rule. In the Middle East, the president's pronouncement was understood as meaning that World War I was being fought in order to help the peoples achieve self-determination. It was heralded as welcome support from a new great power that had never entertained designs on the region and might counterbalance the overwhelming weight of Britain and France and their imperialist ambitions. This was especially welcome coming after the new Bolshevik regime in Russia in December 1917 published the czarist government's secret treaties, revealing among other things the agreements between Britain, France, and Russia to partition the Middle East among them. Known as the Sykes-Picot accords, the agreements eventually became the basis for the postwar division of the region into colonial spheres of influence between Britain and France. This revelation shocked the people of the region and represented the confirmation of their worst fears about the objectives of the two major Western powers.

People in the Middle East could not have known at the

time that in fact Wilson and his advisors were mainly thinking of the peoples of Europe when they talked about World War I as aimed at self-determination of the peoples.[56] Nor could they possibly know that the United States would prove unable to stand up to the machinations of the British and French leaders, Lloyd George and Clemenceau, at the Versailles peace conference; that President Wilson would soon be incapacitated; and that his global policies would be repudiated by the United States Senate and the American electorate. So eager were they to call on the "new world . . . to redress the balance of the old," to paraphrase Canning's famous phrase about the Monroe Doctrine,[57] that in 1919 large majorities of those asked in Syria, Palestine, and Lebanon told an American commission of inquiry, the King-Crane Commission, that they preferred the United States as a mandatory power to any other in helping them in their transition to independence.[58] In the end, these countries, as well as Iraq and Jordan, received Britain and France as mandatories. The two old imperialist powers, with extensive interests and long-standing expansionist ambitions in the Middle East,[59] of course did all in their power to turn the new mandate system established by the League of Nations into a modified version of the old colonial system.

The United States' return to isolation did not harm its standing in the Middle East in the interwar period, when its prestige remained high. Even what thereafter became the momentous involvement of the United States in Saudi Arabia, which began with the 1933 agreements on oil exploration between U.S. companies and the regime of 'Abd al-'Aziz ibn Sa'ud, founder of the kingdom,[60] was initially seen by many in the Middle East in a positive light. It enabled the Saudi regime to decrease its stifling dependence on what had previously been its sole external patron, Great Britain, the power that was correctly perceived by most, inside the Middle East and outside it, as bestriding the region like an imperial colossus. American support of one of the only two quasi-independent Arab countries not subject to European occupation was thus seen as helpful in much of the region.

The entry of the United States into World War II in 1941, which led to a major military campaign in North Africa and the establishment of bases in several parts of the Middle East, was also generally viewed favorably by people across the region. The arrival of a "new" great power with an anticolonialist tradition, and which although allied to Britain and France did not appear to share their imperialist ambitions, was welcomed by many.[61] When the United States rapidly withdrew its forces from most Middle Eastern countries after the war, and helped to force Britain and Soviet Russia to withdraw theirs from Iran, these positive impressions were reinforced. For many years after World War II the United States continued to be seen by people in the Middle East as a potential ally against the old colonial powers, and indeed played such a role in Libya in 1950–51, and during the Suez War of 1956 and the Algerian War of Liberation from France in 1954–62.

But the Middle East's honeymoon with the United States was already coming to an end by this time. Among the crucial factors leading to disillusionment was the struggle over the partition of Palestine in 1947–48, during which the United States championed the founding of the new Jewish state, becoming the first country to recognize it. This was only the beginning of what would be a growing disenchantment with a United States that was assiduous in asserting the rights of Israel, and rarely, if ever, exerted itself on behalf of those of the Palestinians. Equally unpopular was the American drive in the early phases of the Cold War to establish new Western bases (or retain and use for new purposes old British and French bases) in the Middle East as part of the global effort to contain the Soviet Union. What amounted to indirect American support for British efforts to retain Britain's dominant position in the region and its bases in Egypt and Iraq through various U.S.-backed schemes (such as the Middle East Command, the Middle East Defense Organization, and the Baghdad Pact), whose ostensible purpose was opposing Soviet expansion, came to be regarded with deep suspicion by Middle Eastern nationalists.[62] These negative reactions were intensified by Anglo-American connivance in the overthrow of the democratically elected government of Mohammad Mosaddeq in Iran in 1953, and the reimposition of the autocratic rule of the shah.[63]

As a result of these and many other episodes, and as its power in the world and in the Middle East expanded during and after the Cold War, in the eyes of many in the region the United States has gradually changed over the past few decades. It went from being considered a benevolent, disinterested outsider to something quite different: a power with a massive presence in the Middle East, a broad range of interests there, and objectives not always compatible with those of the people of the region. The gap in perceptions is wide on this score: Americans still tend to regard their country as benevolent and disinterested, as acting in the world only for the highest purposes or in self-defense. While most Middle Easterners for the first century and a half of American involvement with their region shared this view, they do so no longer. It is in the context of this wide divergence between the two sides that the post–9/11 American interventions have taken place, with many Americans seeing not only the invasion of Afghanistan but also the much more fraught invasion of Iraq in these high-minded terms, and people in the region generally taking quite a different view.

Blind to the history that has been sketched out here, and ignorant of the culture and politics of the Middle East, in Iraq America's leaders took their country on a perilous adventure among people whose recorded history stretches back longer than any others on earth, and whose memories are very long as well. It may turn out that this adventure will end by doing only a relatively limited amount of damage in Iraq and the Middle East, and to the international system. Today this seems increasingly unlikely, and even at the outset the prospects looked dim to most of those who had any deep knowledge of the region. But "bringing" democracy and the rule of law to a land that has long suffered from the tyranny of the Ba'th regime, but that produced Hammurabi's Code nearly four millennia ago, will be a daunting enterprise. This is not to speak of the alarming degree of arrogance involved in the endeavor. And it will be even more daunting to rule, directly or indirectly, over the people of this complex and heterogeneous country, which the United States alone will be fully and totally responsible for in every respect, from law and order to sanitation, until a sovereign Iraqi government eventually reemerges.

Some of those in the War Party surrounding President Bush, Cheney, and Rumsfeld have been advocating this perilous adventure in Iraq for a long time, and their allies in the media and the think tanks have not hesitated to bandy about words like *empire* to describe what they are launching.[64] The hubris involved is not unprecedented (even if the global reach and power of the United States is): in 1917 General Maude marched into Baghdad and General Edmund Allenby into Jerusalem, and in 1920 General Henri Gouraud entered Damascus, each animated by the same high, global ambitions as are now held by the clique around the president. Of course, many will continue to deny that history repeats itself. But history, starting with Thucydides, teaches us that those who believe themselves to be special, different, and touched by providence, and who ignore history's lessons, may be cruelly surprised by the turn of events.

CHAPTER TWO

AMERICA, THE WEST, AND DEMOCRACY IN THE MIDDLE EAST

Oh ye Egyptians, they may say to you that I have not made an expedition hither for any other object than that of abolishing your religion ... but tell the slanderers that I have not come to you except for the purpose of restoring your rights from the hands of the oppressors. —NAPOLEON BONAPARTE, ALEXANDRIA, JULY 2, 1798

Our armies do not come into your cities and lands as conquerors or enemies, but as liberators. ... It is the hope and desire of the British people and the nations in alliance with them that the Arab race may rise once more to greatness and renown among the peoples of the earth. —GENERAL F. S. MAUDE, COMMANDER OF BRITISH FORCES, BAGHDAD, MARCH 19, 1917

Unlike many armies in the world, you came not to conquer, not to occupy, but to liberate, and the Iraqi people know this. —DONALD RUMSFELD, U.S. SECRETARY OF DEFENSE, BAGHDAD, APRIL 29, 2003

Self-sufficient and secure on the continent—and in the hemisphere—that they have confidently dominated for nearly two centuries, Americans have often looked on the world beyond the seas with some suspicion. Many of their ancestors had left the Old World for good reasons. It was the site of old politics, old values, and old approaches that the New World was thought to have superseded. In consequence of these lingering misgivings about the rest of the world, it has generally required an extraordinary effort, and the call of a noble cause, to persuade Americans that their country should engage in adventures across the seas. This was why embarking on such engagements generally required American presidents to make resounding pronouncements, such as the Monroe Doctrine, the Fourteen Points, the Four Freedoms, and the Truman and Eisenhower Doctrines.[1]

As the administration of George W. Bush tried to answer the objections of its critics to the shifting pretexts it advanced for the radical step of an unprovoked, preemptive war against Iraq, it increasingly turned to the "liberation" and "democratization" of that country as a war aim. In spite of the unprecedented sense of insecurity in the United States resulting from 9/11,[2] even the administration's exaggerated descriptions of the lurid dangers of Iraqi weapons of mass destruction (which later appeared to have existed primarily in the imaginations of those doing the describing) did not succeed in winning over the American people in sufficient numbers to bring them to support the war unreservedly. The Bush team thus invoked the necessity of removing an Iraqi Ba'th regime guilty of abysmal human rights violations against its own people, in order to provide a reason high-minded enough for the United States to launch a war against Iraq. But even simple "regime change" was apparently not enough: presumably only turning Iraq into a functioning democracy would be a goal worthy of American ideals.

THE UNITED STATES' AMBIGUOUS RECORD
IN PROMOTING DEMOCRACY
IN THE MIDDLE EAST

In a February 26, 2003, speech at the American Enterprise Institute (AEI), nest of some of Washington's most outspoken hawks, President Bush made the ambitious plan of democratization his own, outlining a broad agenda whereby Iraq would be only the first step in the transformation of an entire region: "The nation of Iraq ... is fully capable of moving towards democracy and living in freedom.... A new regime in Iraq would serve as a dramatic and inspiring example of freedom for other nations in the region.... Success in Iraq could also begin a new stage for Middle Eastern peace, and set in motion progress towards a truly democratic Palestinian state."[3] With this speech, the president fully endorsed a significant expansion of the original justification for the war. He thereby implicitly embraced a whole set of neoconservative doctrines regarding the Middle East and America's role in the world. He also separated himself from those the world over who might have accepted concerted, forceful international action to deal with Iraqi nonconventional weapons, if they were proven to exist, but who would not embrace America's unilateral redrawing of the map of the Middle East on the pretext that it was intended to bring democracy to Iraq.

Leaving aside for the moment the highly problematic idea of any country actively "democratizing" another, with all the hubris and the arrogance that implies, any serious understanding of democracy would posit that it involves a lengthy organic process of societal, legal, and political development that cannot be short-circuited or imposed. The tortuous process of the emergence of democracy in two of the most economically, socially, and politically advanced countries in Europe and Asia, Germany and Japan, in the eighty to one hundred years before American troops arrived on their soil after World War II, should be a warning against simplistic ideas about American military occupations democratizing other countries.[4] There is also the deeper question of whether there was any real substance or meaning to the slogan of "democratization" that was freely bandied about by those who beat the drums for an invasion of Iraq, given that some of them had evidently adopted it opportunistically.[5] Many of those who had so ardently preached the virtues of democracy in Iraq had never before been known for their concern either for the Iraqis or for democracy in the Arab Middle East.[6]

It is important to recognize that *if* carried out fully and consistently, a policy encouraging progress in the direction of democracy and respect for human rights would, in fact, be in stark contrast with American Middle East involvement in recent decades. As the second Bush administration made its preparations for war with Iraq, there were a few other straws in the wind consonant with its proclaimed change of policy in the Middle East in favor of democracy and human rights. These included the freezing of U.S. aid to Egypt in response to its government's jailing of Sa'ad al-Din Ibrahim, an Egyptian-American academic and critic of Hosni Mubarak's regime, who was later released, and President Bush's demand for reform and democratization of the Palestinian Authority in his June 2002 policy speech on the Middle East. In both cases, though, doubts were raised as to the consistency, the effectiveness, and the real objectives of these new departures in American policy.[7]

To make such a shift toward the encouragement of democracy, and make it consistently, a great deal would have to be changed. Such an approach would not least of all represent a departure in terms of American policy toward Iraq. Starting in the late 1950s, this policy ranged from covert sympathy for the Iraqi Ba'th Party to wholehearted backing for dictatorial Ba'thist regimes at various times from the 1960s through 1990. There were shifts in this policy. At one point, the United States aligned itself more closely with Iran and against Iraq, and then without an apparent qualm abandoned Kurdish rebels it had been financing against the Iraqi central government at Iranian instigation, when the Kurds' primary backer, the shah of Iran, cut a deal with Saddam Hussein in March 1975 at their expense.[8] The Islamic revolution in Iran thereafter ushered in another reversal in American policy, and a honeymoon period of support for Saddam Hussein and his regime that lasted for over a decade—from at least 1980 until the Iraqi invasion of Kuwait in 1990. Some of the details of this tortuous history are worth recounting, if only to appreciate the incongruousness of the Bush administration's statements about the tyranny of the Ba'th Party and its abuses against the Kurds.

At the outset, at least, some of these tergiversations can be understood in terms of long-standing Cold War–driven obsessions of American policy-makers in the Middle East and elsewhere. In the wake of the Iraqi revolution of 1958, the Iraqi Ba'th Party became perhaps the most ferocious opponent of the regime dominated at the outset by a triad—the Iraqi ruler Brigadier General Abdul Karim Kassem, the Iraqi Communist Party, and Arab nationalists who supported United Arab Republic president Gamal Abdel Nasser—that at the time constituted Washington's primary bête noire in the Middle East. In spite of the unsavory nature of the Ba'th Party, U.S. policy-makers therefore adopted it as one of their key tools of influence in Iraq starting in the early 1960s. Even before then, American diplomats had chosen not to warn the Kassem regime of preparations they had learned of in 1958 and 1959 for Ba'thist antigovernment coups, which in the event proved abortive.[9] According to testimony and documents produced during hearings of the Congressional Select Committee on Intelligence headed by the New York Democrat Otis G. Pike held in 1975, the young Saddam Hussein was "among party members colluding with the CIA in 1962 and 1963." The United States thereafter actively supported the Ba'th Party's successful coup of 1963, which led to a slaughter of Iraqi Communist Party members using lists produced by American intelligence sources. The Ba'th then lost power to pro-Nasser Arab nationalists, only to return to power in another American-backed coup d'état in 1968.[10]

There was a hiatus in the American-Iraqi relationship during the 1970s, when the United States aligned itself closely with the shah of Iran in opposing Iraq, whose Ba'thist regime had moved closer to the Soviet Union by signing a Treaty of Friendship and Cooperation in 1972. It was at this time that the United States acceded to the request of the shah and bankrolled a Kurdish rebellion against Baghdad. The shah thereupon cruelly betrayed the Kurds in 1975 when he came to advantageous terms with Saddam Hussein, a betrayal that led to the death of thousands of Kurds.[11] Unaffected by matters like the fate of the Kurds, the American–Iraqi Ba'th relationship warmed in the following decade. This was in large part a consequence of the revolution in Iran, which removed the shah, an American ally on whom Henry Kissinger and Presidents Nixon and Ford had relied heavily to sustain American influence in the region, and brought to power an Islamic regime implacably hostile to the United States.[12] The policy adopted by the Reagan administration and the first Bush administration consisted of directly and indirectly supporting the Iraqi Ba'th regime against the new government of Iran, including backing for the war launched by Saddam Hussein against his Iranian neighbors in 1980. Although this support was generally known at the time, its full extent has now been systematically revealed by probing investigative reporting relying on dozens of declassified government documents from this period.[13]

The Reagan administration's assistance to the eight-year Iraqi war effort was extensive and wide-ranging. It included the provision to the Iraqis of satellite-derived intelligence about Iranian military dispositions, the provision to Iraq by American and European companies of the wherewithal to produce chemical weapons, as well as shipments of military equipment by American companies and by U.S. allies such as

South Korea, the sale to Iraq of American dual-use equipment for the Iraqi nuclear program, and U.S. diplomatic support in the U.N. Security Council to protect Iraq from condemnation for its use of poison gas against Iran.[14] Other sources indicate that the CIA delivered battlefield intelligence to Iraq from AWACS surveillance aircraft, and that the CIA and the Defense Intelligence Agency gave crucial assistance to a major Iraqi offensive on the Al Fāw Peninsula "by blinding Iranian radars for three days."[15]

The United States' close relations, for lengthy periods over several decades, with a regime dominated by a party, the Ba'th, and a leader, Saddam Hussein, that were later reviled by the administration of George W. Bush (and its predecessor), can be explained in the context of a broad, long-standing American approach to the Middle East. This approach has generally been based on studiously ignoring the human rights abuses and/or the undemocratic systems of governments from which the United States stood to benefit in one way or another—a cold, amoral, and cynical policy that won the United States few friends in the Middle East and is part of the baggage America has carried as it has become deeply involved in Iraq. As then–secretary of state Kissinger is reliably said to have declared when an aide protested American abandonment of Iran and the United States' erstwhile protégés, the Kurds, after Saddam Hussein had come to terms with the shah of Iran in 1975: "Covert action should not be confused with missionary work."[16]

There have been a number of lonely voices in the human rights community and among Middle East specialists who have long criticized the human rights abuses and antidemocratic actions of Middle Eastern governments, especially those, such as Saudi Arabia, Egypt, Turkey, and Israel, closely aligned with the United States. Regimes in Saudi Arabia and Egypt have, to differing degrees, at different times, tortured political prisoners, denied their peoples democratic rights, and muzzled the press, unions, and the political opposition. Turkey, which although it now can boast a robust democracy, in the past not only used its army to repress an armed Kurdish rebellion, committing widespread human rights violations in the process, but denied peaceful Kurdish demands for cultural and linguistic rights. Israel, a democracy for its own citizens, is now in the thirty-seventh year of a military occupation of the West Bank and Gaza Strip that has been replete with human rights violations and represents the negation of the democratic right of self-determination for the Palestinians living in those territories.

Before the president's sudden embrace of democracy in the Middle East, the actions of these and other closely allied countries rarely provoked the ire of the Bush administration, or indeed of earlier American administrations. For those who have regularly criticized abuses by these and other governments, a change in American policy to across-the-board support for democracy and human rights—if it were lasting and consistent throughout the region, rather than selective— would be most welcome. It would thus be considerably more encouraging if the same music about human rights and democracy were played in Washington regarding not only traditional whipping boys like Syria and Libya, with their harshly repressive authoritarian regimes, but also close allies like the four mentioned above, where the United States has major strategic and/or energy interests. The U.S. government has been conspicuously silent about the often-serious human rights abuses in these countries, as well as others friendly to U.S. interests, like Morocco, Algeria, Tunisia, Jordan, and the smaller Arab states in the Gulf.

If spreading democracy in the Middle East were to become

a consistent, long-term U.S. objective, as the Bush administration's rhetoric seemed to indicate, that would certainly be a good thing (although it would depend to some extent on the means employed to achieve this objective). It would be especially good if this policy were consistent and lasting, and came to include respect for elected leaders and governments, such as those of Iran, Lebanon, and the Palestinian Authority, even if they operate in deeply flawed systems that are highly imperfect and less than fully democratic, and more to the point, even if they say and do things that may be disagreeable to U.S. policymakers. One is sometimes impelled by the behavior of leading members of the Bush administration to wonder whether by the term *democratic* what they really mean is "doing what we want."

It was particularly instructive in this regard to observe the behavior of senior administration advocates of "democratizing" Iraq during the lead-up to the war as they tried to oblige various democratic states whose peoples and governments were strongly against the war to go along with the United States. Most notably, they attempted to impel the government of Turkey, which had won an overwhelming mandate in a recent election, to go against the clear wishes of the great majority of the country's citizens and allow Turkish territory to be used for the war on Iraq: polls showed that by February 2003, 96 percent of Turks opposed a war against Iraq, up from 80 percent in January.[17] The pique of official Washington (one "administration official" fulminated that "the Turks seem to think we'll keep the bazaar open all night") when Turkish leaders dragged their feet in acceding to U.S. demands, was, to say the least, unseemly. It indicated how shallow the democratic inclinations of leaders of the American administration were when they did not get their way.[18]

While it may be surprising to some, the overall American

record in the area of the promotion of democracy and human rights in the Middle East has in fact been a poor one since the United States became a major power there after World War II. It was certainly not the only great power of which it can be said that democracy and human rights in the Middle East were not a high priority in their policy. Beyond the former colonial rulers' appalling record in this regard, some of the most egregious violations of human rights and the most grotesque perversions of the popular will that have marred post–World War II Middle Eastern history took place in countries that were wholly or partly Soviet protégés from the 1960s through 1990, notably Iraq, Syria, and Libya. The behavior of other regimes aligned with the Soviets for part of this period, such as those of Egypt, the Sudan, Algeria, and North and South Yemen, was frequently hardly better. Nevertheless, as already noted, while in some cases it may have been marginally better, there is little to boast about in the human rights record of regimes aligned with and supported by the United States during the Cold War, including Saudi Arabia, Jordan, Morocco, Tunisia, Turkey, Iran under the shah, Egypt under Anwar Sadat and Mubarak, and Israel in the occupied territories.

Even after the decline of the Cold War rivalry and the collapse of the Soviet Union, which left the United States as the undisputed great power in the Middle East and everywhere else, and which removed the pretext that the United States was too busy fighting communism to support democracy (odd as that pretext might sound), things improved very little. American policy-makers rarely if ever allowed the lack of democracy or the prevalence of human rights abuses to serve as obstacles to relations with friendly governments. Thus, a change by the Bush administration in what has generally been a fairly consistent approach for over half a century, of seeking strategic and material advantage irrespective of the unrepresentative or repressive nature of a given regime, would certainly be a thoroughly new and wholly welcome departure for American Middle East policy.

But several dauntingly difficult issues are raised by such a departure, laudable though it may initially appear. The first is that the United States would be expected to accept the full consequences of dealing in a sensitive, respectful, consistent manner with democratically elected governments, even if they do not do its bidding. Perhaps the best historical example of the problems posed by such an approach is that of France under Charles de Gaulle. When the French president realized that American forces in France under the NATO umbrella were carrying out operations on French territory without the cognizance or consent of the French government, he immediately asked for their removal and was broadly supported in this move by the French people. Of course, France was a major European power and is a long-standing democracy and ally (indeed, the first ally of the fledgling American republic), and the United States immediately, albeit unwillingly, accepted the verdict of the leaders of the French Fifth Republic. Over forty years later, U.S. forces are still not based in France, which nevertheless remains a NATO ally, although the profound divergences over Iraq between the Bush administration and President Jacques Chirac have seriously strained the alliance.

In the current context, this raises some important questions. What if, for example, Saudi Arabia were to become a democracy—perhaps not an immediate prospect, and a seemingly unlikely one, but by no means an impossibility—and what if a democratically elected government were to ask the United States to do something it was unwilling to do? Until recently, the idea of the United States removing its military forces and bases from that country was unacceptable to Washington, although according to most accounts, the U.S. military presence in the kingdom has been unpopular among a broad stratum of the population.[19] In recognition of this fact, the United States has finally moved the forces it stationed in Saudi Arabia after the 1990 Iraqi invasion of Kuwait out of the kingdom, some of them to neighboring Kuwait, Qatar, Bahrain, and Oman.[20] Would Washington take other similar actions it currently deems unacceptable, if a democratic Arabian government (it might no longer be *Saudi* Arabian, or a kingdom, in such a circumstance) were to make such a request?

What if elected democratic governments in Kuwait, Bahrain, and Qatar (all countries that, although they are run by oligarchies, have held elections of some sort recently; indeed, Kuwait has had a parliament, with interruptions, since it became independent in 1960, and has a vigorous, largely free, press) were to follow suit? These are not idle questions, especially now that the collapse of Saddam Hussein's regime in Iraq has removed one of the most frequently invoked pretexts for the presence of U.S. forces in the Middle East.[21] Moreover, these are small countries, with tiny populations, whose citizens are in some cases outnumbered by the foreigners among them; they are concerned about their domestic and internal security in a region dominated by several larger regional powers and highly susceptible to the influence of a superpower like the United States. Would democratic regimes in these countries dare to ask for the removal of U.S. forces, even if public opinion in these states were to demand it? Given the desire of the Pentagon to maintain military bases in the Middle East, the likely answer should such a request come from the Arab Gulf states does not seem very encouraging, nor does the example set in the case of France seem likely to be followed. And judging by the words of James Woolsey, a former CIA director close to the administration (who was briefly considered to head the Iraqi Information Ministry in the Coalition Provisional Authority established by the American occupation[22]), democracy may not be the outcome even in Iraq. "Only fear will reestablish respect for the U.S.," Woolsey told the *Washington Post*, adding ominously that if parties hostile to the United States were to win an election tomorrow, "Well, then perhaps the election should be the day after tomorrow."[23]

THE TRUE VISION BEHIND THE BUSH ADMINISTRATION'S MIDDLE EAST POLICY

To understand why a thirst to see democracy thrive is not really what motivates the Bush administration in the Middle East, one must examine carefully the approaches that have persistently been advocated by a group of neoconservative policy intellectuals who, especially in the two years after 9/11, came to dominate much of the strategic (and to some extent the media) discourse in Washington, and who tightly surrounded the president, Vice President Cheney, and Secretary of Defense Rumsfeld. Members of this influential group have expressed their views in a variety of media for several years, supported by a brace of ultraconservative think tanks in Washington, D.C., notably the AEI, and other ideological supporters of their agenda. These include the Fox television network, owned by Australian mogul Rupert Murdoch, who has placed his ratings-leading news division in the hands of former Republican Party strategist Roger Ailes.[24] Some of the most notable neocon policy intellectuals are associated with the AEI, while the Project for the New American Century (located on the fifth floor of the AEI) and the *Weekly Standard*, edited by William Kristol, are also headquartered at AEI.[25] Their agenda for American Middle East policy is perhaps most clearly apparent from a 1996 report produced for the newly elected right-wing Israeli prime minister Benyamin Netanyahu by a study group sponsored by an Israeli think tank, the Institute for Advanced Strategic and Political Studies.[26]

The chief author of the report was Richard Perle, who was

forced to step down in March 2003 from his influential post as chair of the Pentagon's Defense Policy Board (though Secretary Rumsfeld asked him to stay on as a member of the board). Perle has long been the chief guru among the neocon war hawks.[27] Among Perle's most important allies are Paul Wolfowitz, deputy secretary of defense, and Douglas Feith, undersecretary of defense for policy, the number two and three officials at the Pentagon, and I. Lewis Libby, chief of staff to Vice President Cheney. Besides Perle, the study group included Feith, and David Wurmser, who served as special assistant to John Bolton, the hard-right-wing undersecretary of state for arms control and international security, and then as Cheney's national security advisor for the Middle East,[28] together with other influential figures in the neocon constellation.

The advice these hard-liners gave to the hawkish Netanyahu was robust and muscled, and much of it has since been mirrored in the policies of Ariel Sharon, Netanyahu's successor as head of the Likud Party: abandon the peace process with the Palestinians (the term *peace process* was placed in quotes throughout the report); adopt the right of "hot pursuit" against the Palestinians; "roll back" threats; abandon the principle of "land for peace" in favor of "peace for peace"; and adopt the policy of "peace through strength." Most relevant to the Middle East policies of the United States were the report's recommendations regarding Iraq, Syria, and Iran that its authors and their likeminded associates later championed in their official positions in Washington.

The report counsels Israel to seize the strategic initiative, by engaging Syria, the Lebanese militant group Hezbollah, and Iran via military strikes at Hezbollah and Syrian forces in Lebanon, and if necessary "*striking at select targets in Syria proper*" (italics in original). Further, the report advised "weakening, containing, and even rolling back Syria." This core objective was to be achieved primarily by "removing Saddam

Hussein from power in Iraq," which they stated was "an important Israeli strategic objective in its own right." Here, five years before 9/11 and seven years before the launching of the U.S. war on Iraq, was the kernel of the Iraq strategy that key neocons had been advocating for well over a decade.

Jordan was cited as a vital tool in this process, to be employed by Israel against its enemies in various ways. Insofar as the crucial policy of regime change in Iraq was concerned, this included the placing of a member of the Hashemite royal family that rules Jordan, and before 1958 ruled Iraq, back on the Iraqi throne. In a masterful piece of Orwellian double-speak, the authors advise Netanyahu to state (the report, meant to be used by Netanyahu to drum up support for his policies, is replete with "key passages of a possible speech" in boldface) that "Israel will not only contain its foes; it will transcend them," leaving to the listeners' imagination precisely what otherworldly processes this would entail.

Much about this extraordinary document is worthy of comment, not least of all the ignorance of the history, politics, societies, and religions of the Middle East that pervades it. The lack of basic knowledge about the Middle East exhibited in the report goes beyond misspellings of names and places to its core recommendations. Thus Perle, Feith, Wurmser, and others, part of a group that often seems to have virtually exclusive access to the top decision-makers in the Bush administration,[29] make the suggestion in this report that putting a member of the Hashemite royal family back in control of Iraq would wean Shi'ites in Lebanon and Iraq away from Hezbollah and Iran. This master stroke is possible, the report claims, since "Shia retain strong ties to the Hashemites: the Shia venerate foremost the Prophet's family, the direct descendants of which—and in whose veins the blood of the Prophet flows—is [sic] King Hussein [who was still alive in 1996, when the report was written]."

Perle and his colleagues were here proposing the complete restructuring of a region whose history their suggestions reveal they know very little about. As beginning students of Middle East history would know, the Shi'ites were known as *"shi'at 'Ali"* or the party of 'Ali ibn Abi Talib, the Prophet Muhammad's cousin and son-in-law, and the loyalty of Shi'ites has as a rule been to one specific lineage of the descendants of 'Ali, rather than to all who claim descent from him. The Shi'ites do not venerate other lineages, such as the 'Abbassids or the Hashemites. The latter, while they claim to be related to the Prophet Muhammad through Hashim, Muhammad's great-grandfather, are Sunnis, and as such are often regarded with suspicion by religious Shi'ites. Moreover, the ill will between many Iraqi Shi'ites and the Sunni Hashemite monarchy from its imposition by the British in 1920 until its overthrow in 1958 is well attested.

These are among many basic facts about the Islamic world and the Middle East that are well known to experts and even to those not so expert, but which these "prominent opinion makers," as they describe themselves in the introduction to the report, seem to have missed altogether. They appear to have learned nothing in the interim. Virtually all of the thinking that underlay the planning for the Iraq war by these same individuals and their colleagues—the ideas that all Iraqis would welcome their liberators with open arms, that Iraqi exiles were ready to take over the governance of the country, that order could be maintained in Iraq after the war with a thinly stretched and undermanned contingent of U.S. troops, and that serious preparation for the U.S. occupation of Iraq was not necessary—was blighted by the same enthusiastic ignorance and ideological blindness. To this was added a naive dependence on unreliable sources such as Iraqi dissidents who were happy to reinforce these zealots' preexisting prejudices. For though the Iraqi regime did collapse suddenly after three weeks of lopsided fighting, the initial Iraqi resistance surprised all those who had believed the neocon analysis. Moreover, many months thereafter, the sullen anger of much of the population toward the American occupation, the continuing guerrilla raids on U.S. troops, and the terror attacks against the U.N., the Red Cross, Shi'ite leaders, and other soft targets, showed that the prewar neocon view of Iraq was ill-informed and simplistic at best.

Equally noteworthy in the 1996 report is the perception of a complete identity of Israeli and American interests in the Middle East. It stresses the importance of "a *shared philosophy* of peace through strength," "continuity with Western values," and Israel cooperating "with the U.S. to counter real threats to the region and the West's security." It advises Netanyahu to use language "familiar to the Americans by tapping into themes of American administrations during the Cold War which apply well to Israel." In what sounds eerily like a post-9/11 clarion call, although it was written five years before that event, the report says a "clean break with the past" can be achieved by "reestablishing the principle of preemption, rather than retaliation alone and by ceasing to absorb blows to the nation without response." The similarity of tone between these recommendations and the Bush administration's global strategy is obvious. What should also be obvious is that these prescriptions constitute the template for current American strategy toward the Middle East generally and Iraq in particular, and for a new form of American hegemony over the region, in collaboration with Israel.[30]

This hegemonic vision would almost certainly not be compatible with the freely expressed wishes of the peoples of any new Middle Eastern democracies, since their wishes are likely to include the removal of the many American military bases established with the consent of the Middle East's various nondemocratic oligarchs, autocrats, and dictators. Similarly, they are not likely to welcome domination of the region by Israel acting as a junior partner of the United States. Of course such a response runs directly contrary to the vision of these neocon intellectuals, who speak freely of establishing a long-lasting military presence not only in the fifteen countries in the Middle East and Central Asia where U.S. forces are currently based, but also elsewhere. This raises the rarely asked question of whether American bases in countries where they are not wanted by the population increase or decrease the security of the United States and the American people in the long run, and whether they serve to prevent terrorism or in fact to foster it.

If this question were asked seriously, something exceedingly difficult to do in the atmosphere of Washington, D.C., before and during the invasion of Iraq, and not easy to do even today, it would have revolutionary implications for American strategy and security. I have already argued that there is clearly a profound contradiction between the apparent advocacy of democracy and human rights by the hard-liners around Bush, Cheney, and Rumsfeld, and their long-standing desire to expand both the American military profile in, and America's control over, this part of the world. The underside of their rhetoric about human rights and democracy is a clear volition to change the regimes of several key countries in the Middle East. They thereby intend to refashion the alignment, and indeed the very nature, of the Middle East as it is presently structured. Given the condescension shown by many of these individuals toward the peoples of this region,[31] it is difficult to believe in their protestations that they are motivated by pure, disinterested concern for the democratic and human rights of Arabs and Muslims: the 1996 report cited above never mentions the word *democracy,* and refers to the advancement of "human rights among Arabs" solely as a cynical and opportunistic tactic to isolate and undermine the PLO. Indeed, judging from this report, cynicism, opportunism, and a certain callousness,[32] often combined with breathtaking ignorance, are characteristic of the neocon establishment.

There is little doubt, and indeed ample evidence, that majorities of the people in many Middle Eastern countries thoroughly loathe their governments and would be happy to see them replaced by constitutional democracies that respect human rights. Nevertheless, there is every reason, buttressed by the on-the-spot reportage from the Arab world before, during, and in the aftermath of the Iraq war, to question whether these peoples are eager for that replacement process to be managed by outsiders,[33] or accomplished by massive force and at a high cost in innocent life. In the words of an Iraqi physician treating civilian casualties in Baghdad, "Why all this blood? They came to free us? This is freedom?"[34] And as the history of these countries indicates clearly, there would be strong opposition if that process led to a long-lasting American military occupation of, or even a long-lasting American military presence in and control over, major Arab and Middle Eastern states, as appears to be projected in Iraq. Such an idea would be galling to any country with Iraq's size and regional weight, its glorious history of civilization going back six or seven millennia, and its rapid technical, social, and educational advances before the folly of its Ba'thist regime dragged it into a series of ruinous wars.

HAS EXTERNAL INTERVENTION FOSTERED DEMOCRACY IN THE MIDDLE EAST?

There are solid historical and political reasons for suggesting that war, external intervention, and foreign occupation are far from being ideal recipes for the introduction of democracy in the Middle East. Indeed, there is evidence that such actions retarded the democratic process during the first half of the twentieth century in a number of Arab countries, as well as Turkey and Iran. It is worth once again recalling that both Iran and the Ottoman Empire (which encompassed most of the Eastern Arab countries until 1918) had constitutional revolutions in 1906 and 1908, respectively—the Ottomans in fact adopted a constitution as early as 1876, although two years afterward the autocratic sultan Abdülhamid II suspended it for thirty years. Nevertheless, both states had established parliamentary democracies, albeit marred by many flaws, and had political parties and a free press in the early twentieth century, well before such liberal innovations developed in Russia and much of eastern and southern Europe.

As already discussed, the pre–World War I experience of these two Middle Eastern parliamentary, constitutional democratic regimes with the great parliamentary democracies of the day—Britain and France—was far from happy. To the deep disappointment of Middle Eastern liberals, both Western powers behaved with an imperialist rapacity that was indistinguishable from that of the great Romanov and Hapsburg autocracies. In Egypt, meanwhile, Britain had occupied the country in 1882, in part to short-circuit a nationalist movement that aimed, among other things, to limit the autocracy of the khedive and to move toward parliamentary democracy.[35] The result was a British military occupation that lasted for over seventy years and did much to frustrate and ultimately stifle Egyptian democracy.

After World War I, things got even worse in many respects as far as democracy was concerned, in spite of the self-determination that President Wilson's Fourteen Points promised peoples suffering under foreign rule. Britain prevented the Egyptians from sending a popular delegation to the Paris Peace Conference, thereby providing the spark that ignited the

1919 Egyptian revolution. Even after Britain was forced to concede Egypt a constitutional monarchy and limited independence in 1922, it insisted on keeping bases there, notably in the strategic Suez Canal Zone. The British high commissioner thereafter repeatedly intervened in Egyptian politics in coordination with his local allies in the monarchy and the aristocracy. This intervention ensured that the popular majority party, the Wafd, which most objective observers agreed probably could have won any free and fair election during this period, was kept out of power for eighteen of the next thirty years, until the military-led revolution of 1952.[36]

Similar frustrating experiences faced the parliaments and peoples of Lebanon, Syria, Iraq, and Jordan, where Britain and France for decades maintained a military occupation against the will of the population. As has already been described, both powers forcibly suppressed uprisings in Iraq in 1920 and Syria in 1925 with great loss of civilian life, and repeatedly foiled the will of elected parliaments, in collaboration with local elites that the Western powers were able to co-opt.[37] Whether in Egypt, Lebanon, Syria, Jordan, and Iraq, or in the Sudan (which already had an elected Constituent Assembly when it won its independence in 1956), these parliamentary systems embodied many features of democracy in spite of their elitism, narrow social base, and other flaws. They functioned, and sometimes thrived, in spite of the difficulties of establishing functioning democracies in countries with such high rates of illiteracy and so many other disadvantages.[38] The parliamentary order was overthrown in a series of nationalist military coups in Syria in 1949 (and again in the 1950s, and for a last time in 1963 after constitutional government had twice been reinstated), in Egypt in 1952, and in Iraq in 1958. King Hussein took back power in 1957 from the only elected Jordanian government to seriously challenge the power of the throne,[39] while a 1969 military coup ended parliamentary government in the Sudan.

By the time they had disappeared from the Arab world, with the sole exception of Lebanon, these deeply flawed parliamentary democracies had become largely discredited. This was in part because of their manipulation by entrenched elites, endemic corruption, and a widespread failure to address deep domestic problems, but also because of their inability to end a foreign occupation and to resist Western powers' interventions in these states' domestic affairs. The systems were therefore understandably little mourned by most of their peoples. Thus foreign intervention, which was designed primarily to protect the Western military presence and maintain substantive control over these Middle Eastern countries, repeatedly sabotaged fragile democratic or proto-democratic governments in the Arab world that were unable to achieve full-fledged national independence. These ramshackle parliamentary systems were overthrown one by one and replaced by the nationalist, military-dominated, one-party regimes, the decadent successors of which still blight many Arab countries.

After World War II, aided by the United States, Britain similarly intervened in Iran to frustrate the nationalist program of a democratic, parliamentary government headed by Mohammad Mosaddeq, the last of a series of similar British interventions over nearly half a century aimed at foiling the desire of the Iranian people to take charge of their oil resources and their own destiny. This crucial episode is central to the discussion of Western control over Middle Eastern oil resources, the topic of chapter 3, where it will be treated at length. Chapter 4 will address another case of the Western powers' disregard for the wishes of the indigenous population, in Palestine. There the British foiled the desires of the Palestinian Arab majority for representative democracy for

more than three decades, out of concern for the national aspirations of the country's Jewish minority. The disregard of
the similar aspirations of the Palestinians to national self-
determination first by Britain, and after 1948 by the United
States, still deeply colors how the peoples of the Middle East
regard the Western powers' claims to support democracy and
self-determination.

What lessons can we draw from this summary of the experiences of the Middle East with democracy over the past few
decades? The first is that unwanted foreign military occupation, or even the threat of it, is incompatible with democratization. As might be expected, such an occupation, even when
it takes place in only one country, distorts the course of political development in an entire region, and almost invariably has
the effect of reinforcing chauvinistic nationalism as a defensive
response, as well as provoking and fostering authoritarian tendencies within the target state. Occupation and intervention
by great powers serve as well to stimulate unproductive expenditures on defense and security, which in turn are linked to increased domestic repression. If the Bush administration has
strategic objectives in the Middle East that transcend and con-
tradict its proclaimed desire for a more democratic life for that
region's peoples—and it is virtually impossible to read the
words of key Bush administration policy-makers and their
ideological fellow-travelers without concluding that broad
strategic motives relating to American hegemony in the
twenty-first century are uppermost in their minds where the
Middle East is concerned—then we may be in for a repetition
of an exceedingly ugly phase of the Western encounter with
this region.

Very few people in the United States likely know about or
remember the bitterness with which the Arabs, Iranians, and
in an earlier era, Turks, regarded European intervention and

occupation in their countries. Arabs and Iranians looked similarly on the intensive foreign manipulation of their political systems that followed the end of overt occupation, lasting until the 1950s and 1960s and sometimes later. However, no one in the Arab world and Iran is unaware of these long and unhappy episodes in their history. As previously stated, any citizen over fifty years old, including most Middle Eastern elites, can recall vividly the waning days of the colonial era. For those not old enough to remember it themselves, the history of the struggle for liberation from foreign rule has for decades been amply conveyed to several generations of schoolchildren. Such instruction has instilled in the younger generations the same attitude toward the actions of alien powers as the American educational system does toward the despotic regime maintained in the thirteen colonies by King George III until 1776.

HOW TO BRING DEMOCRACY
TO THE ARAB WORLD

If invasion and occupation, rather than bringing about democracy in the Middle East, are in fact most likely to retard its development, as the historical record strongly suggests, then what can be done to address the abysmal record of most Middle Eastern countries as far as democracy and human rights are concerned? And what are some of the other underlying problems that have retarded the growth of democracy in the past?

The phrase *most Middle Eastern countries* is intended to refer mainly to the Arab states, most of which have a much worse track record with respect to democracy than do Turkey, Iran, and Israel. This is not to say that all has always been rosy and democratic in the latter non-Arab countries of the region. Turkey suffered from the ubiquitous involvement of its military in politics throughout the twentieth century, and from its flawed performance regarding human rights, especially its poor treatment of the country's large Kurdish minority. Iran has had an extremely poor record toward its many religious and ethnic minorities, and currently its partially democratic system has manifested profound weaknesses in the face of the continuing autocratic power of the religious establishment, which still dominates the country. At home, Israeli democracy is marred by the fact that its 1.2 million non-Jewish citizens suffer from aggravated discrimination, while in the West Bank and Gaza Strip, Israel has been a belligerent occupier for more than thirty-six years, in the process grievously violating the Palestinian population's rights, whether human, civil, and national. All three countries nevertheless have functioning democracies in spite of these serious defects.[40]

In the Arab states, by contrast, most of which have been invaded and occupied until relatively recently, the record as far as democracy and human rights are concerned is generally dismal. There is the occasional relatively bright spot in the Arab world, such as the three Gulf countries, Kuwait, Qatar, and Bahrain, which enjoy some aspects of democracy and a free press. On the other hand, in all these countries small oligarchies make most of the key decisions, particularly those regarding their oil revenues, and in the case of Qatar and Bahrain such limited elements of democracy as exist are very new and fragile. There is the remarkable example of Lebanon, whose democracy has weathered two civil wars, one of them lasting for fifteen years, occupation by both of its neighbors, Israel and Syria, and the extraordinary stresses on it that were produced in the period 1968–82 by an unwanted Palestinian state within a state. Finally, there are Morocco, Egypt, Yemen, the United Arab Emirates, and Jordan, each of which has elements of a free press, the rule of law, and some of the forms of democracy, albeit without most of the substance. In none of them, for example, is the head of state, who makes most key decisions, truly accountable to parliament or the people, or subject to replacement by an electoral process. By contrast, dictatorial rule and wholesale denial of civil, political, human, and other rights prevail in Algeria, Tunisia, the Sudan, Libya, Saudi Arabia, Oman, Syria, and, until recently, Iraq.

How can democracy be encouraged to grow both where the buds are already in existence and where the soil appears to be barren? The first thing to recognize is that many countries in the Middle East have some experience with and commitment to a democratic tradition, notably all of the largest of them and a number of others, including Egypt, the Sudan, Syria, Jordan, Iraq, Kuwait, and Lebanon (not to speak of Iran, Turkey, and Israel, non-Arab countries whose internal politics nevertheless have an impact on neighboring countries). This is therefore not a situation in which it is necessary for enlightened Americans or Westerners to bring democracy to benighted "rag-heads" stuck in the Middle Ages who have never experienced it. Yet this is the gist of what is said by all too many of the "experts" who pontificate on this subject in the media.

A second point that must be made is that this "democratic deficit" in the Arab world has absolutely nothing to do with the Islamic religion. Only their ignorance allows so many of the "experts" frequently featured by the media to make such claims, which are belied by the thriving democracies in three of the largest Muslim countries in the world, Indonesia, Bangladesh, and Malaysia, not to speak of Turkey, Iran, and all the Arab countries that once had parliamentary systems. Needless to say, Egypt did not cease to be a Muslim country during the thirty years it experienced parliamentary government, from 1922 to 1952, nor was it because of Islam that democracy failed in Egypt (or elsewhere in the Middle East). It had much more to do with the fact that the parliamentary system and the Egyptian regime in general were so co-opted and undermined by Britain that they were incapable of ending the seventy-two-year-old British military occupation or solving the country's many other pressing problems. It almost seems as if the obsessive and unfounded focus on Islam as the reason for the lack of democracy in the Arab or Islamic world is intended to distract attention from other more obvious reasons, like the incessant interference of the Western powers.

There is plentiful evidence from the Arab world and elsewhere that Islam is no more incompatible with democracy than any other major religion, even though those who would undermine democracy can utilize Islam as a vehicle, just as they can other religions in other countries. Indeed, there exists a significant Islamic modernist tendency that advocates democracy as being completely consonant with the true spirit of Islam,[41] while the trend in favor of liberal democratic parliamentary systems in the late nineteenth and early twentieth centuries was endorsed by much of the Muslim religious establishment at the time. The fact that Islam is capable of producing antidemocratic trends in no way justifies sweeping statements about its incompatibility with democracy, any more than would the powerful monarchical, antidemocratic, and antirepublican trends within French Catholicism in the late nineteenth century justify statements about the incompatibility of Christianity and democracy.

Rather than looking to Islam for the reasons behind the absence of democracy in the Arab world, it would be useful to seek a broad range of historical, social, and political causes beyond the problems of external intervention and occupation already identified. These include foremost a long-standing tradition of strong, unconstrained central states, wielding power arbitrarily and having impunity in violating the rule of law and transgressing the constitution where one existed. This is a much more entrenched tradition in some parts of the Middle East than in any other part of the world, with the possible exception of China, and is rooted in the well over five millennia during which strong, centralized states existed in the region. While it is possible to exaggerate the reach of such constructs,[42] it is clear that in the Middle East, like China, strong, absolutist states have been around for most of recorded human history.

There are exceptions to this tradition of the unconstrained power of the state, even in Egypt, the largest Arab country and site of one of the oldest and strongest states in human history. There, the rule of law has shown institutional resilience, the judiciary is largely independent of the executive, and judges are sometimes able to restrain the power of the state.[43] But even the Egyptian exception illustrates the underlying problem: unable to bend the judiciary to its will, the executive has bypassed it via the imposition of a state of emergency, in force for decades, and via the creation of state security courts that execute the will of the security services against those deemed dangerous by the regime. The Egyptian legal example does not mean that the power of the Middle Eastern state cannot be limited: again, the modern history of the countries of this region testifies to the occasionally successful efforts of their peoples to limit state power and the arbitrary authority of the ruler.[44] However, unlike countries such as the United States, Great Britain, and the Netherlands, where democratic, constitutional systems first arose and where historically there never was a strong central state (before the enormous accretion of power to the state during the wars of the twentieth century), the Middle East is a region where in general the state has always been exceedingly strong.[45]

There were other influences on the power of the state in

the Middle East. These included the Anglo-Saxon liberal tradition of a weak state limited by law that was spread by the educational system in British colonies, by British and American missionary schools, and among members of the elites who obtained education in Britain and the United States. There was, on the other hand, the example of the strong French state, implanted in Egypt via the Napoleonic code that is the basis of the Egyptian legal system, and by French education throughout the Middle East. Then there was the powerful demonstration effect of the colonial state's tradition of trampling on the law whenever it suited its purpose, and its promulgation of manifestly unjust laws that favored European colonial populations. This increased the cynicism of local elites, and reinforced the absolutist tendencies of those who came to head independent Middle Eastern states. These influences also included the strong nationalist desire, after decades of subjugation, for a strong, independent, modern Western-style state that could express the "will of the nation" and limit foreign intervention. And finally, there were the ample pretexts for accretions to state power provided by regional conflicts, foreign intervention, and occupation. In this, Middle Eastern societies were no different from others: wars and external challenges had the inexorable effect of reinforcing the power of the state.[46]

Most modern Middle Eastern states are of relatively recent provenance, with externally imposed frontiers, and were sometimes described as artificial even by their own citizens. It has often been noted that the sovereign model of the nation-state, produced by centuries of European experience, was imposed arbitrarily the world over by the European powers, often causing lingering problems.[47] However, in the Middle East, this process took place in a region that was previously dominated by multiethnic, dynastic states whose legitimacy was derived from religion; a region that thus was not particularly well suited to the European-derived model of the ethnically homogenous nation-state. Iraq, with its Shi'ite, Sunni, and Kurdish components, created out of three Ottoman provinces that had never constituted a single state, is one of the best illustrations of how poorly suited this model was to the region. It exemplifies some of the problems created by the fact that religion and ethnicity often were not consonant with boundaries that were laid down to suit imperial interests. This took place in a series of partitions that were imposed before, during, and after World War I by European statesmen thousands of miles away, who generally had little knowledge of, or concern for, local cultures, history, sensibilities, and desires.

Not all Middle Eastern nation-states fit this pattern: some, like Turkey, Iran, Egypt, Oman, and Morocco were formerly the seats of great empires with a long tradition of "stateness," and after their transformation into nation-states emerged from the colonial era with boundaries that represented a certain ethnic or historical logic. Not surprisingly, they have proven to be relatively stable, unified entities for most of the twentieth century. Some Middle Eastern states, like Tunisia and Yemen, are similarly reasonably cohesive ethnically and in other respects. But in the eastern Arab world, and in particular in the countries that were created out of the Arab provinces of the Ottoman Empire after World War I largely as a reflection of the imperial ambitions of Britain and France— Syria, Lebanon, Jordan, Palestine/Israel, Iraq, and Kuwait and the Arab states of the Gulf region—the nation-state model produced extraordinary stresses throughout much of the past century. Transnational movements like the Ba'th, the Arab Nationalist Movement, and the Syrian Social Nationalist Party advocated the unification of some of these countries on a variety of different bases. Civil wars and ethnic and religious strife ravaged Lebanon; ethnic and political strife repeatedly rent

Iraq; Iraq made repeated claims on Kuwait; and the very existence of all of these states was repeatedly brought into question by their neighbors, and sometimes by some of their citizens.

Remarkably, however, over time the peoples of these new nation-states developed a strong sense of national identity within their artificial, European-drawn frontiers, and these states eventually came to represent the aspirations of their peoples. Today there is a strong sense of Jordanian national identity although Jordan is ruled by an autocratic monarchy dependent on a small, largely East Bank, Jordanian elite, and a majority of its population is of Palestinian origin. Likewise, Lebanese feel Lebanese, Syrians feel Syrian, Iraqis feel Iraqi, and Kuwaitis feel Kuwaiti, in spite of the relatively recent creation of these nation-states. It is clear that over several generations, states that often unsuccessfully battled foreign control and occupation—states that were also weak, and ruled over diverse, divided populations—were nevertheless eventually able to employ the powerful tools of a national educational system, and all the other means available to a modern state for shaping opinion for national purposes. This helped to create loyalty to entities that now have a remarkable solidity, although none of them existed as independent, sovereign units one hundred years ago.[48] Two of the best illustrations are Lebanon, which has weathered extraordinary internal and external stresses but has remained unified and cohesive, and Iraq, which in spite of three wrenching and painful wars in just over twenty years and powerful challenges to its internal cohesion seems to have developed a strong sense of national identity which may now face an ultimate test. It remains to be seen if it can survive the centrifugal forces that may be unleashed in the wake of the crushing of the dictatorial regime that held the country together, often brutally, for thirty-five years.

This brings up the question of how the United States has in recent years come to be so deeply embroiled in the affairs of the countries of the Arab world after decades when nationalism was at work, and eventually succeeded in ending the control exercised by the old imperial powers. Nationalism in the Middle East, for any good it may have done, has generally not contributed much to the rise of democracy. Nor have the nationalist regimes that dominate most of the Arab world brought consistent economic advancement or social progress to their citizens. The best illustrations of this are the modern histories of Iraq and the other countries dominated by regimes that were the degenerate offspring of nationalist parties, movements, and officers' groups: Syria, Egypt, Algeria, and Libya. In the Iraqi, Egyptian, and Syrian cases, we saw that flawed and fragile liberal democracies failed in the face of foreign military occupation and the challenge of regional conflicts like the 1948 Palestine war to be replaced in army coups by radical, nationalist, militarized regimes. In Algeria, a liberation struggle against a ruthless occupation forged a ruthless underground movement, the Front de Libération Nationale (FLN), which has kept an iron grip on power for over forty years, while in Libya a military coup that replaced a feeble monarchy has produced a lasting one-man dictatorship. In all of these cases, aspirations for greater Arab unity, or even a modicum of coordination between Arab states, have gone unfulfilled, as each has charted its own separate, selfish course.

All these regimes clothed themselves in nationalist rhetoric, and indeed were initially able to claim some national achievements. The Egyptian regime created by the revolution of 1952 finally expelled the British in 1954 after seventy-two years, carried out a much overdue land reform, and succeeded in making Egypt a major regional power. These regimes furthered a transformation that broadened access to political power and to social benefits, and enabled people from new socioeconomic groups to supplant the old oligarchy.[49] But all of them developed into new military-civil-party oligarchies, and used the nationalist rhetoric that brought them to power to mask their denial of human and democratic rights and their failure to bring about greater equality and prosperity and true national independence from foreign control.[50] Indeed, in recent decades the Arab world has had a mixed record in terms of economic growth and socioeconomic advancement.[51]

While their hollow nationalist rhetoric has remained unchanged, these formerly radical regimes have become profoundly conservative, and they have converged with the conservative Arab monarchies and other states like Tunisia that did not follow the same trajectory of military intervention and radical domestic social and economic change. The result is that the entire Arab world is blighted by a group of remarkably similar regimes that share several characteristics in common, notably their stagnant political systems and the ubiquitous, brutal efficiency of the means of repression that keep their respective oligarchies safely in power to siphon off and profit from their societies' surplus. In understanding the extraordinary degree of American involvement in the Arab world, these developments, both the undemocratic, oligarchic nature of the regimes, and the waste of so much of their societal resources on the means of repression, play a crucial role.

The only task at which the potent military and repressive apparatus of each Arab state has shown any consistent aptitude is in controlling the restive populations of these countries with an iron hand. Thus Syrian military forces destroyed much of Hama and killed thousands in repressing the revolt of 1982; the Iraqi army crushed the Kurds in repeated campaigns, most recently during the 1980s, and smashed Kurdish and Shi'ite revolts in the wake of the 1991 war; Jordan's army put down both the Palestinian challenge of 1970–71 and periodic uprisings in southern Jordanian towns like Ma'an; Oman suppressed a revolt in the Dhofar region; Yemen's army has fought primarily in civil wars; and Sudan's army has waged a ruthless campaign against separatists in the south of the country. In spite of considerable expenditures on the military, none of these regimes has been successful at war. The disastrous Arab performance in the five Arab-Israeli wars is only one example: Iraq's catastrophic war with Iran, and its crushing defeats in the Gulf wars of 1991 and 2003, the inconclusive Algerian-Moroccan conflict, and the failed Libyan interventions in Chad are others. The extravagant military expenditures of Saudi Arabia, Kuwait, the United Arab Emirates, and Qatar have failed to provide them with any protection against their more powerful neighbors, Iran and Iraq, leaving them almost totally reliant on U.S. power for protection, and thus vulnerable to American dictates.

Sadly, what the nationalist regimes have managed to produce is neither lasting national achievements nor continuing social progress nor protection of the dignity of the individual. Instead they have created a black hole on the map stretching from the Atlantic coast of North Africa to the Persian/Arab Gulf, where by and large democracy is absent and the state does as it pleases, and where power and benefits are passed down within a dominant family, oligarchy, or ethnic group. And the promise of nationalism to free these countries from external control has been betrayed by the dependence of some on the United States for their external and often their internal security, by their waste of resources on armaments, and by their deep disunity. All of these factors in combination have greatly increased the vulnerability of this region to external intervention.

Where does this leave us as far as the nexus between democratization, human rights, and United States policy in the Middle East is concerned? Clearly, external intervention, especially foreign military intervention leading to occupation, exacerbates the situation of the Middle East in general and the Arab countries in particular. This was certainly true of the lengthy and repeated interventions and occupations of the colonial powers. Moreover, the military and covert interventions of the United States in this region over the past few decades have not produced any notable flowerings of democracy, frequently quite the contrary, as in Iran in 1953. Secondly, a strong case can be made that the endemic interstate and intrastate conflicts in the region are major barriers to democratization. The increased power of the state at the expense of civil society throughout most of the Middle East has been born of many factors, but the region's many internal and external conflicts have been important among them. Needless to say, resolving these conflicts will not be easy. They include not only the Palestine-Israel conflict, but also lingering disputes between Iraq and Iran and between Iraq and Turkey, the Cyprus and Western Sahara disputes, as well as several other conflicts internal to the countries in question, notably in Turkish and Iraqi Kurdistan, the Berber regions of Algeria, and the southern Sudan.

However, while resolving these disputes will not automatically bring democracy, failing to resolve them, allowing them to fester, or making them worse virtually guarantees the constant creation of new obstacles to democratization and respect for human rights. In the case of some of these conflicts, far from resolving them, the United States has in the past often exacerbated them. The U.S. supported Iraq against Iran during the Iran-Iraq War,[52] strongly backs Israel and prevents any international pressure from being exerted on it for a just compromise settlement with the Palestinians, and provides more arms to Middle Eastern states than any other country,[53] while itself dominating the region with what looks like will be a huge long-term military deployment that itself is not popular in many parts of the region and thereby contributes to heightening tensions. If the United States is not to continue constituting an obstacle to democratization in the Middle East, it must help to resolve regional conflicts rather than exacerbating them.

Ultimately, these conflicts are for the people of these countries to resolve for themselves. All external actors can do is to limit their own intervention, help resolve disputes such as those between Israel and the Palestinians or over Cyprus that they have helped to complicate by their past policies, and contribute to civil society's self-assertion in the face of the enormous power of the state. We have already noted that the Nile and Mesopotamian river valleys, home to the first and some of the longest-lasting civilizations in human history, have a long tradition of strong states that continued with the Islamic era, culminating in the more than five-hundred-year trajectory of the Ottoman Empire, one of the most advanced and developed of the early modern states. At the same time, the Middle East was home to some of the greatest products of mankind's individual genius and prophetic vision, which can be set against this powerful tradition of state power.

Tragically, many artifacts from the world's best collection of these earliest products of human civilization disappeared when the National Museum of Iraq in Baghdad was looted on April 9 and 10, 2003. This occurred in the chaos that ensued after the city was abandoned to lawlessness for days following the entry of American troops. John F. Burns, one of the first reporters on the scene afterward, said it was "likely to be reckoned as one of the greatest cultural disasters in recent Middle Eastern history." Burns quotes a heartbroken Iraqi archaeologist employed at the museum: "A country's identity, its value and civilization resides in its history. If a country's civilization is looted, as ours has been here, its history ends."[54] These initial reports proved exaggerated, and some items were returned or recovered, although five months later UNESCO experts reported that thirteen thousand artifacts were missing, and archaeologists pointed out that uncontrolled looting at ar-chaeological sites all over the country may do more damage than the losses to the museum.[55] The failure of U.S. forces, who had been in control of Baghdad at that point for many days, to protect the museum, and their continuing inability to stop the ongoing looting of archeological sites, constitute violations of the Fourth Geneva Convention, according to whose terms the occupying power is fully responsible for the security of lives, property, and cultural sites in territory under its control.

In view of the ancient traditions represented by the priceless collection of the National Museum of Iraq, traditions that had existed for several millennia when Europe was still sunken in barbarism and ignorance, perhaps Westerners should be a little humbler in their treatment of this region, afflicted though it currently is by some of the most miserable regimes and most intractable conflicts in the modern world. An approach emphasizing humility, and a consciousness of the not-entirely-positive record of Western powers regarding constitutionalism, the rule of law, and human rights in the region, would perhaps go further in moving the Middle East toward greater democracy and respect for human rights than the Bush administration's trumpeting about bringing democracy to the Arabs, if necessary by force, heard since it decided to invade Iraq and remake the Middle East.

CHAPTER THREE

THE MIDDLE EAST:
GEOSTRATEGY AND OIL

——————

It is distinctly in the interest of the United States to encourage industry to promote the orderly development of petroleum resources in ... areas such as the Persian Gulf.... The buying power of the United States ... will depend in some degree on the retention by the United States of such oil resources.... Indeed the actual expansion of such holdings is very much to be desired.
—JAMES FORRESTAL, U.S. SECRETARY OF THE NAVY, 1944

Since the heyday of the earliest imperial states of ancient Mesopotamia, Egypt, and Anatolia, the area we have come to call the Middle East has always had extraordinary geostrategic importance.[1] This centrally located region stretches from the Atlantic coast of North Africa to the western edges of central Asia, and lies between the southern littoral of the Mediterranean and the northwestern shores of the Indian Ocean. It should be clear why it was so strategically vital when the "known world" was restricted to the Asia/Europe/Africa landmass. This was because the Middle East contained or bordered on the land bridges, passageways, and narrows—the Sinai Isthmus, the Caucasus, the Strait of Gibraltar, the Dardanelles, Bab el Mandeb, and the Strait of Hormuz—and the sheltered seas—the Mediterranean, the Black Sea, the Caspian Sea, the Red Sea, and the Persian/Arabian Gulf—that provided the best routes connecting the different extremities of the vast

Eurasian/African continent.[2] In addition to that unique asset resulting from the location of this region, the land in the rich river valleys of Egypt and Mesopotamia—which came to be known for good reason as the Fertile Crescent—was so productive that, in the case of Egypt, it constituted the granary of empires from the Roman to the Ottoman, and was an important source of cotton for the British and French textile industries well into the twentieth century.

GEOSTRATEGIC IMPORTANCE OF THE MIDDLE EAST

The Middle East was historically vital to inter- and intraregional trade, manufacture, the passage of armies and fleets, finance, and the transit of people and ideas. The growth of the world's first cities was made possible by the wealth produced by the region's rich agriculture, and most importantly because of its central position astride a series of important passageways and choke points. It was thus not surprising that a sequence of major states and empires grew up in and around this region. These started with the first known states, which produced some of the greatest empires in early human history, in Mesopotamia, Egypt, and Anatolia, and continued through the apogee of the Phoenician, Persian, Greek, Carthaginian, Roman, Byzantine, and Islamic empires,[3] all of which aspired to dominate the Middle East, whether in terms of trade or conquest. The area was of particular interest to those powers located outside the region that had ambitions of global hegemony.

However, the Middle East was not just an arena favorable to the extension of the power of the state or to the establishment of empires, or where the entrepreneurship, wealth, and opulence of the traders, merchants, artisans, and manufacturers of the ancient world thrived. Because of the lengthy development of its urban civilizations, the power of its centralized states, its vast natural wealth and diversity, its geographical centrality, and the ease of access to and through this region, the Middle East was also the cradle of important works of law, religion, the sciences, and the arts: some of the greatest products of the human mind and spirit. The three monotheistic religions, and much of the science, philosophy, literature, and art of the ancient world originated here, and spread throughout this region, and from it eventually to other parts of the world.

However, after the modern era began with the circumnavigation of the globe, which made possible the establishment of the first truly global empires starting at the turn of the sixteenth century, the importance of the Middle East briefly waned. For the first time in recorded history, it was no longer necessary for those in western Europe to pass through the Middle East to get to and from Africa and South and East Asia. The states and merchants of the Middle East had for millennia enjoyed a near-monopoly of international transit and trade between the different extremities of the Eurasian/African landmass. After the Portuguese and Spanish naval discoveries of the turn of the sixteenth century, their comfortable monopoly suddenly disappeared. With it went the profits, and some of the prosperity, that this transit and trade had engendered, producing long-lasting effects for Middle Eastern and Mediterranean economies and states. Some historians have indeed ascribed important aspects of the decline of these states and the economies they dominated to this lasting shift in world trade routes.[4]

Whereas states and empires based in the Middle East had previously dominated much of the known world, now the rising western European world powers one after another attempted to take control over the newly developed worldwide system of seaborne trade and the land bases needed to sustain it. This new international trading network rapidly replaced the Middle East's now extinct near-monopoly over trade in and through the central parts of the eastern hemisphere. Trade through the Middle East and the Mediterranean of course continued, though producing reduced prosperity for ports like Genoa, Venice, Izmir, Istanbul, and Alexandria. By contrast, vast benefits accrued to Portugal, Spain, Holland, France, and Britain in succession, as their dominance of the seas and superior technology enabled them not only to control world trade, but also to enslave, annihilate or subjugate, and seize the wealth of the native populations of four relatively isolated continents: North and South America, Australia, and Africa south of the Sahara.

In combination with the resulting appropriation by the European colonial powers of a substantial share of the world's surplus, the development of capitalist agriculture, and of modern industrial manufacturing, global financial networks, and other pillars of the new world-system produced the entrepreneurship, the capital, and the technology that gave Europe a decisive edge in its ultimately successful effort to dominate the globe more thoroughly than had ever before been possible.[5] The end result was an unprecedented integration of the world economy, and a hegemony of modern capitalism based in western Europe and its North American and other offshoots that has only grown more all encompassing through the present day.

In spite of the vast resulting shift in the global balance of power that followed on the emergence of the modern world system and the concomitant decline in the importance of the trade routes that ran through the Middle East, it did not take long for the significance of this region to reassert itself; indeed, this significance may have increased in some respects. For Europe's domination of several regions of the globe, and European-dominated world trade, were both in some measure a function of unimpeded access to and through the Middle East. By the end of the eighteenth century, this region bordering the two great European land-based empires, those of the Romanovs and the Hapsburgs, and athwart the route to India, had become a crucial focus of inter-European rivalries, much as had been North America, the Caribbean, India, and the Indian Ocean earlier in the eighteenth century.[6] Among the evidence of the quickening of this new rivalry in the region, and of the continued strategic importance of the Middle East, was the irruption of a Russian fleet into the Mediterranean in the early 1770s, Napoleon's 1798 expedition to Egypt, and the subsequent British campaign to expel French forces from there. But no longer was the Middle East the seat of self-sufficient world-empires that dominated much of the known world from their position at or near its center. By the nineteenth century it was becoming just another periphery of a vast new world system whose "center" lay somewhere far away in the North Atlantic between Europe and North America, albeit a periphery containing a number of states that retained a strong residual ability to resist outright conquest.

This "peripheralization" of the Middle East, and its concomitant incorporation into the new world economy, was only a prelude to its ultimate country-by-country subjugation by the European colonial powers.[7] In part because of the stubborn resistance to European expansion put up by the peoples and states of the Middle East, and the surprising strength of the Ottoman state in particular, this was one of the last regions of the world to be formally and fully incorporated into the great European empires that by the end of the second decade of the twentieth century had engulfed virtually the entire inhabited surface of the eastern hemisphere.

But there was another reason for this delay in the incorporation of the Middle East into formal European spheres of control and domination, in spite of the fact that its pivotal strategic position made it a rich prize. This was the coincidental fact that alone among major regions of the world, it bordered directly on Europe, and was thus an object of the dueling and contradictory ambitions not only of the two greatest global empires of the age, Britain and France, but also of the neighboring Russian and Austro-Hungarian empires, as well as of nearby Italy, and fellow imperialist latecomer Germany, after their respective unifications in 1870.

The result was a peculiar diplomatic dance starting early in the nineteenth century, whereby none of the great powers was able to stake a preponderant claim to the lands of the major Middle Eastern states or do more than nibble at their peripheries. This occurred largely because each of these powers hesitated to provoke the collapse of the states of the region for fear that their rivals would profit from the scramble that would thereafter ensue, and thereby obtain a decisive strategic advantage. Thus, paradoxically, the same geostrategic centrality that had made the Middle East a locus of empires in earlier eras now helped to preserve it temporarily from full control by the great powers of the new era. In particular, several of the European powers were highly sensitive to control by their rivals of the Turkish straits, the Sinai Isthmus (and after 1869 of the newly constructed Suez Canal), and of the Strait of Hormuz, as well as numerous lesser strategic features that made this region so important.

There thus developed serious rivalries throughout the Middle East between the various imperialist powers, some of them of very long standing. These included disputes between Russia and Austria in different parts of the Balkans, between Britain, France, and Russia over the straits, between Britain and France over Egypt, Syria, Oman, the Sudan, and many other subsidiary points, between Russia and Britain over Persia and Afghanistan, between France and Italy over Tunisia, between Italy, France, and Britain over Libya, and between Germany and France over Morocco, to name only some of the most important of these contentions between European colonial powers. In a sense, the very number of competitors over such a long period was a factor in perpetuating these rivalries and in preserving the temporary autonomy of several Middle Eastern states, especially the Ottoman Empire, in spite of its nickname, "the sick man of Europe."

Only in the first decades of the twentieth century were the great powers able to come to final terms over a partition that allocated to each their respective domains in the Middle East. This became possible as a result of three main sets of understandings: the Anglo-French and Anglo-Russian ententes of 1904 and 1907, which allocated Egypt to Britain and Morocco to France and devised spheres of influence for Britain and Russia in Iran and Central Asia; the "railway partitions" just before World War I, which gave each major European power an exclusive sphere of influence within the Ottoman Empire;[8] and the Sykes-Picot and subsequent accords for the final partition of the empire during and after the war and following the disappearance of the Hapsburgs and Romanovs and the defeat of Germany. Besides the distribution of the few colonies Germany had managed to acquire, this was the main outcome of the First World War as far as the division of what remained of the world between the colonial powers was concerned. It marked the apogee of the process of Europe securing direct control over the globe.

When the smoke of war and partition had finally cleared in the Middle East in the post–World War I era, only a few states had escaped full-scale European occupation and domination. These were the new Turkish republic, which fiercely, and ultimately successfully, resisted attempts by Britain, France, Russia (before its revolution in 1917), Italy, and Greece to divide up the Anatolian core of the Ottoman Empire; Iran, which had been occupied during the war by British and Russian forces, but managed thereafter to assert a precarious independence, benefiting from the temporary weakness of Soviet Russia; and Yemen and Saudi Arabia, both too remote and rugged to be occupied and directly controlled, and in the initial estimate of the European powers, bereft of any resources that would make the effort to do so worthwhile.

The discovery of oil in Saudi Arabia changed that estimation, producing a far-reaching impact on the international relations of the entire Middle East, and on the post–World War II world economy. The oil and gas that were eventually produced in significant quantities in a dozen Middle Eastern countries suddenly became a significant new focus of interest in a region that was already considered supremely important. Oil transformed and considerably enhanced the already great geostrategic importance of the Middle East. The story begins with the painful experiences of the first Middle Eastern oil producer, Iran.

OIL AND FOREIGN INTERVENTION: THE IRANIAN TEMPLATE

There is no better example than Iran of how oil and foreign intervention were intertwined in the Middle East. This was a country that had long suffered from external intervention, a problem that only became more acute as a result of the discovery of unsuspected riches beneath its soil. Iran was the first place in the Middle East where oil was exploited industrially in commercial quantities. It was thus the first Middle Eastern state to experience a new kind and a new level of interference in its affairs, designed to ensure lasting foreign control of this extremely valuable commodity. The pattern established in Iran came to be followed elsewhere in the region, partly because the powerful British-government-controlled monopoly corporation that commanded its oil industry for so long (the Anglo-Persian Oil Company), soon came to dominate that of several of its neighbors.

The Iranian case thus in many ways served as the template for the asymmetrical relationships that developed between powerful Western oil companies and their great-power patrons on the one hand, and the weak regimes of a number of Middle Eastern countries on the other. A pattern of unequal relations, overbearing Western behavior, and local resentment was thus created in Iran that persisted for well over half a century in the oil-producing countries of the Middle East. This imbalance in turn engendered a nationalist reaction that after many setbacks and zigzags, notably in Iran from 1950–53, ultimately led to the successful nationalization of the oil industry in all Middle Eastern countries during the 1970s. However, the memory of the previous unequal relationship remains a vivid one for many in the region, among elites and the general public alike, and continues to this day to have significant weight in the politics of countries like Iran, Iraq, and Saudi Arabia.

Since earliest antiquity, oil had been known to exist beneath the ground in Iran and Mesopotamia, as can be seen from archaeological evidence found at sites all over the region dating back several millennia.[9] Petroleum products had long been extracted in small quantities by preindustrial methods in both regions, but the significance of oil increased exponentially in the early twentieth century.[10] This was a function of the many entirely new uses to which petroleum products were being put as part of a complete revolution in transportation, as they came to provide power for older means of transport such as ships and trains, as well as entirely new ones, like automobiles and airplanes,[11] made possible by the availability of these products and by the invention of the internal combustion engine. The significance of Iranian oil in particular was a result of an apparently minor strategic transformation with major consequences that occurred in the years immediately before World War I.

This transformation had to do with the principal strategic instrument of the global hegemony of the greatest power of its day: Britain's Royal Navy. For decades, the fleet had relied on coal to power its ships. High-quality steam coal, plentifully available in Britain, was a major strategic asset, utterly reliable because of the availability of guaranteed, secure supplies. But coal had disadvantages as a source of energy. It was bulky, required large numbers of sailors to move aboard ship, and did not produce as much thermal power as oil. By contrast, oil was easy to store and move, produced more power for its weight than coal, and its use freed up sailors for other duties. Oil-fired ships could accelerate and move considerably faster than coal-burning ones, had much greater range, and could carry more guns and armor and much more fuel. Because of this greater range, a shift from coal to oil meant that Britain would require fewer coaling stations and therefore fewer bases in far-flung places. There was only one problem: Britain had no oil at home, and little of it was known to be located in its vast empire. Thus, until 1912, oil was used only to power lighter ships that needed maximum speed. The big-gun dreadnought battleships, the fast battle-cruisers, and the swift cruisers that were the heart of the Royal Navy and the decisive weapons systems of the era, were all powered by coal.

This is where Iran came in. For in 1901 a British businessman, William D'Arcy, had obtained from the Iranian government a sixty-year concession that gave him the "exclusive privilege to search for, obtain, exploit, develop, render suitable for trade, carry away and sell" Iranian petroleum products.[12] This concession, covering half a million square miles, the entirety of Iran except for the five northern provinces bordering on Russia, was obtained for only £20,000 in cash, £20,000 in stock (plus bribes to various courtiers[13]), and the promise of a mere 16 percent of company profits, plus a nominal annual rent. Partly with oil in mind, Britain was careful to ensure its position in Iran via the 1907 entente with Russia, which gave Britain an exclusive, recognized sphere of influence in the southeastern part of the country. The concessionaires soon discovered commercially significant quantities of oil, and began production in 1908. The following year, the Anglo-Persian Oil Company was formed in London to exploit the new concession, with the assistance of the British Admiralty. The Admiralty had earlier helped D'Arcy to diversify his financial backers and to find the funds necessary for the costly work of exploration and production of oil in the difficult terrain of southwestern Iran.

At this point the new first lord of the Admiralty, Winston Churchill, made a momentous decision. This involved the crucial question of the construction of a new generation of dreadnought battleships in the midst of a deadly Anglo-German naval race. Churchill had to decide how to mount heavy, newly developed, larger fifteen-inch guns in these ships, without robbing them of vital armor or equally vital speed. In technical terms, there was no question about the right choice. In Churchill's words: "In equal ships oil gave a large excess of speed over coal. It enabled that speed to be attained with far greater rapidity. It gave forty per cent greater radius of action for the same weight of coal. It enabled a fleet to refuel at sea with great facility."[14] In view of these facts and the fevered state of the naval rivalry with Germany, it was decided that the new ships must be oil-powered. Churchill thereby did three things: he ensured the building of the fastest and best-armed battleships of their era; he produced a naval revolution, as all other battleships were suddenly rendered obsolete and other powers were obliged to power their new ships with oil and arm them with bigger guns; and most importantly, he made Britain profoundly dependent on oil, a commodity that, unlike coal, had to be imported.

Once this decision was made, there could be no turning back, for Britain or for its rivals. Whereas oil had previously been important, it suddenly became a strategic commodity absolutely vital to the maintenance of Britain's naval supremacy over Germany, in view of the powerful challenge of the German High Seas Fleet. Oil therefore overnight became crucial to Britain's global hegemony, intensifying its attention to Iranian oil and vastly enhancing the strategic importance not just of Iran but of the entire Middle East. This was the most promising region of the world for new sources of oil, and of all the great and not so great powers, none but the United States and Russia had significant quantities of oil in their own territory, and few even had known sources of oil in their colonial possessions.

Long before the discovery of oil, Iran's feeble central government had proven itself incapable of preventing encroachments on its sovereignty or the annexation by its powerful Russian and British Indian neighbors of adjacent territories to which it had long-standing claims.[15] Since the time of Peter the Great, Russia had been advancing southward in the Caucasus and Transcaspian regions, and British power, ensconced in India, constantly pressed at Iran's southeastern frontiers with Baluchistan, while inexorably expanding its paramount presence in regions on both sides of the Gulf that had long been dominated by Persia.[16]

With the rapid growth of the oil industry in Iran under the impetus of the Anglo-Persian Oil Company's intensive development of the D'Arcy concession, and the suddenly increased strategic importance of oil—and Iranian oil in particular—to the greatest power of the age, Iran was faced with a new kind of encroachment on its sovereignty. For Britain was now necessarily intent on obtaining absolute security of supply for a commodity that was vital to the maintenance of its naval superiority. Security of supply meant that two things were necessary. The first was ensuring British control of the southern coastal regions of Iran where the Anglo-Persian Oil Company was already producing oil. In these regions, security for exploration and production came to be provided by units of the British Indian army's Bengal Lancers and the locally recruited, British-officered South Persia Rifles, which gave Britain quasi-sovereign power over the areas where Anglo-Persian operated.

The second necessity was ensuring permanent British control of the company that produced the oil. The company could not be allowed to fall into foreign hands, any more than could the region where the oil was located, and this operation required a different kind of intervention by the British government. In London, where after an official commission (headed, naturally, by a rear admiral) had carefully examined the situation on the ground in Iran, the British cabinet in 1913 authorized the governmental purchase of 51 percent of the stock of the Anglo-Persian Oil Company for £2 million. This was a momentous step, for it meant that Britain was now directly involved in ownership of Middle Eastern oil. Needless to say, this lucrative investment more than repaid itself over the years, both financially and strategically.

Britain now had physical control over the area where oil was located, and the company's sixty-year concession gave it the right to extract Iranian oil for a pittance. By 1914, Anglo-

Persian's fields were producing 273,000 tons of oil annually (and by 1920 over five times that quantity).[17] On the eve of World War I, it remained for Britain to ensure the uninterrupted production of Iranian oil in circumstances of a gathering world conflict in which the neighboring Ottoman Empire, a state far stronger than Iran, risked falling under the influence of the Triple Alliance headed by Germany (and eventually did, joining the war on Germany's side). The fear was that Ottoman forces, backed by Germany, might invade Iran in order to interrupt the crucial flow of oil to the Royal Navy, and this not unrealistic fear engendered countermoves, including the British invasion of Ottoman-controlled Iraq.

Thus was unleashed a new cycle of external intervention in the Middle East, motivated not just by the strategic character of the region but by the new factor of oil. This cycle obviously was about far more than control of Iran or Iraq or other parts of the Middle East, which just happened to be the arena where the strategic interests of the great powers collided. In consequence, Iran and its people rapidly became little more than pawns in a situation where a vital element of world supremacy was at stake, the inevitable fate of peoples and states in a strategic region when they are no longer capable of defending themselves or their sovereignty. The discovery of oil, and the British Admiralty's momentous prewar decisions, thereafter made the region considerably more important, and rendered these peoples and states all the more vulnerable to external influence.

In consequence of this vulnerability, Iran suffered a continuing British occupation of the south of the country during World War I, and a matching Russian one in the north. As soon as the war broke out, British troops were landed in the oil-producing areas of Iran, reinforcing British forces already stationed there. In part to protect the Iranian oil fields, British troops were landed as well at Basra in Ottoman-controlled Iraq, marking the beginning of the ill-fated British march up the Tigris that ended in disaster at Kut in 1916.[18] But even after Russian troops evacuated Iran in the wake of the Bolshevik Revolution, and British troops were later on obliged to leave by a combination of Iranian resistance and British war-weariness and money problems, the foreign presence embodied by the Anglo-Persian Oil Company only grew more powerful.[19] Controlling the port of Abadan and a network of installations including oil rigs, pipelines, storage tanks, housing for its employees, and a fleet of barges, exempt from Iranian taxation, guarded by British Indian troops that were at its beck and call, and firmly backed by the British government, which held a controlling interest in its finances, the company was a towering state-within-a-state in the southern part of the country.

Even a forceful new Iranian ruler, Reza Shah Pahlavi, who ousted the Qājār monarchy and strengthened and centralized the Iranian state, could not loosen the company's hold. Cancellation of its concession in 1932, which provoked Britain's recourse to the Permanent Court of Justice at the Hague and the Council of the League of Nations, only persuaded the company to increase the share of profits it paid the Iranian state from 16 to 20 percent.[20] The council was unimpressed by the Iranian argument that the original concession had been granted by an unrepresentative, unconstitutional government acting under foreign pressure.[21] Reza Shah's failure served as the backdrop to the abortive attempt in the early 1950s by the elected government of Mohammad Mosaddeq to nationalize Iran's oil resources, bringing them under control of the parliament representing the Iranian people.[22] This incident had all the hallmarks of the struggle over oil throughout the Middle East: efforts by governments influenced by nationalist pressures to retake assets they perceived to be theirs; the resistance of the foreign companies, backed by governments willing to intervene to protect their interests; and the equivocal role played by leaders, often installed by foreign powers, who proved more responsive to the wishes of these powers than to those of their own people.

After the Allies removed Reza Shah during World War II because of his pro-German sentiments, they installed his son, Mohammad Reza Pahlavi. In a familiar move, Russian troops once more occupied the north of the country, and British forces (supplemented by American troops) again took control of the south, as Iran became a vital corridor for lend-lease aid to the Soviet Union. Although the tripartite occupation ended after the war (the United States pressed Britain to withdraw to avoid giving the Soviets a pretext to stay), Iran had once again become a political football between the great powers, with Stalin's Russia again putting pressure on the country from the north, and Britain doing the same thing from the south. The two new factors in this familiar pattern were the entry of an entirely new power onto the Iranian stage, the United States, and the further post–World War II enhancement of the importance of oil resources, control of which had played a vital role in the Allied victory, and the absence of which were central to the defeat of Germany and Japan.

Seeming to step right into the boots of the czars after more than two decades during which the Soviet Union had not bullied its southern neighbors,[23] Stalin made alarming territorial demands on both Turkey and Iran immediately after the war. He supported the abortive Kurdish Mahabad Republic in northern Iran and renewed claims to lapsed Russian oil concessions in the country while provocatively reopening with Turkey the dossiers of the straits and old Russian claims on the border regions of Kars and Ardahan, which the USSR had left dormant for two decades. These southward probes, which were crucial in the genesis of the Cold War, were rebuffed, but one consequence of the denial of Russian claims for oil concessions was the reopening in Iranian politics of the question of the status of the Anglo-Iranian Oil Company. There were big strikes and demonstrations against the company in 1946, and demands in the newly empowered Iranian Parliament (stronger now that the wartime Allies had replaced the autocratic Reza Shah with his son and were now divided among themselves) for a more equitable deal with the oil giant. By 1949, mass student protests in Teheran against the AIOC concession were commonplace.

Late the next year, a parliamentary committee under Mosaddeq began to consider a radical solution to the problem: nationalization of the oil industry. Panicking, the AIOC suddenly changed its long-standing position and offered a fifty-fifty profit split, but it was too little, too late after decades of the AIOC lording it over the Iranians. In April 1951 Parliament passed a bill nationalizing the industry, and in May the popular Mosaddeq became prime minister, winning a unanimous vote of confidence two months later. The Iranians argued that the nationalization was perfectly legal, citing as a precedent the recent nationalizations of a wide range of companies in Britain by the Labour government only a few years before.

Negotiations with AIOC proved fruitless, with the British company arrogantly demanding compensation not only for its physical assets but for future profits on probable underground reserves, something that was unacceptable to the Iranians. At the same time, the company massively increased oil production in Iraq and Kuwait, whose oil industries it controlled completely, while instituting a worldwide boycott of the production of the newly nationalized Iranian oil industry. This boycott was scrupulously respected by the other major companies, which were worried about the same thing happening to their assets elsewhere, especially after the "bad example" of Mexico's oil nationalization of 1938.[24] In support of the actions of the AIOC, the governments of Britain and the United States resolutely opposed the nationalization, began to concert their diplomatic and covert activities in Iran, and started encouraging the opposition to Mosaddeq in the Parliament and from the young shah they had installed a few years earlier. At first these efforts were futile, as Mosaddeq was able to appeal to Iranian public opinion, which supported his measures wholeheartedly, enabling him to win a resounding victory in a popular referendum.

But in time Parliament, Mosaddeq, and the disparate coalition that supported him were worn down by the pressure of the economic boycott, combined with the collusion between foreign powers determined to prevent Iran from succeeding with its audacious gesture, and members of the Iranian elite, headed by the shah, determined to preserve their prerogatives in the face of the advance of popular power. Finally, in August 1953, the Iranian military, which had been advised by American officers since World War II, carried out a coup inspired and organized by the British MI6 and the CIA.[25] The resulting reimposition of the shah's absolute power at the expense of the powers of the elected Parliament thus represented yet another example of the old, cavalier contempt shown by democratic Western powers for constitutionalism and democracy in the Middle East when they perceived their interests were threatened.

The other result of the coup represented a new factor: for the shah's new government, headed by a reliable senior general, proceeded to return the Iranian oil industry to its old state of subservience to Western oil companies. The sole difference from the pre-1951 situation was that the major American oil giants obtained a 40 percent share (in effect compensation for American participation in the overthrow of Iranian democracy) of the new arrangement, which once again vested full control of the production and sale of Iranian oil in foreign hands. The AIOC, now renamed British Petroleum (BP), got the rest, in a deal described less than a decade later as "one of the most attractive contracts to the oil industry in the Middle East, as far as terms of payment are concerned."[26] For the next quarter of a century, and in spite of seismic changes in the Middle Eastern oil industry as successful nationalizations finally took place, it appeared that as a result of their determination to maintain their control of the Iranian oil industry, the Western powers had imposed a lasting new order in Iran. The volcanic Iranian popular revolution of 1978–79, which drove out the shah and was fueled in part by lasting, bitter resentment over ceaseless oil-driven Western meddling in Iranian politics culminating in the 1953 coup, proved that these appearances had been deceiving.

IRAQ, A COUNTRY SHAPED BY OIL

While Iran (or Persia, to use its premodern name) had long existed within much the same frontiers, albeit as an empire rather than a nation-state, this was not true of two of the other major Middle Eastern oil-producing states, Iraq and Saudi Arabia. There never had been a state, empire, or nation of Iraq before British statesmen created it in the wake of World War I. Iraq was the term used by the classical Arab geographers for this region, and continued to be the common Arabic name for Mesopotamia down to the modern era. For millennia, it had been the seat of vast, powerful empires, from those of the Assyrians and Babylonians in antiquity to that of the Abbasids in the Islamic era. Iraq per se, however, had never been a single political unit, and certainly not a nation-state, and during the Ottoman era was divided into three separate provinces.[27]

Soon after the war ended, a gathering in Damascus of Iraqi leaders had called for the creation of such a state under a Hashemite prince as part of an Arab federation.[28] This had an impact on British imperial planners when they deliberated about the country's future. But the well-known presence of oil in Iraq since antiquity, reinforced by the near-certainty of contemporary geologists that it was present in commercially significant quantities, had much to do with Iraq's creation in the form it has retained until the present day.

In the "railway partitions" of the Ottoman Empire just before World War I, whereby the powers recognized one another's claims to spheres of influence via understandings about areas where each was free to build (or prevent the building) of railways, Britain had established its primacy in the southern part of Iraq.[29] This claim was related primarily to a desire to control the communications of southern Mesopotamia with the Gulf and India, and between there and the Mediterranean, although it was known that there was oil in both the south and the north of the country. This prewar recognition of a paramount British interest in southern Iraq was expanded in the 1916 Sykes-Picot accords between the Allied powers into a zone where Britain was to have direct and exclusive control. Another zone to the north, stretching from the Iranian frontier west to the Mediterranean and including Baghdad, was to be indirectly controlled by Britain. Thus Britain would dominate the shortest course from the Mediterranean to the Gulf that was later used for land and air routes and an oil pipeline. These accords gave France similar zones of control in Syria and allotted it paramount influence in the Mosul region. Britain thereby created a buffer zone between their possessions and those of its old rival, Russia, which had secured recognition from its allies of its paramount interest in eastern Anatolia and at the Straits.

The fall in 1917 of the government of the Romanov czars,

the party to these secret deals, and an accentuated perception in London after the war of the strategic importance of oil, led the British prime minister Lloyd George to renegotiate this deal with the French premier Clemenceau. This took place just before the outset of the negotiation of the post–World War I peace treaties in Paris in 1919, when Clemenceau was in London. In an expansive mood after receiving a rapturous reception from the normally phlegmatic British public, the grizzled French leader graciously acceded to his British colleague's request that France give up its claims to Mosul in favor of Britain with the magnanimous words, "You shall have it. Anything else?" (he thereafter granted another request from Lloyd George to cede French political claims in Palestine).[30] The only quid pro quo Clemenceau asked for in Mesopotamia was a share for France of the oil that was known to be present in large quantities in the Mosul region. Thus in a few moments did the two men dispose of the future of northern Iraq, its people and its resources.

These Anglo-French deals were the cornerstone of the edifice of the modern Iraqi state, and prefigured the final determination of its frontiers. The specific internal form this state would take, however, was influenced by two factors. The first was jockeying between different centers of British imperial power, and the second was the resistance of the Iraqi people to British control of the country. When British troops first marched into southern Iraq in 1914, they instituted a military occupation, which applied the methods of Britain's Indian empire, whence came most of the officers and administrators who conquered and governed Iraq. Britain's Indian Raj was by tradition a semi-independent unit of the empire, with its own viceroy, government, army, and fleet, and its own well-established forms of governance, although the viceroy of course reported to the secretary of state for India and the cabinet in London.

It was only as their troops approached Baghdad in the spring of 1917, in a campaign delayed by the catastrophic defeat by Ottoman troops of a British corps at Kut in 1916, that British ministers gave serious thought to political coordination of their action in Iraq with their parallel military campaign in Palestine and their support of the Arab revolt in the Hijaz. The British high commissioner in Cairo, who reported to the foreign secretary in London, directed the political aspects of these efforts. The high commissioner had working under him an extraordinary body of intelligence officers and scholars, concentrated in the Arab Bureau.[31] This group, "nominally owned by the Foreign Office, funded by the War Office, and effectively controlled by the Admiralty," influenced the perspective not only of Cairo, but also of London.[32] Its patron there was the new secretary of state for war (until his death in June 1916), Lord Kitchener, who had immense authority on "Eastern questions." If anyone could be said to "know the East," it was Kitchener, and it was he who in 1912 in Cairo had started the talks with Arab leaders that during the war led to the Arab revolt, and in London had first authorized their continuation, later carried on from Cairo under supervision of the Foreign Office.[33]

Although the secretary of state for India and the foreign secretary and their permanent officials in London were in regular contact, their subordinates in India and Egypt and in the field had different training and perspectives, and were affected by different institutional imperatives. In consequence, it transpired before, during, and after World War I that Britain's right hand was not only frequently unsynchronized with its left, but that they sometimes engaged in bouts of arm wrestling with one another. (This is a relevant precedent for understanding the squabbling between the different wings of the Bush administration, resulting in its confused handling of

the Middle East before, during, and after the 2003 Gulf war.[34])
When it came time to decide what announcement to have the
commander of British forces make upon the capture of the
fabled Islamic capital of Baghdad, one of the first major Allied
victories of the war, there were conflicting views among British
officials in India and Egypt that were reflected in the debate
that took place in London, in both the Committee of Imperial
Defense (CID) and the cabinet.

The firmly held view of the British Indian government was
that Iraq should be ruled directly by British officials, that no
attention whatsoever should be given to the wishes of the Arab
population, and that the potentially rich territory of Iraq
should become a field for Indian business, enterprise, and
possibly colonization by landless Indian peasants. In effect,
some of them wanted Iraq to be in effect a full-blown possession of Britain's colony, India, or as Colonel A. T. Wilson, later
senior political officer in Iraq, put it early in the war: "I should
like to see it announced that Mesopotamia was to be annexed
to India as a colony of India and Indians."[35] This was an expression of "the desire of Indian officials to receive their due,
India's due, for sacrifices made in Mesopotamia."[36] They thus
meant Iraq to be a sort of "reward" for India's sacrifices in
World War I, when hundreds of thousands of Indian troops
fought and many died (for the greater glory of the British
Empire, of course).[37] There was not a little of the traditional
attempt to aggrandize the sphere controlled by British officials
in India in all of this, talk of rewarding the Indians themselves
notwithstanding.

Something of the same motivation operated in that other
pole of British imperial power, Egypt. British officials in Egypt,
who had fostered and encouraged the revolt of the Arabs, saw
them as a valuable ally against the Ottomans, and as potentially useful in the future. As we have already seen, at the insti-

gation of London they had already committed Britain to support of Arab independence within vaguely defined boundaries, in a correspondence with the ruler of Mecca, Husayn ibn 'Ali. By any reading of this highly ambiguous and much disputed correspondence, most of Iraq was included within those boundaries.[38] The officials in London and their subordinates in Cairo who had advocated support of Arab aspirations insisted that the announcement to be made by General Maude, the commander of British forces advancing on Baghdad, reflect these commitments. This argument was anathema to British Indian officials in Iraq or in India, and to their superiors in the India Office, but in the end they were overruled.

The declaration that General Maude finally made in Baghdad in March 1917, cited at the beginning of chapter 2, although drafted by Sir Mark Sykes, an inconsistent advocate of the principle of Arab independence (he advocated Kurdish independence and Zionism equally inconsistently, but defended his country's interests doggedly), was resonant with lofty rhetoric, but very short on specifics. The Iraqis were to have institutions "in consonance with their sacred laws," meaning that the shari'a, Islamic law as derived from the Koran, would not be infringed upon; they "were to participate in the management of [their] civil affairs in collaboration with the representatives of Great Britain who accompany the British Army"; the Arab race would hopefully once more "rise to greatness," whatever that meant; and the British were of course "liberators," not conquerors; but the words *independence, statehood,* and *self-government* did not occur in the declaration.[39]

As is often the case, events on the ground were to have a determining effect. Cairo was far away, London even farther, and those who made the decisions in Iraq were deeply influenced by the paternalistic colonial traditions of British

India and determined to run things their way. They were able to do so for a while, creating a semicolonial administration that denied the Iraqis any say in their future or any hand in their own affairs. These British officials, used to ruling directly and without hindrance over the fringes of the vast British Indian empire, dealt with a heavy hand with those who opposed their plans. Thus, the former deputy for Basra in the Ottoman Parliament, the powerful regional leader Sayyid Talib al-Naqib, who insisted forcefully and with some local support that the Iraqis were ready for self-government, was summarily exiled to the Seychelles Islands, the Guantánamo Bay for political prisoners of its day. This did not stop others from taking up this cause.

The inevitable result of such blind policies was a popular revolt in 1920 that nearly took on nationwide dimensions before it was crushed through the ruthless employment of air-power against the civilian population in the areas of southern and central Iraq that had managed to throw off British control. The revolt finally tipped the scales against those, such as Colonel Arnold Wilson, the British political officer at the outset of the occupation, who had advocated and implemented a modified form of British direct rule in Iraq. In view of the amplitude of the revolt, and given Britain's precarious postwar financial circumstances and how thinly stretched were British forces around the world, it was clear to the cabinet in London that a less heavy-handed, less expensive, and less personnel-intensive means of ruling Iraq and protecting British interests there would have to be found.

Thus in 1921, at the Cairo Conference presided over by Winston Churchill, now colonial secretary, one of the decisions taken was to reorganize thoroughly Britain's presence in its new League of Nations mandate in Iraq.[40] This was to be done by instituting indirect rule of the country, through installing the Hashemite prince Faisal, recently expelled from Syria by the French, as king of a new, "independent" Iraqi state. After a rigged plebiscite, briskly arranged by the freshly appointed British high commissioner, Sir Percy Cox, with the able assistance of Gertrude Bell and other Arabists, all was in order. Thus originated an Iraqi regime that lasted until 1958, and through which Britain preserved its military bases and influence in Iraq, albeit at the cost of further alienating the Iraqi people.

One of the most crucial matters to be negotiated with the new Iraqi government was an agreement to explore for and produce oil. Oil had been the chief reason for the inclusion of the Mosul region within the area controlled by Britain, for Mosul was where the richest deposits were known to be located since before World War I, although considerable quantities of oil were eventually discovered in the Basra region of southern Iraq and along the Iranian border. The British were intent on excluding from this promising field of enterprise companies that had obtained prewar concessions for exploration and production from the Ottoman Empire, and others representing competing powers, notably the United States. The British authorities in Iraq naturally favored instead the holder of a prewar concession for the provinces of Mosul and Baghdad from the Ottoman Empire, the Turkish Petroleum Company (TPC), which was dominated by the government-controlled Anglo-Persian Oil Company.

Its name notwithstanding, the Turkish Petroleum Company was a prewar foreign consortium originally including major British, Dutch, and German oil interests (with the latter's share later going to the French in fulfillment of the Clemenceau–Lloyd George deal of 1918[41]) that had not managed to begin exploration and production before 1914. Although the negotiations took nearly a year and half, after the customary strong-armed intervention an agreement between the new Iraqi government and the TPC (which in 1929 became the Iraqi Petroleum Company) was initialed in March 1925. This accord was along the lines of the disadvantageous terms of the agreements with Iran, and was similarly unpopular in Iraq. When brought before the Iraqi cabinet for ratification, two ministers resigned in protest, although the agreement was finally approved, rushed through before an Iraq parliament could be elected.

Parliamentary rule was one of the features the British were obliged to accept as part of their shift to indirect rule, and in keeping with their commitments to the League of Nations, whose Covenant enjoined the mandatory powers to develop representative institutions. The Iraqi Parliament, although it later on came to have a reputation as a rubber stamp for the measures proposed by the monarchy and its British overlords, was not an entirely tame body at the outset. The first issue facing the newly elected Parliament was a treaty with Great Britain, which consecrated its position in the country, regularized its military presence, and formalized Iraq's subordination (including obliging Iraq to accept the "advice" of the high commissioner "on all matters affecting the international and financial obligations" of Britain).[42] Earlier governments had resigned in protest against the treaty, and the high commissioner had governed the country with emergency powers for years, until he could put together a cabinet that would ratify the draft treaty. However, the newly elected deputies raised furious objections to the unequal provisions of the treaty, and there were large street demonstrations against its terms and against the British. It was only through employment of the most rigorous measures of compulsion, such as a draft law produced by the high commissioner giving the king the power to dissolve Parliament, that that body was eventually compelled to vote for the treaty. In the event, it passed with only thirty-seven votes in favor, with twenty-eight against and eight abstaining. This was a highly inauspicious start for an Anglo-Iraqi relationship that was to continue to be rocky, particularly on matters involving oil.

Iraq rapidly became a major producer of oil, with its rich fields eventually connected to the Mediterranean via a pipeline across British-controlled Jordan and Palestine terminating at Haifa, and another across Syria and Lebanon terminating at Tripoli and Sidon. Britain had thus acquired the oil of Iraq on advantageous terms, and the means to transport it to the sea. France and the United States had been mollified with 23.75 percent shares of Iraqi production for their oil companies.[43] This deal was in fulfillment of Lloyd George's 1918 promise to Clemenceau, and in grudging recognition of the prior oil rights in Iraq that American companies had had via old Ottoman concessions, and persistent American demands for an economic open door in League of Nations mandates (which Lord Curzon in 1920 had initially disingenuously dismissed by stating that "in any case, the resources of Iraq would belong not to Britain but to the future state to be founded there," words whose echoes could be heard in the declarations of American officials after the occupation of Iraq in 2003).[44]

The Iraqi people were not so fortunate in the results of these deals, and although Iraq received a certain amount of revenue from its oil, the lion's share of the benefits went to the foreign companies that effectively controlled production in Iraq, as they did in Iran, and later on in Kuwait and Bahrain. In the first three it was Anglo-Persian (later AIOC, and thereafter BP) in various guises that towered over the local governments, with its position in the three countries enabling it to shift production to the others in order to exert pressure on any government that got out of line, as in Iran during the 1951–53 oil crisis there.

A few years later, the 1958 Iraqi revolution led by Brigadier

General Abdul Karim Kassem appeared to place these valuable British interests in jeopardy, but in fact it was not until many years later that any fundamental change took place in the relationship between the British oil company and the Iraqi government. In the interim, Iraqi popular bitterness about foreign control over the country's oil, and the insufficient benefits accruing to Iraq from its most valuable resource, continued to grow. Exploiting this resentment became the stock-in-trade of Iraqi political parties, and it was to play a major role in the popularity of the Ba'th government when it finally nationalized the Iraqi oil industry in 1975.

SAUDI ARABIA: DYNASTIC POWER, RELIGION, AMERICA, AND OIL

While it was once commonplace for states to be identified by the dynasties that rule them, Saudi Arabia (together with the Hashemite Kingdom of Jordan) today constitutes something of an anomaly in this regard. However, given the central role of the ruling dynasty in the founding of the modern Saudi state (and its eighteenth- and nineteenth-century predecessors), this anomaly is easily explained. The Kingdom of Saudi Arabia in large measure owes its existence to the personality of its founding ruler, and the father of its succeeding four kings, 'Abd al-'Aziz ibn Sa'ud (best known as Ibn Sa'ud).[45] It was he who, over the first three decades of the twentieth century, brought the Saudi dynasty back from its early-nineteenth-century nadir, after it had lost control of its historic heartland in the eastern Arabian region of Nejd, by recapturing the capital, Riyadh, in 1902, and thereafter conquering neighboring regions, establishing the kingdom within its present frontiers, and creating the basic structures of the Saudi state.

The forceful personality and personal capabilities of Ibn

Sa'ud, or those of earlier Saudi rulers, do not entirely explain the success of the Saudi dynasty in repeatedly establishing its hegemony over most of the Arabian Peninsula for a period of more than two hundred years. Crucial to this success was its alliance with a puritanical religious reform movement founded by a late-eighteenth-century preacher, Muhammad ibn 'Abd al-Wahhab, which came to be known to outsiders as the Wahhabis (a term abhorred by the movement's adherents, who prefer the term muwahhidun, or unifiers, in reference to the oneness of God). This group gave the Saudi family the means to mobilize residents of the Nejd region in a way transcending the usual tribal connections, and enabled them to wield power that proved far superior to that of all of their local rivals.[46] The Wahhabi movement was revived and welded into an even more formidable force under the aegis of his dynasty by Ibn Sa'ud in the first decades of the twentieth century.

But while this formula explains the eighteenth- and nineteenth-century successes of the Saudi royal dynasty, it took more than an able and ambitious dynast and a dynamic religious movement providing him with a potent source of support to sustain the present-day Kingdom of Saudi Arabia in the treacherous international environment of the first decades of the twentieth century. Crucial to its creation and expansion was the support extended first by Britain, before, during, and after World War I, and the even more important support extended a few decades later by the United States. This was a complicated story. It involved in the first instance the strange phenomenon of Saudi and Hashemite forces, both armed and financed by Britain during World War I, supposedly in order to combat the Ottomans, fighting a series of pitched battles with each other. It involved secondly the extraordinary loss of Britain's paramount position in the Arabian Peninsula to a brash newcomer that was not even a regional power, the

United States, as a result of a historic oil exploration deal signed in 1933.

We have already seen in the case of Iraq how Britain's right hand in the Middle East often did not know, or approve of, or support, what the left hand was doing. Events in the Arabian Peninsula during and after World War 1 provide perhaps the most remarkable illustration of how this bureaucratic infighting and institutional narrow-mindedness complicated the British war effort and British policy in the region generally, often leading to entirely unexpected and unintended results. Since the occupation of Egypt in 1882, Britain had dealt with the affairs of the Hijaz and the Red Sea region from Cairo, although British India was considered to have significant interests in the pilgrimage and other Hijaz-related matters due its need to consider the sensibilities of the millions of pious Indian Muslims who were subjects of the Raj. Thus it was that before World War I, Britain's representative in Cairo, Lord Kitchener, had been in contact with Abdullah and Faisal, the sons of the Hijazi ruler, Sharif Husayn, and once the war broke out authorized from London the Husayn-McMahon correspondence. This led eventually to the Arab Revolt, and to a military effort on the eastern flank of Britain's campaign against Ottoman forces in the Sinai and Palestine.

On the Eastern side of Arabia and in the Gulf, as we have also seen, it was Britain's other arm in India that was paramount. The Indian Foreign Service, Army and Navy had a dense network of treaty relationships, agents and bases in Oman, the so-called Trucial States (today's United Arab Emirates), Bahrain, Kuwait, and along the Persian coast dating back to the eighteenth century. It was from India that political agents had been sent out into the interior of Arabia to assess the rising power of the new Saudi state after it had been reestablished in Riyadh in 1902. British India had had a long

and not entirely happy series of experiences with earlier itera-
tions of this Saudi state, which a century earlier had come to
dominate the entire Peninsula in a dramatic fashion marked
by the sack of Karbala in 1802, and the seizure of Mecca and
Medina in 1803 by the ferociously orthodox Wahhabis, and
their subsequent eruption into the Gulf, where they interfered
with shipping and trade.

These agents reported that this state was again a formidable power, and once World War I broke out, an envoy, Capt
W. H. I. Shakspear, was stationed in Riyadh until his death in
battle in 1915. Thereafter, a treaty of friendship with Britain
was negotiated by India's paramount regional representative,
Sir Percy Cox,[47] and subsidies and arms were extended to 'Abd
al-'Aziz ibn Sa'ud, in the hope that he would direct his formidable military capabilities northward against the Ottomans
and their local allies. In spite of a few desultory campaigns in
this direction, Ibn Sa'ud's main concern was not the Ottomans
and their clients, but the consolidation of his power and his
traditional rivals in the Hijaz to the west, the Hashemites,
whom he knew to be receiving even larger British subsidies
and far more arms than he. Skirmishing between the forces of
the two Arabian principalities soon developed into open war-
fare, and to the astonishment and chagrin of London and
Cairo, which had poured resources into the Hijaz in support
of their clients there for many years, the Hashemite forces
were crushed in battle after battle. In January 1926 Ibn Sa'ud,
already sultan of Nejd and ruler of most of the Arabian
Peninsula, was proclaimed king of the Hijaz in the Sacred
Mosque of Mecca. Soon thereafter virtually the entire peninsula had been unified and renamed the Kingdom of Saudi
Arabia.

Although the bemused representatives of British India,
who had been supporting Ibn Sa'ud for over a decade, could

not have been unhappy to see the Hashemite protégés of their British rivals in Cairo brought low, Britain was unable to obtain permanent advantage from the resounding victory of one of its clients over another. For the establishment of Saudi power in Arabia was followed by an even more important development. This was the irruption in the 1930s of the powerful American oil industry, backed by an otherwise isolationist government in Washington, into what had hitherto been the virtually exclusive Middle Eastern preserve of British-government-owned and -backed British Petroleum. The story of how this came to pass, and how Britain, after an unbroken string of successes in acquiring access to and control over Middle Eastern oil, failed to win what in the end proved to be the largest prize in the world of oil, access to the vast oil reserves of Saudi Arabia, is a strange one indeed.

In suffering this reverse, Britain may have been the victim of its own success, or of the arrogance of power that emanated from men like Sir Percy Cox, or of the perceived slights it had inflicted on the proud Saudi ruler, whom it had tried to keep on a tight leash even while lavishing funds and equipment on his hated Hashemite rival. Or perhaps Britain's luck had begun to run out in the Middle East, and the shrewd Ibn Sa'ud understood the advantage to be gained from balancing the overwhelming power of Britain, which surrounded the Arabian Peninsula, with that of the distant but formidable rising star of the United States. The British had already seen one American upstart, Gulf Oil, gain a foothold in Bahrain, part of what they considered their own private preserve. In the Saudi negotiations, the British were more interested in denying access to Saudi oil to the Americans than they were in exploiting it themselves, and their offer was considerably lower than that of their rivals. Moreover, one of Ibn Sa'ud's closest advisors, H. St. John Philby, was working as a paid consultant to the Americans, even as he advised the British. Whatever the explanation, when the moment came for Ibn Sa'ud to offer the much coveted concession to explore his vast territories for oil in 1933, he awarded it to an American company, Standard Oil of California (Socal). Three years later Socal joined its Middle Eastern operations with those of Texaco, bringing together two of the giants of the American oil industry, an industry that dominated the global oil market in spite of its feeble share of Middle Eastern oil. It was this concession, to a group that came to be named the Arabian-American Oil Company (ARAMCO), which permanently transformed that minimal American presence, making American companies the dominant force in the world of Middle Eastern petroleum resources.[48] In 1947 Standard of California and Socony (formerly Standard of New York, later Mobil) joined in the ARAMCO consortium, thus bringing together three of the main components of J. D. Rockefeller's Standard Oil empire that had been broken up by American antitrust laws.

As shrewd geologists suspected, in view of the considerable quantities of oil that had been discovered in adjacent Iran, Iraq, and Bahrain, and its comparable geologic formations, Saudi Arabia was rich indeed in oil. Although significant production only began during World War II, when Saudi Arabia provided a major share of the petroleum products used by American forces in the vital Middle Eastern and Mediterranean theater of the war, this country was a major prize indeed. Beyond its copious oil reserves, which soon proved to be the largest in the world, Saudi Arabia provided two other assets of inestimable value to a power aspiring to a major role in the Middle East. The first was great strategic advantage, lying as it did along major air, sea, and land routes through and within the region, and with direct access to both the Red Sea and the Gulf. The United States soon took advantage of this position to establish a major air base during World War II at Dhahran, in eastern Saudi Arabia, which was utilized by strategic bombers and transport craft for two decades. The second was that unlike Egypt, Syria, Iraq, Tunisia, and other Middle Eastern states with major Western military and naval bases, in Saudi Arabia there was no strong nationalist opposition to a foreign military presence, at least not at this stage. Indeed, without newspapers, universities, or a modern educational system, the kingdom was not characterized by the mass-based nationalist political movements that were already the bane of British and French policy-makers in other countries in the region.

For although the Saudi dynasty had founded the kingdom in part by relying on a movement that represented one of the most chauvinistic, narrow-minded, intolerant, and xenophobic tendencies in modern Islamic history, the Wahhabis, Ibn Sa'ud had forcibly crushed the extreme faction of this movement in the 1930s when it threatened to embroil him in problems with his British patrons by launching unauthorized raids across the Iraqi and Jordanian frontiers. The regime thereafter kept the Wahhabi movement on the tightest of leashes, carefully monitoring its behavior and rigorously circumscribing its actions to specific spheres such as preaching, education, and the administration of justice. Much later, this proved to be a devil's bargain, as the unintended consequences of this restriction of Wahhabi activities, combined with the impact on Saudi society of previously undreamed-of oil wealth, were to lead to a worldwide expansion of fundamentalist Wahhabi proselytism. But in the mid-twentieth century all of this was far in the future, and by keeping American troops and oil workers strictly segregated from his xenophobic subjects, Ibn Sa'ud and his successors were able to offer the United States advantages unavailable elsewhere to its great power rivals.

The concession to ARAMCO involved terms that changed the pattern that BP had heretofore used its monopoly position to impose in Iran, Iraq, and Kuwait: instead of a derisory share of profits, or a per-ton royalty or tax, ARAMCO offered a fifty-fifty split on profits. While a major improvement, and a precedent that BP was soon after obliged to follow, this was not as good as it looked, since the oil companies could still play with the books (as BP had long done in Iran and elsewhere[49]). Moreover, both oil production levels and world prices were determined not by the producing countries, but by the international oil cartel—the so-called Seven Sisters—dominated by American companies.[50] These companies, in brazen defiance of American antitrust law, were allowed to collude for these ends by a government in Washington that was exceedingly compliant toward the oil industry.[51]

Once the American companies grouped in ARAMCO had control of Saudi oil and had made the vast investments necessary to build up that country's production capacity, it became possible for them to use the capacity of what became the "swing producer"—the only country with the ability to rapidly increase its production by an extra million or two barrels per day of oil—in order to affect prices in the international oil market.[52] Prices were thus kept very low—they were at $1.80 per barrel in 1963, down to $1.20 in 1969[53]—thereby fueling the enormous expansion of the economies of the United States, Western Europe, and Japan from World War II onward, and ensuring that the revenues of the oil-producing countries, whose natural resources made this bonanza possible, were considerably smaller than they would have been, had they controlled production themselves. This situation began to be transformed with the establishment in 1960 of the Organization of Petroleum Exporting Countries (OPEC), of which Iran, Iraq, Kuwait, Venezuela, and Saudi Arabia were founding members. After a series of moves in the late 1960s and early 1970s by producing countries to assert their control over their own resources, and after the Arab oil boycott of 1973 in the wake of the October War, prices of oil came to be set by a producers' cartel rather than by one representing the economies of the major consumers of oil. Prices in consequence shot up, producing enormous increases in revenues for the producers, massive increases in prices for consumers, but strangely enough causing little harm to the position of the companies themselves.

While this revolutionary development marked the end of the long absolute reign of the oil companies in the world oil market, it did little to crimp their profits. The companies still dominated the "downstream" aspects of production, including shipping, refining, and marketing, and had incomparable expertise in exploration for oil, not to speak of access to considerable amounts of capital to invest in new oil discoveries. They could thus find new sources of oil and begin production in them, while refining and marketing the end product in the consuming countries. All of this continued to be vastly profitable for them, especially as prices rose. Nor did it affect the paramount position the United States had acquired in Saudi Arabia, a position that became even more advantageous after the flood of new oil revenues into the Saudi treasury. For the American oil companies continued to enjoy a privileged position in their relations with the Saudi oil industry (these companies were now operating in partnership with the nationalized Saudi company that came to be called Saudi ARAMCO), while the United States continued to enjoy its strategic privileges in the country, such as rights to military bases. In addition, American industry and services also had great advantages in access to the lucrative Saudi market, which in light of the new oil wealth was insatiable in its demand for construction, consumer goods, and most profitably of all, expensive weapons systems far too complex to be used without the very expensive training and maintenance provided by willing American companies. Little could any of the many American beneficiaries of the last few decades have dreamed in 1933 what benefits would flow from the oil concession magnanimously offered to Socal by Ibn Sa'ud in that year.

The new dispensation in the oil industry was not all positive for the peoples of the oil-producing countries of the Middle East, however. Having thrown off the iron grip of the oil companies and their great power patrons, they found themselves facing a velvet-covered mailed fist wielded by regimes that were now, thanks to the massive oil revenues they controlled, infinitely richer and considerably more powerful than they had ever been before.

THE MIXED BLESSING OF INDIGENOUS CONTROL OVER MIDDLE EASTERN OIL

The story of how the oil-producing countries won control of their own oil production, and with it control over the world oil market, and thereupon significantly raised the price of oil, bringing themselves manifold increases in revenue, is a Rashomon-like tale that has as many versions as it has narrators. To unreconstructed nationalists in the producing countries, and some elsewhere, it is a stirring and uplifting tale of little Third World Davids slaying the Western neocolonialist Seven Sisters Goliath. To consumers in the prosperous world of the three-car garage, it is a mournful story of their expulsion in 1973 from a paradise where they paid pennies per gallon to fill up their gas-guzzling behemoths. To consumers in the developing world, it is a pitiful tale wherein larger and larger amounts of their scarce hard currency reserves had to be diverted from other essential needs in order to buy more and more expensive petroleum products. For old and new imperialists (whether those who long for the days when the colored races knew who was boss because a Sir Percy Cox could bring them to heel with a word or two, or an RAF bomb or two, or the neo-imperialist wannabes in Washington) it is a tragedy which the occupation of Iraq should soon rewrite, putting those who dared to challenge the old dispensation back in their places. None of these perspectives needs much elucidation, as they are almost self-explanatory.

One perspective that does need clarification, however, is the sad tale of how the untold new wealth resulting from the OPEC price increases starting in the early 1970s ended up in what were by and large the wrong hands, and led to only limited benefits and many dire consequences for those to whom these oil resources really belonged: the peoples of the Middle Eastern oil-producing countries.

Originally dominated by J.D. Rockefeller's Standard Oil trust, and later by a number of giant companies (the Seven Sisters), the oil industry had changed little over the first seven or eight decades of the twentieth century. Once they had come to terms with one another and had carved up the world of oil, the companies essentially decided what would happen in terms of production and prices, and their governments backed them up, with the threat of force or covert intervention if necessary, while generally protecting them from any antitrust or price-fixing charges. In this situation, the producer countries had very little choice but to obey the dictates of the oil companies, with the terrible example of Iran to discourage them from disobedience. However, once a sufficient number of countries had nationalized their oil industries and banded together in OPEC, everything changed. For once the producing countries ran their own oil industries (which they found they could do with relatively little difficulty), decided on production levels, and agreed with one another within OPEC on their respective quotas, they found that their producers' cartel could dictate prices just as easily as had the cartel run by the oil companies. If they were unable to agree, Saudi Arabia, still in the role of swing producer, imposed an agreement on them by virtue of its ability to flood the market with oil, or withhold production from it.

The only fundamental difference between the old cartel of the oil companies and that of OPEC was that these oil-producing countries wanted to maximize their own revenue, and found that in a market where demand constantly grew, that was very easy to do. Prices shot up in consequence, spurred by the fortuitous coincidence of the Arab oil boycott at the time of the 1973 war,[54] and so did the producing countries' revenues, to previously unimaginable levels. The producers were now not only getting a much higher price per barrel—prices went from under $2 in the 1960s to an average of $25 at the end of the 1970s[55]—but they were also receiving the lion's share of that price per barrel, rather than a tiny fraction, as before.

However, nationalization of the oil industry meant that greater power, and vastly greater revenues, flowed into the hands of the elites who controlled the oil-producing states. Even before the post-1973 bonanza, these states and these elites had of course been the prime beneficiaries of the much smaller oil revenues produced in the pre-OPEC era, as all the oil-producing countries were characterized by top-heavy, paternalistic, and undemocratic political systems centered on a powerful ruler. This trend was only accentuated in the post-OPEC era. For it was naturally not Arab or Iranian private companies that now controlled the oil, nor was the private sector in any of these countries the primary beneficiary.

Companies controlled by the state now ran the oil industry, all of whose revenues flowed to the state, which then had absolute power over their allocation. The net result was that new state structures were created where none had existed before, already-strong states grew even stronger, and already-entrenched elites became even harder to remove. It is probably not a coincidence that in the three decades since the oil boom the entire Middle East region, which up until the early 1970s had been known for the instability of its regimes, has not seen a single significant regime change, with the sole exception of Iran.

Needless to say, none of the oil-producing states in the Middle East that enjoyed these enhanced revenues was a democracy, although as we have seen, some of them, like Iraq, Iran, Bahrain, and Kuwait, had once been at least aspiring democracies, with some of the trappings of constitutionalism. They ranged from Algeria under the sclerotic one-party rule of the FLN from after liberation up to the present, to Libya under the erratic, absolute dictatorship of Qaddafi, to Saudi Arabia, Iran under the shah, and the other entrenched Gulf family autocracies—or kleptocracies, according to some—where the ruling family in effect owned the state and its resources, to the brutal Ba'thist dictatorship in Iraq. Far from encouraging change, the increased flow of oil revenues to these authoritarian states reinforced what have historically been among the worst tendencies in Middle Eastern societies: toward the absolute power of the ruler, toward the strengthening of the state at the expense of society, and toward supporting the dependency of citizens on the state. Worse, all of this took place in states that were in many cases deeply dependent on the West to support them against their local rivals and protect them against their peoples, while others were until 1991 aligned with the Soviet Union, which was only too happy to supply them with expensive weapons that they could pay for with their newly acquired hard currency.

The end results were eminently predictable. Instead of this flood of oil money going mainly toward human or infrastructural development, it ended up supporting a vast system of patronage and corruption that upheld the dominant elites whether in allegedly "socialist," and "progressive" states like Algeria, Libya, and Iraq or in the conservative monarchies of the Gulf. Popular acquiescence in a nonrepresentative, politically repressive system was purchased by these elites with marginal improvements in the quality of life for the masses, although in some cases, like Algeria, the elites were so greedy and so inefficient that there were no such improvements. Meanwhile, the elites appropriated for themselves a considerable proportion of the new surplus, raising conspicuous consumption to new heights and becoming an international byword for nouveau riche vulgarity and profligate waste. What was not used for these purposes was squandered on expensive weapons systems that were either never used and rusted in the desert, since they were far too sophisticated for the capabilities of these societies to absorb them, or were utilized in brutal regional conflicts that served as a distraction from the serious, unmet challenges of societal development.

Thus, instead of making possible real independence, and new possibilities for these societies, the new oil revenues instead created a whole new culture of dependency, both of citizens on the state, and of these societies on the developed world. And while external powers, both in the West and the Soviet Union, could be blamed for profiting by selling unnecessary weapons systems, or for supporting unpopular regimes because they served their selfish interests, the societal deformities and political distortions that ensued within these states can be laid entirely at the door of the rulers and regimes of the oil producers of the Middle East. In the end, winning control of their oil resources, a sort of magic grail for several generations since the early years of the twentieth century, proved to be a cruel disappointment for the peoples of these societies. For while some good came of this, whether in education, infrastructure, or the eventual budding of aspects of democracy in a very few cases like Bahrain, Kuwait, and Qatar, this had to be set against many missed opportunities. Had the investments in education, health care, housing, technology, and social services been as great as or greater than those on useless weapons, the apparatus of domestic repression and the bank accounts of the rulers, their families, cronies, and hangers-on, how different might the outcome have been. Among the worst consequences of what did transpire was the growth of behemoth-like states that had fattened on oil revenues and that came to dominate society and the economy in the decades since the rise of OPEC, blotting out in many cases the possibility of real steps toward a more open society such as popular participation, limitation of the powers of the ruler, and real democracy.

But it is worth noting that however much some may have regretted these lost opportunities, and the reinforcement of the patronage-wielding, all-powerful state, there were no voices in the Middle Eastern countries that regretted the principle that they should have control over their own oil resources. The tragedy was that it was not the peoples, but the unrepresentative regimes that ruled them, that really controlled these resources. Clearly, no one longed for the day when foreign companies, backed by arrogant Western diplomats and gunboat diplomacy, dictated oil production, gave the producing countries a pittance, and battened on these countries' natural riches. And whatever problems these societies faced as a result of the misuse of their oil revenues by narrowly based, unrepresentative, dictatorial regimes, no one dreamed that the clock might be turned back, and that the producer countries might lose control over their oil resources.

With the American occupation of oil-rich Iraq, however, the specter of foreign control over Middle Eastern oil emerged once again. As the new American occupation regime in Iraq took its first steps to reorganize the battered Iraqi oil industry, fear of foreign control, born of decades of bitter experiences of being forced to watch others dictate the disposition of their countries' most valuable resource, spread throughout the country and the region. In an ominous sign of which way things were going, persistent news reports indicated that the Iraqi oil ministry, under its new American-appointed directors, seconded by their American advisors headed by a former senior executive of Shell Oil, was contemplating operating independently of OPEC, as a step toward breaking the power of the cartel. This proved not to be true, and indeed, OPEC accepted a delegation representing the U.S.-appointed Iraqi Governing Council as an observer at the first OPEC ministerial meeting after the American occupation of Iraq.[56] Even more ominous were reports about the "privatization" of Iraqi oil,[57] or joint production agreements that would give foreign companies absolute control over a share of Iraqi oil production, or "mortgaging" Iraqi oil revenues into the future to help pay the costs of the American occupation.[58] Although Paul Bremer, head of the Coalition Provisional Authority, was reported to have opposed this last idea proposed by other Bush administration officials, on the grounds that it "has the disadvantage ... of making it look as if we are in some way taking a lien against oil revenues, and therefore that's why we fought this war," he also said of the Iraqi Governing Council's reluctance to privatize the country's oil industry that he was "encouraging the Iraqi government to change that policy."[59] A new era seemed to be dawning in Iraq that looked suspiciously like the good old days of Sir Percy Cox.

CHAPTER FOUR

THE UNITED STATES
AND PALESTINE

Zionism, be it right or wrong, good or bad, is rooted in age-long traditions, in present needs, in future hopes, of far greater import than the desires and prejudices of the 700,000 Arabs who now inhabit that ancient land. —ARTHUR JAMES BALFOUR,
AUGUST 11, 1919

The Palestinians must be made to understand in the deepest recesses of their consciousness that they are a defeated people.
— MOSHE YAALON, ISRAELI ARMY CHIEF OF STAFF,
AUGUST 30, 2002

As with many other unresolved issues in the modern Middle East, it was Great Britain rather than the United States that initially created the problem of Palestine. But in Palestine, as elsewhere, it has been the lot of America, Britain's successor as the Western power with undisputed hegemony over the Middle East, to contend with this problem and its seemingly unending sequels. The outlines of the problem can be simply stated: with the Balfour Declaration of November 2, 1917,[1] Britain threw the weight of the greatest power of the age, one that was at that moment in the process of conquering Palestine, behind the creation of a Jewish state in what was then an overwhelmingly Arab country.[2] Everything that has followed in that conflict-riven land has flowed inevitably from this decision.

As previously discussed, the United States was not, in 1917

and for several decades thereafter, a power with significant interests in the Middle East, beyond relatively modest cultural, educational, and missionary concerns. Nevertheless, some of the same religious and romantic factors that led many European Protestants to extend their fervent support to Zionism affected American Protestants, with the same potent political results. Beyond what they knew from tales from the Bible, Americans in the early twentieth century knew very little about Palestine, and this biblical knowledge generally served to obscure almost completely the realities of the contemporary Middle East. Americans knew considerably less about the region than did Europeans, who had long been engaged in trading with, invading, and visiting it. Moreover, in consequence of these lengthy contacts, several European countries, notably Britain, France, Germany, Russia, the Netherlands, Italy, and Spain, had developed a high degree of scholarly expertise about aspects of Islam and Middle Eastern languages, history, and culture, with knowledge following power and thereafter serving as its handmaiden, as so often it does.[3] There was little such expert academic knowledge about the Middle East in the United States, which did not even have a permanent foreign intelligence service until after World War II.[4]

There were other reasons beyond the potent influence of the Bible for Americans to be attracted by the lure of Zionism. Because of their own pioneer heritage, Americans were even more apt than Europeans to identify with lurid images of brave, outnumbered settlers of European stock taming an arid land in the face of opposition from ignorant, fanatical nomads—wildly distorted and unrealistic (albeit lasting) though these images were.[5] For these and other reasons, soon after the beginning of the modern political Zionist enterprise around the turn of the twentieth century, many American politicians declared themselves strongly supportive of it. Like European political leaders, they were swayed mainly by their own beliefs, which tended to reflect the biblically induced pro-Zionist sentiment prevalent among their Protestant constituents. At the outset at least, this sentiment was probably more significant than the views of their less numerous and far less influential American Jewish constituents, most of whom in any case were anti- or non-Zionist until the rise of Nazism.[6] This Christian support for Zionism continues to be politically important, with increasing weight recently among Evangelical and fundamentalist Protestant congregations.

Woodrow Wilson was the first American president to support Zionism publicly, and his backing was crucial to the awarding to Britain of the League of Nations mandate for Palestine.[7] This in turn led to the inclusion in the terms of the mandate of the text of the Balfour Declaration, committing the entire international community to establishing a Jewish national home in a country that was in fact at that time almost entirely Arab (but that was named as neither Arab nor Palestinian in the terms of the declaration and the mandate). Wilson extended American support to Zionism in spite of the misgivings of some of his expert advisors, and in spite of the results of the King-Crane Commission. This body had been sent to the Middle East at the express wish of the American president, and in spite of the distinct lack of enthusiasm for the idea by the British and French, in order to determine the wishes of the populations concerned. The commission discovered the majority Arab population of Palestine to be overwhelmingly opposed to the establishment of a Jewish national home—which they rightly feared would inexorably develop into an exclusively Jewish state in their homeland and at their expense.[8] Not for the last time in the framing of U.S. Middle Eastern policy, political and personal considerations overrode the advice of the experts in the framing of Wilson's decision.[9] Although the United States withdrew from active involvement in the League of Nations and from many other aspects of international politics soon afterward, the impact on Palestine of these key post–World War I decisions was to be lasting. Under the protection of the British mandate, and with its invaluable support, by 1939 the Zionist movement had created the nucleus of a viable, independent Jewish state, bearing out the fears that the Palestinians had expressed to the King-Crane Commission.[10]

It was thus in keeping with what was to become an American tradition that a few decades after Wilson's original intervention, at critical moments for the fortunes of the Palestinians and the Zionist cause, President Truman overrode the views of most of his foreign policy advisors on the Palestine issue.[11] He did so to decisive effect in supporting the Zionist movement when it came into confrontation with the British after World War II; in supporting a 1947 U.N. plan for the partition of Palestine that was exceedingly favorable to the Zionists;[12] and in extending American recognition to the new Jewish state immediately after it declared its independence on May 15, 1948. Justifying his support for Zionism in spite of the objections of his officials, Truman famously remarked: "I'm sorry, gentlemen, but I have to answer to hundreds of thousands who are anxious for the success of Zionism; I do not have hundreds of thousands of Arabs among my constituents."[13]

This sums up one aspect of the conundrum of American power as it has affected the Palestinians. Unable to appeal to the Bible for religious and historical justification of their claims (although many of them are Christians), as could the Zionists, unable to claim that they had strategic value to the United States, as Israel was able to do, especially during the

Cold War, and unable to marshal a powerful lobby to support them domestically, as Israel has been exemplary in doing, the Palestinians have consistently failed to gain a fair hearing for their cause in the United States. This has been especially harmful as the United States has grown increasingly important in determining outcomes that affected them. Their failure was partly a function of the Palestinians' continuing ignorance, from the 1940s until the present day, of how American politics worked, and of the political ineffectiveness of a largely first-generation Arab-American community that initially was not very focused on the question of Palestine, and since has failed to make an impact on the American political system. The task of both Palestinians and Arab Americans was made all the harder by the fact that they were up against a vivid narrative rooted in biblical themes familiar to most Americans, and which took on added poignancy from the terrible, recent memory of the Holocaust.

For decades the way in which the United States has treated the Palestine question has had a powerful and enduring impact on how America was regarded in Middle Eastern public opinion. Most Arabs, Middle Easterners, and Muslims, as well as increasing numbers of others in the rest of the world, have come to regard the American attitude toward the Palestinians as an important standard by which the United States should be judged as a great power.[14] By the same token, it must be admitted that over its many decades of unstinting and generous support for Israel, the United States has been remarkably successful in persuading Arab governments that, appearances notwithstanding, it was not completely biased in favor of Israel, or even if it was, such a bias should simply be ignored.

As American policy has increasingly converged with that of Israel, this process of persuasion has grown more difficult for

United States policy-makers. Absent such persuasion, there have been increasing internal difficulties for Arab governments perceived by their own citizens to be supine before a United States totally biased in favor of Israel. Moreover, in the wake of the murderous suicide attacks of September 11, 2001, on New York and Washington, the convergence between the policies of the Bush administration and the government of Prime Minister Ariel Sharon has reached the point that they are virtually indistinguishable in a number of realms, notably as regards what has become their shared rhetoric on the topic of "terrorism." Nowadays, Palestinian militant groups like Hamas and Islamic Jihad are lumped together with al-Qa'ida in the statements of the Bush administration and the Israeli government, and increasingly appear to be the object of similar attention in U.S. law and as a target of law enforcement agencies. While these two Palestinian groups have repeatedly killed civilians, as have most other European, South Asian, and Latin American groups on the government's list of terrorist organizations, they have not actively targeted the United States and American citizens, as has al-Qa'ida. Nevertheless, like al-Qa'ida, but unlike many other groups on the government's list of terrorist organizations, Hamas and Islamic Jihad and their alleged adherents and supporters in the United States have been the object of sustained, serious attention from federal prosecutors.[15]

It remains to be seen how much of an impact this American-Israeli convergence and the identification of the United States with Israel will have on America's standing in public opinion in the Middle East, or with regional governments, or on these governments' standing with their own peoples. For most people in the Middle East insist on distinguishing between groups like al-Qa'ida and what they see as Palestinian movements of resistance to occupation. Even if they morally disapprove of the targeting of Israeli civilians, as many (but certainly not all) do, most believe that Palestinian violence against Israeli civilians can only be understood in the context of the Israeli occupation and its intense, systematic violence against Palestinian civilians. Middle Easterners understand, as most Americans do not, that while civilians constituted a majority of the over eight hundred Israelis killed in the three years after the second *intifada*, or uprising, began in September 2000, they also were a majority of the over twenty-four hundred Palestinians killed.[16] In view of the Bush administration's almost exclusive focus on Palestinian violence directed against Israeli civilians, and its inattention to the far greater toll among Palestinian civilians, the perception among Middle Easterners that the United States cares about innocents only if they are Americans or Israelis, and pays no attention to them if they are Palestinians or Arabs, is hard to efface. In the eyes of many in the Middle East, it appears that some civilian lives have much more value than others in U.S. policy.

U.S. POLICY: FROM EVEN-HANDED TO PARTISAN

It has not always been thus. Indeed, American policy has changed considerably over time, as has the image of the United States in the Middle East with respect to the question of Palestine. At the outset, even the decisive American support for the establishment of Israel in 1948 did not spoil the generally good state of American relations with Middle Eastern countries and peoples. This was partly because Britain was still seen as the dominant Middle Eastern power and was largely blamed for the Palestine tragedy, partly because the United States still benefited from its aura as an anticolonial force, and partly because both rulers and public opinion in most Middle

Eastern countries still had relatively little experience with the U.S. in the 1940s and early 1950s. Moreover, the 1956 Suez Crisis, when the United States stood firm against the tripartite aggression against Egypt launched by Britain, France, and Israel, and then peremptorily forced Israel to withdraw from the occupied Sinai Peninsula and Gaza Strip in January 1957, significantly enhanced America's image in the Arab world and the rest of the Middle East.

Until the intrusion of Cold War considerations in the years that followed, in fact, the United States' position on Palestine did little harm to its standing with important segments of Middle Eastern public opinion and to its relations with many governments in the region. In any case, with a few notable exceptions (the oil boycott instigated by the Saudi king Faisal after the 1973 war being one) pro-Western governments like those of Saudi Arabia, Jordan, Libya (before 1969), Tunisia, and Morocco have consistently allowed their appreciation of American support for them in their regional disputes, or other benefits that flowed from good bilateral relations with Washington, to outweigh any concern they might have over the American position on Palestine. Saudi Arabia's King 'Abd al-'Aziz ibn Sa'ud, the founder of the kingdom, for example, stressed the injustice of establishing a Jewish state in an Arab land during his 1944 meeting with President Franklin Roosevelt aboard an American cruiser in Egypt. Both Roosevelt and his successor, Harry Truman, promised Ibn Sa'ud that the United States would do nothing as regards Palestine without consulting its new Arab ally, but the Saudi monarch was able to do nothing when this promise was ignored.[17]

Indeed, during most of the 1950s the American position on Arab-Israeli issues was relatively balanced, in spite of a deep American popular sympathy for Israel based on the biblical and other factors already mentioned, reinforced in the meantime by potent and successful public relations efforts to enhance the new state's image with the American citizenry. Nevertheless, in addition to forcing Israel out of Sinai, during the 1950s the United States also repeatedly voted in the U.N. Security Council to condemn Israel for its savage reprisals, such as the October 1953 raid on Qibya in the West Bank, to avenge the killing of three Israeli civilians. In this raid, fifty-four Palestinian civilians were killed when they were pinned inside their homes with gunfire, after which soldiers of the infamous Unit 101, commanded by Ariel Sharon, dynamited dozens of structures over the heads of the victims.[18] It could certainly be said that until the mid-1960s the United States acted more as an honest broker in the conflict than as a dedicated ally of Israel.[19]

For most of this period, too, the attacks by Palestinians on Israelis for which Israeli raids were supposed to be reprisals were by and large not supported or condoned by Arab governments, which were restrained by their British patrons (in the case of Jordan), or intimidated by the power the Israeli army had demonstrated during the 1948 and 1956 wars.[20] Through the mid-1950s there were in fact repeated initiatives to resolve the nascent Arab-Israeli conflict, mainly by the United States but also by other mediators, on the basis of territorial compromise and the return of some of the 750,000 Palestinian refugees who were driven from or fled their homes in 1948.[21] The principle of peace with Israel on the basis of these ideas was accepted at different times by several Arab governments, but was rejected by Israel, largely because of the refusal of Israel's first prime minister, David Ben-Gurion, in particular to contemplate either territorial concessions or the return of refugees.[22] Ben-Gurion and his followers, such as Moshe Dayan, disagreed with a minority of Israeli leaders like Moshe Sharrett in considering a large, strong Israel more important than peace on these terms. Notwithstanding these realities, which were soon forgotten by American public opinion, if it ever properly registered them, it was the Arabs alone who got a reputation as rejectionists when they refused compromise with Israel in the 1960s. The United States, although it had advocated such a compromise in the 1950s, eventually allowed the matter to drop when it was rejected by Israel. This eventually constituted another pattern in U.S. policy: giving up on American initiatives when Israel raised objections.

Although the United States provided Israel from the outset with considerable economic aid, that aid did not become significant until the late 1960s and only reached astronomical levels beginning in 1973, when it numbered in the billions of dollars annually, putting Israel ahead of all other American aid recipients. Moreover, the United States did not sell Israel significant quantities or the most modern kinds of arms until the 1960s, when President Kennedy decided to provide the Jewish state with Hawk antiaircraft missiles and President Johnson sold Israel Skyhawk fighter-bombers.[23] From the early 1950s until the 1967 war it was France rather than the United States that furnished the key weapons systems to the potent Israeli arsenal, as well as the Dimona nuclear reactor, which thereafter enabled Israel to transform itself into a significant nuclear power (France ceased to supply arms to Israel after the June 1967 war). The United States was thus not the foremost military or diplomatic backer of Israel until after 1967. It was the superimposition of Cold War rivalries on the Arab-Israeli conflict that revolutionized both the conflict and American relations with the region.

The Cold War had entered the Middle East much earlier, indeed from its very beginning, with the immediate post–World War II crises between the Soviet Union and Iran and Turkey leading eventually to the issuance of the Truman

Doctrine in 1947. However, at the outset the Cold War mainly affected the region's non-Arab peripheries bordering on the Soviet Union. It was not until the mid-1960s that the leading Arab states surrounding Israel, Egypt and Syria, became increasingly identified with the Soviet Union as a result of their inability to remain nonaligned between the two great blocs, and their need for large quantities of weapons in light of their military defeats by Israel in 1948, 1956, and 1967. Thereafter, the United States began to offer significant military, and later economic, assistance to the Jewish state.

The deepening American involvement in Vietnam in the late 1960s contributed to the imposition of Cold War patterns on the Middle East, as American policy-makers came to see the alignment with the Soviet Union of several Arab states, notably Egypt and Syria, through Cold War lenses. Especially after it routed the Arabs in 1967, and as the war in Vietnam turned uglier, a potent Israel came to be attractive to the United States as a proxy stick with which to beat Soviet proxies in the Middle East. Ironically, there is much evidence that most of the leading Arab states were not interested in confrontation with Israel before 1967. It is now known that they were dragged into it during the spring of that year by attacks on Israel by Palestinian groups based in Syria and the zeal of the radical neo-Ba'th regime in power in Damascus.[24] They thereafter were incapable of escaping this confrontation after the territory of three of their number, Egypt, Syria, and Jordan, had been occupied as a result of their defeat in 1967. Once the Arab states and Israel, and their respective superpower patrons, had been thus involved, there was no getting out of the rigid symmetries imposed by the Cold War, at least for a time.

This began what might be called the classic phase of the Arab-Israeli conflict, one that concluded only with the collapse of the USSR and the end of the Cold War. This phase encompassed the 1967 war, the so-called war of attrition along the Suez Canal ending in 1970, the 1973 war, and the 1978 and 1982 Israeli invasions of Lebanon. The Arab parties engaged in the conflict, notably Egypt and Syria, the newly established Palestine Liberation Organization (PLO),[25] and to a lesser extent Iraq, were seen as aligned with the Soviet Union, which was perceived as calling the shots. This was an idea false in every respect,[26] but which was the product of an era of distorted perceptions when American policy-makers even saw Vietnam and China as proxies of the Soviet Union. The Soviets posed as the disinterested and generous patrons of the Arabs, although there was much evidence of deep and bitter rifts between the two sides over the rigid limitations that the Soviet Union placed on its military and economic support, out of fear of being dragged into uncontrollable confrontations with the United States by what Moscow saw as irresponsible Arab governments.[27]

Although the United States backed a broad range of Middle Eastern states, including Iran, Turkey, and several Arab countries, its support for Israel from the late 1960s onward was increasingly both quantitatively and qualitatively different from that it extended to any other country in the Middle East. Not only did U.S. aid to Israel eventually surpass that extended to any other country in the world, it also came to include advanced weapons systems no other client or ally, even NATO allies, received, and which sometimes were delivered to the Israeli military at the same time as they reached the U.S. armed forces. Thus, by the last phase of the 1968–70 Egyptian-Israeli war of attrition along the Suez Canal, which continued despite a failed 1968–69 initiative to stop the fighting by Secretary of State William Rogers, the United States was delivering to Israel several top-of-the-line F-4 Phantom fighter-bombers per month right off the McDonnell Douglas assembly lines, although the advanced war-planes were badly needed in Vietnam at that time.[28]

By 1970, the conflict had grown much more intense, with an increasingly salient role for the superpowers. As Israeli F-4 Phantoms bombed targets deeper and deeper inside Egypt, Israeli pilots were shooting down the most advanced interceptors in the Soviet arsenal, Egyptian MiG-21J's, flown by Soviet pilots. Soviet-supplied SAM-2 and SAM-3 antiaircraft missiles were being installed closer and closer to the Suez Canal, threatening to establish a no-fly zone for Israeli planes over Israeli positions on the east side of the canal. Finally, by August 1970, losses of Israeli F-4 Phantoms to Egyptian antiaircraft fire became greater than the United States' ability to replace them, given how stretched production of them was due to the Vietnam War.[29] At this stage, the United States made a determined effort to lower the level of violence, partly out of fear that the situation would get out of control and eventually embroil the superpowers. Rogers managed to obtain a cease-fire along the canal, which lasted for three years, although the political element of the Rogers Plan, involving negotiations between Egypt and Israel, became a dead letter because Israel refused to enter into serious negotiations, citing alleged Egyptian violations of the terms of the cease-fire.

The end result was a temporary calming of Israel's Egyptian front, at the expense of an explosion on the eastern front, for the Rogers Plan provoked divisions between the Arab parties that accepted it, Egypt and Jordan, on the one hand, and the Arab parties that rejected it, Syria, Iraq, and the PLO.[30] In the end, the fractious PLO paid the highest price for its rejection, being eliminated from Jordan by the Jordanian army in a series of campaigns beginning with the bloody Black September fighting in Amman in 1970 and continuing until the spring of 1971, when Palestinian fighters were finally routed in Northern Jordan. A coup in Syria in November 1970 led by Hafez al-Asad against the wing of the Syrian Ba'th Party that had most strongly supported the Palestinians, and the elimination thereafter by Iraqi strongman Ahmad Hassan Bakr and his deputy and relative Saddam Hussein of those Iraqi Ba'thist leaders most sympathetic to the Palestinians, left them in a weak position, isolated in Lebanon and without significant Arab government support. The PLO nevertheless had reestablished Palestinian nationalism, in eclipse since the 1948 war, as a force to be reckoned with.

Until this point, the United States had done little to resolve the Palestine problem per se: beyond timid efforts to persuade Israel to accept partial refugee repatriation and territorial compromise in the 1950s, it had ignored the Palestinians, focusing instead on its relations with the Arab states, and preeminently on its rivalry with the USSR. The U.S. at best engaged in conflict management, as in its interventions of 1956 and 1970, which both reestablished the *status quo ante bellum*, or pursued a policy of interested benign neglect, as in 1967, when it gave what amounted to a covert green light to Israel's preemptive attack on Egypt, Syria, and Jordan. Henry Kissinger, who soon after 1970 had taken control of American Middle East policy (and of most other aspects of American foreign policy and strategy), and by 1973 had replaced Rogers, pursued the benign-neglect approach until the 1973 war. Only then did the Egyptian-Syrian attack on Israeli forces in the occupied Sinai Peninsula and Golan Heights oblige him to devote his attention to this problem. Again, the solution chosen was to focus primarily on obtaining strategic advantage vis-à-vis the USSR rather than peacemaking per se, with the main American aim being to win Egypt into the American camp and away from the Soviet one. Kissinger did this with a series of disengagement accords that ultimately, under the Carter administration, led to the Camp David agreement and the Egyptian-Israeli peace treaty of 1979.

Kissinger paid the minimum of attention necessary to the Syrian-Israeli front, where the post-1973 crisis was defused by a disengagement accord that was still in force over thirty years later. Throughout, the secretary of state paid even less serious attention to Jordan or the Palestinians (except to extend support, overtly in Jordan and covertly in Lebanon, to the opponents of the latter). President Carter and his advisors eventually followed the same approach of ignoring the Palestinians, although this was not their initial intention. In 1977 Carter attempted to initiate comprehensive Middle East settlement negotiations including the Palestinians, made a pioneering statement about the need for a Palestinian homeland, and initiated contacts with the PLO through his ambassador to the U.N., Andrew Young. Carter soon drew back from all of these exposed positions, under intense pressure from the powerful Israeli lobby. It was not U.S. policy, but rather Egyptian president Anwar Sadat's 1977 initiative of traveling to Jerusalem, that eventually led to Camp David and a separate Egyptian-Israeli peace. The Carter administration was in any case soon preoccupied by the Iran hostage crisis, and thereafter by the Soviet invasion of Afghanistan, and was consequently distracted from Middle East diplomacy.

The Reagan years saw an unprecedented American warming to Israel, with the first appearance in foreign policy-making positions of the muscular nationalists like Dick Cheney and Donald Rumsfeld and the neoconservatives like Richard Perle and Paul Wolfowitz who would later dominate the Bush Administration's foreign policy. Under such influences, American benign neglect of the Palestinians became more and more malignant, as the Reagan administration turned a blind eye to increasingly aggressive Israeli settlement policies that were steadily swallowing up land in the West Bank. This had become a critical issue beginning in 1977 with the advent to power in Israel of right-wing Likud governments,[31] which were committed to keeping control of what they called "Judea and Samaria" (the West Bank, to the rest of the world) and began a settlement-building campaign to make sure this would happen that has hardly flagged since then. Beyond this, the Reagan administration gave a covert green light to Israel's invasion of Lebanon and its expulsion of the PLO from Beirut in 1982,[32] and thereafter helped Israel to create a puppet Lebanese government that was brought to sign a short-lived peace treaty on Israeli terms. The only concrete result of this ill-fated and foolish American initiative was to alienate the overwhelming majority of Lebanese and to provoke a series of lethal attacks on American marines, diplomatic facilities, and academics in Beirut. Although Reagan's last secretary of state, George Shultz, opened up direct, public contacts between the U.S. government and the PLO for the first time, after the Palestinians met a number of American conditions, in the end this initiative did little to resolve the Palestinian-Israeli conflict, which by the end of the Reagan years had erupted into the first Palestinian intifada. It was left to the first Bush administration to launch the first serious multilateral effort to resolve the Arab-Israeli conflict, including its Palestinian dimensions, in the wake of the U.S. war to expel Iraq from Kuwait in 1991.

Starting at Madrid in the fall of that year, Secretary of State James Baker managed an achievement unprecedented since the Balfour Declaration in 1917 had created an international conflict over Palestine.[33] This was to seat virtually all parties to the Arab-Israeli conflict, and all the relevant international actors, around one table, albeit only for one short meeting, after which the proceedings broke up into bilateral negotiations in Washington, D.C., between Israel and its neighbors, as well as multilateral sessions on a number of issues of common interest. Unfortunately, the ground rules that the United States, acting under Israeli pressure, imposed for the functioning of the bilateral Palestinian-Israeli negotiations that went on in Washington for the next twenty months nullified many of the advantages thereby achieved.[34] They also affected the subsequent talks between the two sides that started secretly at Oslo and elsewhere in 1992 and 1993 on the margins of the Washington talks. These ground rules explicitly excluded immediate direct Palestinian-Israeli negotiations over the major problems between the two sides, the so-called final-status issues. These issues were left for negotiations scheduled for several years later, but which were repeatedly postponed, provoking the fury of the Palestinians. Instead, at Madrid and in Washington, the Palestinians initially were obliged to accept the fiction of a Jordanian-Palestinian joint delegation, and were not allowed to choose their own representatives, with Palestinians from Jerusalem, from outside the occupied territories, or identified with the PLO all excluded, although some individuals from these categories (myself included) were allowed to function as "advisors" to the Palestinian delegation.

Most seriously, the Palestinians were forced to accept what ended up being an indefinite deferment of the negotiation of all the most important final-status issues between them and the Israelis: sovereignty, statehood, final borders, settlements, Jerusalem, refugees, and water. All the Palestinians were allowed to negotiate with the Israelis, by these restrictive ground rules, was an interim accord for self-government. This process ultimately produced the Palestinian Authority (PA), which eventually obtained extremely limited control over 17.2

percent of the West Bank and the Gaza Strip, divided into seventy-five "islands," all isolated from one another by swaths of Israeli-controlled territory and dozens of military checkpoints. In the meantime, while protracted negotiations ensued, these ground rules enabled Israel to maintain its occupation and its control of most of the occupied territories and of the most important aspects of the life of the 3.5 million Palestinians under occupation. Most importantly, all the while, Israel was able to continue expanding its illegal settlements and the strategic roads that connected them, which at the same time divided the West Bank and Gaza Strip into scores of easily controlled and isolated parcels.

The highly respected head of the Palestinian delegation to the Madrid and Washington negotiations, Dr. Haidar 'Abd al-Shafi, said at the time and has repeated publicly since, that it was a grievous mistake for the Palestinians to continue to negotiate under such onerous conditions, when the unceasing expansion of illegal Israeli settlements in the occupied territories and the building of roads to connect them continued devouring the very land that was supposed to be subject to negotiation. He added that the Palestinians should have withdrawn from the talks when the United States failed to insist that Israel respect the terms of reference for the Madrid process (terms that were highly favorable to it), and in particular when the United States failed to honor the commitments contained in its Letter of Assurance to the Palestinians.[35] The latter in particular stated that the United States would oppose actions that were "prejudicial or precedential," would "make negotiations more difficult or preempt their final outcome," or that would "predetermine" final-status options. Seeing the American failure to do anything about Israeli actions such as the constant building of settlements that contravened these guidelines, the entire Palestinian delegation agreed with the position of Dr 'Abd al-Shafi and insisted on a Palestinian withdrawal from the talks, only to be overruled by Yasir Arafat and the rest of the PLO leadership in Tunis, which was calling all the important shots throughout the negotiations.[36]

From this fatal mistake flowed much else: notably the mounting fury of ordinary Palestinians as repeated American-imposed deadlines were allowed to fall by the wayside (in spite of the statement in the Letter of Assurances that "negotiations should proceed as quickly as possible toward agreement"),[37] as year after year of frustrating negotiations led to thousands more acres of land being confiscated and hundreds of more miles of settler-only roads being built, and as the Israeli settler population in the occupied territories doubled from two hundred thousand in 1991 to four hundred thousand in 2000. This ominous precedent was repeated again and again as negotiations continued in different venues, but with similar disappointing results for the Palestinians.

The negotiations that started at Madrid went on fruitlessly in Washington for ten sessions, stretching from October 1991 through June 1993. Eventually, after the election of Yitzhak Rabin at the head of a Labor government in 1992, Israel decided to start indirect and then direct back-channel negotiations with the PLO itself in Oslo and elsewhere. While this meant that a major Palestinian demand—direct negotiations with the PLO—had been met, it had an important downside. Now, the negotiations were no longer mainly in the hands of an increasingly competent delegation of West Bankers and Gazans, with intimate knowledge about the situation under occupation, with a popular constituency back home that they had to report to periodically. This group over time had developed a certain amount of expertise in negotiating with the Israelis—and with the American "honest brokers," who were often harder to deal with than the Israelis themselves.[38]

Instead, the negotiations were now carried out in secret, mainly at Oslo, by a group of PLO officials apparently chosen primarily for their loyalty to Arafat and his colleagues in the PLO leadership, with limited knowledge of English (the language of the negotiations), no legal background, no firsthand knowledge of the situation in the occupied territories, no negotiating experience with Israelis, and no direct knowledge of how the twenty months of Madrid and Washington discussions had gone.

These weaknesses of the Palestinian negotiating team were reflected in the disappointing terms for the Palestinians of the resulting Oslo accords. These accords were the basis for the Israeli-PLO Declaration of Principles signed on the White House lawn on September 13, 1993, in the presence of Yasir Arafat, Yitzhak Rabin, and President Clinton.[39] As fleshed out by a series of subsequent interim agreements, these accords eventually produced the misshapen map of scores of isolated islands of territory over which the newly established PA "ruled," and the political, legal, and diplomatic straitjacket within which the Palestinians have found themselves ever since.

THE OSLO PROCESS AND
ITS CONSEQUENCES

While most people the world over naturally thought that peace had been achieved with the ceremony on the White House lawn in September 1993, for ordinary Palestinians the Oslo accords began a process that went downhill almost from the beginning. For in keeping with the Madrid ground rules, nothing of any importance to the two sides had yet even been negotiated, let alone agreed upon. By the Oslo accords, the PLO formally recognized the state of Israel (it had in fact already done so once before, de facto as part of the Palestinian Declaration of Independence in 1988). While Israel now formally recognized the PLO as representing the Palestinians, it did not recognize the right of the Palestinian people to statehood, self-determination, or sovereignty, or that they had the right to borders, or where those borders were. While in consequence of Oslo, Israel got acceptance and recognition from the Arab world and developed commercial or political or indirect relations with a majority of Arab countries, by contrast the Palestinians were forgotten by their supporters in the Arab world and elsewhere, who mistakenly thought that they had finally achieved their national objectives. They could be forgiven this impression, given the overly optimistic tone of PLO and PA statements.

Much more seriously, the lives of most Palestinians got considerably worse after Oslo: a series of "closures"—crippling Israeli restrictions on movement—were imposed, first around Jerusalem, cutting the Arab eastern part of the city off from its immediate hinterland in the adjacent parts of the West Bank (again in violation of the Madrid ground rules, and again without provoking as much as a peep from the American sponsor of the "peace process"), and then in other areas. After having enjoyed virtually complete freedom of movement in and through the entirety of Israel and the occupied territories for the first two decades of the occupation, after Oslo, Palestinians found themselves in a situation where their movement was more and more restricted. A vast network of so-called bypass roads were built after the Oslo accords and as a direct consequence of them, ostensibly to connect Israeli settlements to one another and to Israel, but that had two devastating effects as by-products. First, they cut off adjacent Palestinian areas from one another, producing discontinuities of space and jurisdiction; and second, they demonstrated to

Palestinians, with thousands of tons of newly poured reinforced concrete, that the ever expanding Israeli settlements
were there to stay and that Palestinian dreams of statehood
and sovereignty in the entirety of the West Bank, Gaza Strip,
and East Jerusalem were not going to be realized.

Meanwhile, Palestinian GDP per capita continuously
declined, unemployment rose as labor flows were interrupted
because the movement of Palestinians was more and more
restricted, and the daily travel of ordinary citizens in, to, and
through the occupied territories and between the dozens of
islands of territory "controlled" by the new PA set up by the
Oslo accords, grew more and more difficult. On top of these
problems created by Israel and the Palestinian-Israeli accords,
the newly established Palestinian Authority proved corrupt
and ridden by debilitating cronyism. Its newly elected president, Yasir Arafat, appointed thousands of his trusted retainers
to make-work jobs in the bloated bureaucracy and security
services, he obstructed much of what was done to create a rule
of law, the elected Legislative Assembly was steadily deprived
of its powers, and insufficient aid or investment arrived to
improve the situation of ordinary Palestinians. Over the years,
angry mass dissatisfaction with the PA's incompetence, in-
efficiency, and poor performance in negotiations with Israel
grew in the West Bank and Gaza Strip, to the point that the
popularity even of the national leader, Yasir Arafat, began to
suffer.

Within a few years after Oslo, especially after the assassina-
tion of Yitzhak Rabin by an Israeli right-wing extremist in late
1995, negotiations between the two sides bogged down.
Tragically, little effort was made by the United States to resolve
the basic differences between Palestinians and Israelis in the
mid-1990s, when the Oslo accords were perhaps still salvage-
able, although American diplomats, and occasionally Pres-

ident Clinton himself, at times became involved in the negotiation of minute issues separating the two sides. Instead of
pressing for the immediate launching of final-status negotiations to resolve the major problems separating the two, the
Clinton administration allowed Israel to drag out and delay
the negotiation and implementation of further interim self-
government accords. Nearly a decade after negotiations started
in 1991, these accords left the Palestinians in partial control of
scores of isolated pockets of territory in less than 20 percent of
the West Bank and about 60 percent of the Gaza Strip, and no
nearer their objectives of ending Israel's occupation and settlement of their land and creating a viable, independent, sovereign Palestinian state.

Not surprisingly in view of these results, despair and anger
spread among ordinary Palestinians as their daily life grew
harder and harder, the high hopes of the early 1990s evapo-
rated, and the network of Israeli settlements, army checkpoints, strategic bypass roads, and the military occupation
that protected them grew more and more entrenched. From
here to the outbreak of the second Palestinian intifada in
September 2000 was but a very short step, although ignorant
outside observers purported to be shocked that such a thing
could have happened, and others claimed that it had been pur-
posely ignited by Arafat.

The uprising began after the Clinton administration let
most of its eight years in office go by without making any substantive effort to begin detailed negotiations on the complex
final-status issues between the Palestinians and Israelis such
as settlements, borders, Jerusalem, refugees, water, and sovereignty. Even by the dilatory Madrid/Oslo schedule, these negotiations could and should have been started much earlier in
Clinton's term. Clinton's own advisors, the Palestinians, and
others had warned the president that none of the extensive

necessary preliminary groundwork relating to these sensitive and complex issues had been done at the working level to prepare for a summit meeting. Nevertheless, just four months before the November 2000 elections, Clinton succumbed to the importuning of the Israeli prime minister, Ehud Barak, and convened a summit meeting with him and Arafat at Camp David in July 2000; taking place with utterly inadequate preparation (normally top leaders only meet to finalize details of accords subordinates have largely worked out), the summit was doomed to fail, and duly did so.[40] However, after having forced the Palestinians to attend a summit they argued had been insufficiently prepared for, and after the U.S. president promised that he would not blame any party if it did not succeed, instead of Clinton and Barak sharing the blame for its failure with Arafat, both leaders wrongly placed all the blame on the Palestinian leader.

At Camp David, Barak made a stingy take-it-or-leave-it offer to Arafat that was predictably rejected. The offer, which would have divided the West Bank into three disconnected segments, and gave Israel complete control over the borders of a state that would thereby have been much less than sovereign, was ludicrously described in the ensuing mythology that grew up around Camp David as "generous."[41] Nevertheless, Barak seems to have exerted more effort (until the end of his mandate in February 2001) on demonizing Arafat than on attempting to salvage the failed Camp David negotiations. As elections loomed in Israel, Barak thereby obtusely seemed to be doing the work of the Israeli right-wing parties for them by decrying Arafat for being unwilling to make peace—which raised the question of why Israeli voters should put their confidence in a man who had had previously campaigned on a peace platform and had just spent much of his mandate in negotiating with Arafat. In fact, although Arafat typically showed little adroitness in responding imaginatively to Barak's unsatisfactory offer and his slanderous attacks, the Palestinian and Israeli negotiators continued serious talks during the ensuing months.

Ironically, during several weeks of negotiations at the Egyptian resort of Taba in January 2001, senior Palestinian and Israeli negotiators, working from an improved version of the proposals discussed at Camp David that was put forward by President Clinton in December 2000, made significant progress on many of the key issues between the two sides. They came very close to agreement on frontiers,[42] sovereignty, and other questions, and significantly narrowed the gap even on the hardest issues of Jerusalem and refugees. But it was already far too late by this point: the disputed November 2000 presidential election had been decided in George W. Bush's favor, and Clinton was well beyond being a lame duck; Barak had already lost his majority in the Knesset and was about to suffer a resounding defeat in the February 2001 elections to Sharon; and Arafat, who had won over 80 percent of the vote for the position of president of the PA in a reasonably fair election in 1995, had over five years lost the confidence of most Palestinians, with his popularity according to reliable polls declining to well below 30 percent.[43] Most importantly, the much-tried patience of the Palestinian people had finally given out, and all that was necessary to ignite it was a spark. Once Ariel Sharon had provided that spark by his provocative visit to a Muslim holy site in Jerusalem accompanied by a huge phalanx of security personnel,[44] demonstrations and confrontations with Israeli occupation troops soon gave way to the second intifada, fatally compromising for the moment any possibility that negotiations could succeed.

The violence that started in September 2000 and has followed with little interruption has been the subject of almost as much mythology in the United States as the nursery fable of Barak's "generous offer" at Camp David. It came to be generally believed by those who got their information from the American mass media that the Palestinians launched the intifada at the instigation of their leadership, and that Yasir Arafat in particular was primarily responsible for the violence that followed, although most of it has been perpetrated by his most deadly political rivals in Hamas and Islamic Jihad. In fact the intifada started as an unarmed, popular mass protest against the provocative visit of Ariel Sharon to the Haram al-Sharif, but his visit was only the trigger. After years of disappointment with a seemingly endless negotiating process that had produced mainly negative results for most Palestinians, who still lived under Israeli military occupation, and that had delegitimized Arafat as well as the PLO and the PA, the situation in the West Bank and Gaza Strip was primed for an explosion.

When it took place, stone-throwing by unarmed Palestinian youths was met in the first five weeks of the uprising by lethal automatic weapons and sniper fire by the Israeli security forces that killed as many as ten demonstrators a day and maimed dozens. Little attention was paid in the American media to the horrendous casualties inflicted daily by Israeli troops on these unarmed Palestinian demonstrators, well before there were any significant Israeli casualties, and weeks before the first Palestinian attack on Israeli civilians during the intifada.[45] In time, armed Palestinians joined haphazardly in the one-sided fighting, provoking and justifying an even higher level of organized Israeli repression against the mainly unarmed Palestinian demonstrators and making it possible to portray the conflict as one in which two equal military forces were battling it out, a ludicrous misrepresentation. This escalation in turn led Palestinian militant groups to their own escalation, in the form of terror attacks on Israeli civilians.[46] Little of this filtered through the American media screen. Nor did the American media generally report what was routinely reported in the Israeli press: that the Israeli army had been planning and training assiduously for years for an all-out assault on Palestinian built-up areas that had been "ceded" to the PA, and that its high command was eager to wipe out the impact of its humiliating withdrawal from Lebanon the previous May by teaching the Palestinians a harsh lesson.[47]

In its reporting of the intifada, much of the American and Israeli media placed primary emphasis on suicide attacks by Hamas, Islamic Jihad, and other Palestinian militant groups on Israeli civilian targets. These devastating attacks on civilians in buses, restaurants, and markets in Israeli cities were truly horrific, and rightly shocked Americans. They did not know, however that they only started after the intifada had been raging for over five weeks, during which time horrendous casualties among Palestinian civilians were accompanied by relatively few casualties on the Israeli side, virtually all of them soldiers (20 Palestinians were killed on the first two days of violence at the end of September, and another 121 in October, almost all of them unarmed civilians, before the first Israeli civilian was killed on November 2, 2000).[48] There was thereafter scant mention in the U.S. media of the devastating impact of Israel's routine use from the outset of battlefield weapons like long-range sniper rifles, tanks, missiles, helicopters, and fighter-bombers in heavily built-up Palestinian civilian areas. Moreover, even attacks on Israeli troops inside the occupied territories became "terrorism" in the media, mimicking the Israeli government's practice of calling all opposition to its illegitimate rule terrorism, and assimilating Palestinian resistance to its military occupation to the kinds of attacks on unarmed civilians that Americans ordinarily, and rightly, associate with that term.

The violence since September 2000 has been perceived by many in the United States and Israel as having resulted primarily in Israeli civilian victims of Palestinian suicide attacks in Israeli urban areas. By contrast, the extremely high Palestinian civilian casualty toll received relatively little attention in the United States. In fact, over the course of the first three years of the intifada, the number of Palestinians killed and wounded (26,053) was nearly four times the number of Israelis (6,752), with the majority of the casualties on both sides being unarmed civilians.[49] Further, the psychic and emotional hardship imposed on Israelis by thirty-six months of bloody attacks in public places, which was exceedingly heavy, was extremely well chronicled and personalized, in stark contrast to the virtual imprisonment for most of this period of the entire Palestinian population of over 3.5 million in their cities, towns, and villages, with psychic and emotional effects that could only be guessed at, as they were little reported.[50]

This lopsided and essentially reversed image of what was actually happening on the ground in Israel-Palestine was brilliantly spun for the media, Congress, and policy-makers by the Sharon government and Israel's lobby in the United States, headed by the formidable American Israel Public Affairs Committee (AIPAC) and affiliated think tanks like the Washington Institute for Near East Policy. Not surprisingly, especially after the shock of the 9/11 attacks, which had disturbing but superficial similarities in that suicide bombers apparently motivated by Islam were involved in both (Hamas and Islamic Jihad are of course Islamic movements, but other attacks were carried out by secular Palestinian groups, some of them by women), this false image had a profound impact on the media, on public opinion, and especially on the thinking of the Bush administration. The reality, that Hamas and Islamic Jihad, far from being in league with the PA, were its fiercest rivals, and were trying to undermine it and the negotiating approach it espoused, was hardly reflected in the American media, any more than was the curious fact that for at least the first two years of the intifada, most of Israel's response to attacks by these militant groups was directed not at them but against their rival, the PA.

The dominant neoconservative elements in the administration were already predisposed to accept a hard-line Likud analysis that said that Oslo was a mistake, Arafat was irredeemable, the PA was a nest of terrorists, and force was the only possible response. This was not surprising, since these neocon "Sharonistas" in official and unofficial Washington had long espoused extremist Likud views,[51] which were grounded in willful ignorance and misinterpretation of the history, politics, and culture of the Middle East. They were predicated on the argument that by "unleashing" the intifada, Arafat had revealed his essential nature as a terrorist, which was the core message of Barak's self-defeating denunciations of Arafat. These were gleefully picked up and amplified thereafter by the Likud-dominated governments that replaced Barak's, and served to reinforce the argument that all Israelis were in agreement on this analysis. The logical conclusion to such a line of thinking was shared by the Bush administration's ascendant neocons and the new Likud government in early 2001: given that in principle force was the only way to deal with terrorists, the Israeli army was fully justified in all that it did, even against the PA and Palestinian civilians. The ideological convergence over terrorism in the wake of 9/11 clinched the argument being made by these neocons, who called for enthusiastic support for the line of blind military repression coupled with an obstinate refusal to negotiate seriously that was followed by Ariel Sharon and the governments he headed from February 2001 onward.[52] With the zigs and zags characteristic of Bush administration foreign policy, this eventually became the official line in Washington.

It was only after well over two years of carnage in Palestine and Israel that had thus been tacitly sanctioned by the Bush administration, and in the aftermath of the capture of Baghdad in the spring of 2003, when Washington felt the need for some evidence to show the Arabs and the rest of the world that it was not totally hostile to Arabs and Muslims, that a change in policy toward the Palestinian-Israeli conflict became manifest. This took the form of very belated administration support for the "road map" produced by senior representatives of the United States, Russia, the European Union, and the United Nations, so-called the "Quartet" but mainly reflecting the views of its American drafters. Originally prepared for presentation in mid-2002, it was delayed again and again at the behest of the Sharon government, which used a variety of pretexts to prevail on the Bush administration to postpone action.

The Israeli government's true objective was to gain more time for its army to impose a military solution, in pursuit of the mirage of a "defeat" of the Palestinians. However, the aim of the Israeli army general staff was not just the defeat of Palestinian militant groups carrying out attacks on Israeli civilians inside Israel and on Israeli troops and settlers in the occupied territories. It was rather the defeat of the entire Palestinian people, via the imposition of draconian collective punishment on the whole population of over 3.5 million men, women, and children in the West Bank and Gaza Strip. This involved curfews imposed on tens of thousands of people at a time for days and even weeks, the enforced closures of scores of villages and towns, over a hundred checkpoints that prevented normal movement, all of this combined with punishing raids on heavily populated built-up areas by Israeli troops and armored vehicles in which civilian casualties frequently exceeded the number of militants killed, wounded, or captured. The objective of this campaign was clearly evidenced by the statement of Israeli army chief of staff Moshe Yaalon: "The Palestinians must be made to understand in the deepest recesses of their consciousness that they are a defeated people."[53]

By the spring of 2003, however, something had changed. Although hard-line elements on both sides may have wanted to continue the fight, both Palestinian militant groups and the Israeli army high command and its extremist supporters in the Sharon government were operating under new constraints. Public opinion on both sides reflected utter weariness with respect to the unending violence, and anyone with any sense on either side could see that their own side's violence had failed to bring their opponents to their knees: instead it had more strongly unified both peoples and made them more resistant to making concessions. Moreover, the decision-makers in the Bush administration, largely for reasons having to do with the administration's sagging popularity over Iraq, had finally decided to throw the weight of the president himself into Middle East policy-making. This was the environment in which it at last became possible for the road map to be formally put forward and accepted by both sides, and for the Palestinian militant groups on June 29, 2003 to initiate a unilateral three-month cease-fire mediated by the chief of the Egyptian security services. It was believed, incorrectly as it turned out, that Israel had agreed to halt its assassinations of Palestinian militants, although it did briefly withdraw some troops from areas of the Gaza Strip and the town of Bethlehem.

The resulting lull was a function of all of these factors, as well as of the state of exhaustion on both sides. But there was no guarantee that this would be any more than a temporary respite, or that any progress would be made toward resolving the underlying issues between the Palestinians and the Israelis. For a serious transformation of the situation much more was necessary than simply halting the violence. As long as Israeli settlements continued to expand, as long as the basic structure of the Israeli military occupation remained in place, as long as the Israeli military and Palestinian militant groups remained committed to a military solution to the conflict and were unrestrained by political authority on either side, and as long as there was not a fixed timetable for compliance with the respective obligations of both sides, no progress toward a real settlement of the conflict could take place.

In keeping with the prevailing slant of Bush administration policy, the road map did not take a dispassionate or even-handed approach to these problems, instead laying overwhelming stress on halting *Palestinian* violence, with no mention of halting the much greater violence of the Israeli occupation, not to speak of the routine brutalities and indignities that it inflicted daily. While the road map laid out obligations for both sides, it was clear very early on that it included no mechanism to ensure that Israel would halt expansion of existing settlements and dismantle those built after September 2000, and indeed there never was a let-up in this relentless process. There was even less assurance that the short-lived government of PA prime minister Mahmud Abbas, or those of any of his successors, could crack down on Palestinian militant groups, given that support from the U.S. and Israel, in the form of meaningful reciprocal actions, was unlikely to be forthcoming. The expectation that Palestinian leaders would launch a civil war against militant groups attacking Israel while Israel simultaneously continued attacks on the Palestinian leadership, continued to expand settlements, and strengthened its military presence—all of this in the absence of any concrete assurance that minimal Palestinian aspirations would be met—was always unrealistic. Not surprisingly, the June 2003 cease-fire was broken less than two months later in a hail of fresh Israeli assassinations of Palestinian leaders and "collateral" civilian casualties, fresh Palestinian suicide attacks, and mutual recriminations.

A NEW APPROACH FOR THE U.S.

After the experiences of the first Bush, Clinton, and the George W. Bush administrations, it should by now be clear that if there is ever to be any substantive progress in Palestinian-Israeli peacemaking, the approach taken by these three administrations must be completely reversed. Instead of endlessly deferring negotiations on the important issues, as Madrid and Oslo did and as the road map—if it is ever implemented—is likely to do, talks on these issues must be started immediately. Instead of letting Israel continue to gobble up the pie that the two sides must ultimately agree to share, as it was allowed to do under Madrid/Oslo and is allowed to do under the terms of the road map, there must be an absolute and immediate freeze on any provocative actions, whether as regards settlements, Jerusalem, water, or any other issue that must be the subject of negotiations if there is to be peace. In other words, the United States must insist not just on a cessation of violence by both sides (the violence of the occupation as well as the violence of Hamas, Islamic Jihad, and others), but even more importantly that there be a halt to all actions that are "prejudicial or precedential" or that preempt the final outcome of negotiations, to use the language of the ground rules for the Madrid negotiations. Honored only in the breach, impartial implementation of these ground rules is the only way to level the playing field and establish a basis in good faith for successful negotiations, rather than the brutal imposition of a fait accompli on the weaker side, which cannot lead to a just or lasting peace.

Of course in the end, only the two sides can bring serious

negotiations, if they are ever started, to a successful conclusion. There is deep doubt among most competent observers
about whether the current leadership on either the Israeli or
Palestinian side is capable of providing the vision and states-
manship necessary to start and complete the process. Both
Arafat and Sharon are mired in the mind-set of the time, a
half-century ago, when they were formed politically. More
importantly, Arafat and his colleagues of the PA have no vision
for their people, no means of achieving their aims, and no
hope of controlling the Palestinian militant groups that preach
a violent solution, while Sharon and his generals hold out to
their people only the distant prospect of a crushing military
victory over the Palestinians that is as illusory as it would be
bloody. While decisive action to start negotiations and force
movement on all concerned might break the logjam, it is clear
that the American approach thus far has served only to reinforce the existing immobility and the intransigence of actors
on both sides.

It may be that the settlement since 1967 of well over four
hundred thousand Israelis in the occupied West Bank, Gaza
Strip, and East Jerusalem—a process that was always ultimately aimed at ensuring permanent Israeli control over most
of these territories and making the creation of a viable, sovereign Palestinian state alongside Israel impossible—means that
a completely new approach will have to be found, since these
Israeli actions have rendered such a two-state solution all but
obsolete. But whatever the basis for negotiations that ultimately emerges, only a dispassionate, impartial, and fair
arbiter can help bring the two sides to mutually acceptable
terms. The United States has only rarely played such a role over
the past few decades. If there is to be peace between
Palestinians and Israelis, the U.S. must begin to act in this fashion, or it must allow another party to do so.

CHAPTER FIVE

RAISING THE GHOSTS OF EMPIRE

We are in for many more years of turmoil and misery in the Middle East, where one of the main problems is, to put it as plainly as possible, American power. What America refuses to see clearly, it can hardly hope to remedy. —EDWARD SAID, 2003

Soon after the twentieth century began, Britain and France, through force of arms or other means, completed their imposition of direct or indirect control over virtually all of the Middle East. Their domination of the region was total, whether in the military, economic, or technological spheres. Similarly, as the twenty-first century opened, the United States had conquered and was engaged in an indefinite military occupation of one of the most important Arab countries, Iraq, immediately following its lightning conquest and occupation of Afghanistan. Like Britain before it, the United States towered strategically over the entire region, from the Atlantic to central Asia, with both significant military, naval, and air deployments in numerous countries and a dominating economic and cultural presence.

Much is different in the situations of the two powers, although perhaps not as much as might appear at first glance. Although Britain was the hegemonic power during the century and a half ending in World War II, it never enjoyed the unfettered status of unique superpower that the United States has held since the end of the Cold War.[1] Like the Ottomans, Portugal, Spain, Holland, France, Austria-Hungary, and Germany, in controlling a European-based world-empire in the modern era, Britain always had to deal with a multipolar, or at least bipolar, world. By contrast, the United States, since overcoming the considerable competition provided by the Soviet Union (a formidable rival, although its power was often exaggerated by its foes), has been vastly more powerful than any other state. This is a situation unseen since the premodern heydays of Tang China, the Mongols, and the Roman Empire. Since American domination encompasses the entire globe, it is in many ways unprecedented in human history, yet this domination is not total, nor does it mean that American power has no limits.

The unease, confusion, and uncertainty of many American statesmen, policy-makers, and intellectuals about how to deal with the overwhelming military and economic superiority of their country in the world, especially since the end of the Cold War, has only made even more salient the self-assurance of those, inside and outside the Bush administration, who affirm a doctrine of untrammeled and assertive American primacy, what some of them call "benign American hegemony"[2] and others are unashamed to call empire. However, not all those who regard this brave new post–Cold War world with equanimity are advocates of American imperial triumphalism. In works representing disparate disciplines and perspectives, sober voices like those of John Mearsheimer, Joseph Nye, Neil Smith, and Clyde Prestowitz warn against the shallow, simplistic, naive, and ahistorical arrogance of such a perspective.[3] They stress the ongoing relevance of great-power competition even in this new era, the need for the United States to understand that its hegemony is not unfettered, and the continuities in American imperial behavior between the beginning of the twentieth century and the beginning of the twenty-first. From Europe, most notably from France, come other critical reflections on the new era that belie the simplicity of the

American triumphalist worldview, such as those of Alain Joxe, Etienne Balibar, and Emmanuel Todd, arguing that a hegemonic United States plays a destabilizing role in the world, one that must be balanced by other powers.[4]

There were other major differences between the situation of the United States at the beginning of the twenty-first century and that of the European colonial powers in their heyday. In the wake of World War I, the aspirations for independence of numerous nations unwillingly subjected to foreign control were greatly encouraged by Woodrow Wilson's enunciation of the Fourteen Points (which their author primarily meant to apply to European countries, but which had a profound resonance elsewhere nonetheless). Many in the colonized world were also heartened by the initial promise of the Bolshevik Revolution to free peoples who had suffered under the czarist yoke. In consequence of these and other factors, imperialism and colonialism had begun to acquire a bad name internationally, and even at home in some quarters in the centers of the great European colonial empires.

Nevertheless, the will of the European elites to rule over "lesser peoples" remained undiminished for at least another generation, and European imperialism dominated most of the world until World War II. Although ostensibly barred from the front door, it managed to enter some of the last unoccupied areas in the Middle East through the back door, in the form of League of Nations mandates. Indeed, the interwar period constituted the high-water mark of the traditional colonial order in the Middle East and in much of the rest of the world, marked as it was by the new neocolonial League of Nations mandates, and by Italy invading Ethiopia and Japan Manchuria. This remained the case even as a new era of resistance to colonialism and of intense pressures for decolonization was gathering strength.

By contrast, today imperialism is thought to be a thing of the past, at least in most branches of American popular culture and among American politicians, many of whom insistently repeat the refrain that unlike other great powers, the United States has never sought and does not seek an empire.[5] Claims that the United States might be engaging in imperialist behavior meet indignant rejections in these quarters, usually leavened with insults about the "anti-Americanism" and lack of patriotism of those making these assertions. Paradoxically, the imperial idea is today enjoying a fashionable revival among certain segments of the American intelligentsia, who seem intoxicated by the appearance of unlimited American power.[6] Nevertheless, complications are created by the entirely healthy American popular allergy to empire: as Niall Ferguson, an enthusiastic booster of an overt American imperial role, regretfully notes, "Americans ... have always been reticent about their nation's global role;"[7] or as another author puts it, there is "a strong diffidence towards exercising world leadership ... as a continuing element in American political culture."[8] As a result, even those in the Bush administration who might harbor a private wish for a world order organized obediently around a triumphant and hegemonic United States, who are clearly seduced by the intellectual pied pipers who urge them to embrace freely America's imperial burden, and whose policy pronouncements are redolent of imperial pretensions, are usually careful to eschew the appearances of overt domination.

It was thus that officials in positions of responsibility in Washington were careful to proclaim before, during, and after the third Gulf war (the 1980–88 Iran-Iraq War being the first, and the 1991 war following Iraq's invasion of Kuwait the second) that Iraq was the property of the Iraqis, and that Iraqi oil belonged solely to the Iraqi people. These officials even showed an initial allergy to using the term *occupation* to describe the American military presence in Iraq after the conquest of that country. They insisted that what was taking place was "liberation," not "occupation," and commentators—on the FOX News Channel and in much of the rest of the media—duly repeated this claim. Mercifully, reality finally overcame the tireless spinning of the Bush administration on that issue, at least (although on little else regarding Iraq, until the yawning gap between the truth and the Bush administration's exaggerated or fabricated prewar claims about Iraq's nuclear and other unconventional military capabilities and its links to al-Qa'ida finally began to be publicly apparent months after the war's end). In the end, "occupation" was grudgingly accepted by the Bush administration as the only possible term to describe this imposed American military presence in a foreign country.

There were other differences between these two episodes of the West intruding militarily in the Middle East at the beginning of consecutive centuries. Whereas Britain created its new post–World War I structure of control in the Middle East with the help of explorers, geographers, scholars, linguists, archaeologists, and other experts, many of them grouped during the war in the Arab Bureau, at the turn of the twenty-first century the United States had nothing similar to this body of eminent regional experts closely advising top policy-makers. Of course, numerous skilled, highly trained, linguistically competent Middle East specialists worked in different branches of American government service, whether in the State Department, the CIA and other parts of the intelligence community, or the uniformed military. However, according to Robert Baer, a former covert operations officer of the CIA, many of these experts suffered from disadvantages: "In general, few American officials are still in contact with 'the Arab street,' which requires a knowledge of the language, as well as years of study and travel. There is no shortcut to understanding the Middle East."[9] This could not be said of most of the British experts who advised their government soon after the turn of the twentieth century: one might dispute the prescience of their policy recommendations, but they had spent much of their lives in this region, were deeply immersed in its politics, and had considerable knowledge of its culture.

Perhaps even more important, from early on during the second Bush administration, career officials and military officers with real Middle Eastern expertise had rapidly learned to lay very low in a Washington world dominated by influential, aggressive, and highly opinionated political appointees. These zealots tightly surrounded Secretary of Defense Donald Rumsfeld and Vice President Dick Cheney, the leading actors defining the administration's foreign and security policies, while their like-minded fellows had received appointments in many other key parts of the government bureaucracy. A recently retired U.S. Air Force officer, Lieutenant Colonel Karen Kwiatkowski, who until April 2003 worked in the office of Undersecretary of Defense for Policy Douglas Feith, perhaps the epicenter of this group and the individual currently in charge of the reconstruction of Iraq, described how its members "tended to work with like-minded political appointees in other agencies . . . rather than with those agencies' career analysts or the CIA." She added: "What I saw was aberrant, pervasive and contrary to good order and discipline. If one is seeking the answers to why peculiar bits of 'intelligence' found sanctity in a presidential speech, or why the post-Saddam [Hussein] occupation [of Iraq] has been distinguished by confusion and false steps, one need look no further than the process inside the Office of the Secretary of Defense."[10]

Members of this powerful network of like-minded political appointees had strong and highly biased views on the

Middle East, but most had little real knowledge of the region. This was seen in the case of the gross misinformation about the Hashemites and the Shi'a—two major fixtures of Middle East reality for the past dozen centuries at least—contained in the report coauthored by the influential Richard Perle, the sponsor of many of these young neocons. If such people could get these sorts of basics wrong, there was precious little in the Middle East that they could be said to be experts about. In the eyes of these suddenly "expert" advisors, moreover, the actual, real-world expertise embodied by the U.S. government's trained Middle East specialists, except for a few ideologically tested individuals, was inherently suspect and was taken as a prima facie indication of grave political unsoundness.

Indeed, the very term *Arabist* became a nasty epithet inside the beltway, to the point of scaring qualified officers at the CIA and State Department away from the field.[11] This was the result of a concerted, systematic campaign by these officials in concert with hawkish policy advocates with unassailable perches in a network of handsomely funded conservative think tanks like the American Enterprise Institute, the Hudson Institute, and the Washington Institute for Near East Policy.[12] Notwithstanding the palpable lack of real Middle East expertise of most of these pundits—as one wag put it, they "couldn't find their way from the airport to the Hilton in most Middle Eastern capitals without a minder"—such people had unlimited access to the TV airwaves dominated by cable market-leader FOX News, and to newspapers and magazines owned by moguls like Rupert Murdoch, Conrad Black, and others with similar views. Through these media, they successfully spread a miasma of bias and misinformation about the Middle East that was the essential precondition for the success of the policies espoused by their ideological soul-mates within the administration.

It is certainly the case that the experts within the ranks of the permanent bureaucracy in Washington have not always been farsighted or accurate about the Middle East. Most of them failed to anticipate the Iranian revolution, and more generally they underestimated the importance of the rise of radical Islamist political movements in the Middle East and elsewhere in the Islamic world since the late 1970s, failings that applied to many experts in academia as well. Other mistakes and misreadings can be attributed to government experts on the Middle East. But these permanent officials generally were more sinned against than sinning in their disputes with the political appointees who were their superiors. This is a well-established pattern in Washington, since the days of the Iran-Contra scandal during the Reagan administration, when a senior intelligence official and noted expert was obliged to pay the price for the failure of the absurd schemes dreamed up by Colonel Oliver North and his amateurish fellow-conspirators.[13] Similarly, government Middle East experts counseled against the Reagan administration's blind support of Israel during the 1982 invasion of Lebanon and afterward, when U.S. forces intervened in support of Israel's protégés in Lebanon. They were overruled by the decision-makers at the top, with disastrous consequences for American Marines and diplomats in Lebanon, some of whom paid with their lives for these terrible mistakes of their superiors.[14]

This pattern of blind zealotry overriding expertise was clearly apparent in the approach of the Bush administration in the build-up to the 2003 Iraq war. It is increasingly accepted by fair-minded observers that the Bush team simply ignored those few intelligence experts and professionals who might have had the courage to put forward data that contradicted their expressed views. Indeed, they and their fellow travelers in the media and right-wing think tanks directed constant abuse at those professionals who dissented from the orthodoxy they had imposed.[15] Thus, this administration simply dictated the "intelligence" conclusions regarding Saddam Hussein's regime that fit its fixed preconceptions, ranging from Iraq's possession of nonconventional weapons to its links with terrorism.[16] They spun the intelligence the way they had successfully spun so much else, expecting naively that reality would oblige by conforming to their ideologically inspired imaginings, and that there would be no consequences to deal with. The outcome thus far in Iraq is evidence of how wrong they were, with American soldiers, international civil servants, and Iraqi civilians paying a very high price for their follies.

It might be argued that the Middle East experts in Washington in this administration have had to do no more than deal with the problem common to permanent officials in all major democracies, that of telling their political masters what they might not want to hear. But this has been a particularly acute problem with the second Bush administration where foreign policy generally was concerned, because those George W. Bush appointed to high office generally wanted to hear only one specific, ideologically determined note, rather than a more complex melody better reflecting reality. And where the Middle East in particular was concerned, it was clear that many of the most senior officials in this administration had passionate feelings, and deep, long-standing biases that made them virtually impervious to facts or opinions that contradicted their strong views.[17]

By contrast, as the edifice of the British imperium in the Middle East was completed during and after World War I, the senior British decision-makers—Asquith, Lloyd George, Grey, Kitchener, Churchill, and Curzon—were closely advised both by men from within their own ministries with considerable expertise about the region, and by men (and one or two women) both inside and outside the permanent bureaucracy who had spent many years living and working in the Middle East. One may fault individuals who played such senior advisory roles like T. E. Lawrence, Gertrude Bell, Percy Cox, Commander D. E. Hogarth, Colonel Gilbert Clayton, and H. St. John Philby for their prejudices, their adherence to a British imperial vision, and their many mistakes. But it was undeniable that they had a lengthy, immediate, firsthand knowledge of the Middle East, its languages, peoples, and history. Some of them produced works of scholarship and literature about the Middle East that can still be profitably consulted today.[18]

Moreover, rather than seeing their views diluted and buffered by layers of bureaucracy, as in Washington today, these experts often reported directly to, and were consulted personally by, the cabinet ministers who had the ultimate responsibility for foreign policy decisions, and who themselves in many cases had wide personal experience of the Middle East. Among the members of the British cabinets that reshaped the Middle East during and after World War I, Kitchener, Churchill, and Curzon all had spent considerable parts of their lives in the Middle East and Central and South Asia, and had researched and written extensively about these regions.[19] All three men were notable imperialists in the fullest sense of the word, and could not be said to have put the interests of subject peoples above those of Great Britain, but at least they had firsthand experience of many distant parts of its empire. The contrast could not be starker with the situation of the Bush administration, most of whose senior decision-makers have no significant or lengthy firsthand experience of the world beyond the frontiers of the United States (Colin Powell is the major exception), and who were carefully insulated from hearing any expert advice that contradicted their ideological preconceptions.

While in hindsight it might seem as if the Arab Bureau and

other British experts did not do such an outstanding job, in fact their contribution was essential. We have seen how British power managed to dominate and control the Middle East for decades, but also how Britain was under constant pressure from local nationalists, culminating in numerous embarrassing revolts. A school of neoimperialist Middle East historians, the most prominent of whom is the late Elie Kedourie, castigated British officials in London for the sin of listening to their expert advisors, and for the latter's weakness in taking seriously Middle Eastern nationalisms that he saw as weak, artificial, and ill-suited to their societies. The sympathy for imperialism of such authors, and their antipathy toward the Arabs, is barely concealed: in their view Britain should have ruled the region directly and unashamedly, without regard for negligible considerations like Arab public opinion.[20] Strong echoes of this contempt for what the Arabs may think and say still permeate American public discourse, as well as the attitude of many senior Bush administration officials.[21]

Most of Britain and France's problems in their dealings with the peoples of the Middle East did not arise from an over-reliance on expertise, or from the excessive sympathy of their experts for the peoples of the region or their nationalist aspirations. They arose rather from the complete incompatibility between their countries' imperialist aims and the aspirations of the growing number of politically active citizens in the Middle Eastern countries they dominated. Pace Kedourie and his latter-day neoconservative acolytes, modern politics, with all the messiness that it entails, had arrived in the Middle East by the turn of the twentieth century. In consequence, Britain and France had no choice but to deal with nationalist, democratic, and egalitarian aspirations, however sincerely or insincerely these may have been conveyed by the educated politicians and middle-class newspapermen, writers, and educators so manifestly despised by British and French colonial officials, and writers who echoed them like Kedourie.[22]

British Arabists argued for a constitutional monarchy in Iraq in 1921, and however transparently Sir Percy Cox and his successors may have manipulated this system thereafter, it was clearly superior (in terms of British interests) to the completely unworkable old-style colonial direct rule it replaced.[23] Britain was similarly forced to concede nominal independence to Egypt in 1922, here too abandoning the heavy-handed forms of control that were so congenial to the British colonial mentality, largely on the advice of the same Arabist experts. It is highly debatable whether the kind of regime that resulted in both cases—a very limited democracy hobbled by an imposed monarchy and external intervention in a country with heavily compromised sovereignty—was in the long run a good thing for either Iraq or Egypt. Nor were the arrangements that resulted in other cases in the Middle East necessarily much better. One of the arguments made in chapter 2 is that the negative results of this bitter experience discredited democracy for many years in the region.

But it is likely that the solutions devised by these British experts made possible the prolongation of some forms of external control, which probably would have collapsed in the new post–World War I atmosphere, had the rigid old methods of direct colonial control been retained. And while the objective of these British and French experts was the prolongation of their respective countries' domination over the Middle East, it was also the case that some of them had a certain respect and sympathy for the aspirations of the people of these countries, and that the solutions they devised were meant to allow for some of these aspirations to be realized, even if that may not have been the ultimate outcome.

The basic problem in the British and French cases, however, was neither a lack of expertise nor excessive reliance on experts, nor was it a lack of respect on the part of decision-makers for the advice that they received. These decision-makers often listened carefully to those with experience in the Middle East, although sometimes only after ignoring it had done great damage.[24] The problem was rather the irresoluble contradiction between the imperial center's absolute need for control, whether of vital transit routes or natural resources, or simply for the prestige attendant on the mastery of exotic lands abroad, and the irrepressible desire of the peoples of the Middle East to throw off that control. No number of solemn statements about respect for the rights of the peoples concerned, and no amount of tinkering with a system devised to deny the indigenous populations control over the basic decisions that concerned them, could resolve that basic contradiction. In consequence, the edifice of imperial power in the Middle East in the interwar period was necessarily shaky, in spite of its imposing air. As soon as the international environment shifted in the wake of World War II, with the entry of the United States and the Soviet Union into the Middle East as superpowers overshadowing the old colonial powers, the days of the neocolonial systems that these older powers had devised were numbered. All of these systems in fact disappeared within just over two decades after World War II, albeit leaving lasting effects on the societies in which they had been established, and on relations between these societies and the West.

Similarly, the problem the United States faces today is not one of expertise alone—although it now seems manifest from the problems facing the U.S. occupation regime in Baghdad that thus far in the Iraqi episode real expertise has been sorely lacking in the highest councils of the U.S. government.[25] It is rather one of the contradiction between the dynamic unleashed by the Bush administration's headlong rush into the occupation and domination of Afghanistan, Iraq, and other countries of the region, and the natural desire of peoples not to be dictated to by foreigners, even ones who may have rid them of despised regimes. No amount of rhetoric about democratization, even if it is occasionally sincere, and no amount of harping on the all-too-real evils perpetrated by the Taliban and the Ba'th that were mercifully ended by the intervention of the United States can outweigh this potent contradiction. As a general rule, people do not want to be ruled by others from far away, even if those rulers are well intentioned. Americans, whose very independence resulted from a similar sentiment, should be able to appreciate this simple fact.

What seems most painful to those with any real knowledge of the region is the apparent unwillingness of those in power in Washington to accept that in this vast region of the world the United States is wittingly or unwittingly stepping into the boots of earlier imperial powers, and that this cannot under any circumstances be a good thing and cannot possibly be "done right."[26] Similarly, there seems to have been a deep reluctance on the part of most senior Bush administration policymakers thus far in the Iraqi adventure to engage in a careful reading of the history of the Middle East, or to pay serious attention to the region's political dynamics. Taking these Middle East realities as seriously as they deserve, rather than responding to the urgings of influential zealots within and without the administration who have been purveying an ignorant, ideologically driven fantasy version of Middle Eastern reality, would have spared the region, the United States, and the world much anguish. Doing so today could yet prevent even worse outcomes.

However much may have changed in the world as a whole from the early twentieth to the early twenty-first centuries, and however powerful the United States may be, any deep reading of the history of the Middle East would show that it is impossible to erect a Western system of domination there in the twenty-first century—whether one calls it empire or not—that will not face resistance by its subjects. It is impossible to march into the Middle East proclaiming good intentions and to ignore the fact that the locals have a longer sense of history than most Americans, and will recall vividly that over the past two centuries they have been reassured several times by their conquerors that they had the best of intentions. Napoleon, Lord Dufferin in Egypt in 1882, General Maude in Baghdad in 1917, General Gouraud in Damascus in 1920, and many others offered the same reassurances, which in every case turned out to be worthless.

Even if the intentions of the Bush administration regarding the establishment of democracy in the Middle East were as pure as the driven snow, even if this administration and its powerful friends in the oil business had not the slightest rapacious aspiration toward the fabulous potential bonanza of Iraqi oil, even if there existed every sincere intention in the Pentagon to remove all American forces and bases from the entire Middle East as soon as possible—even if all these dubious hypotheticals were granted—Middle Easterners have every reason on the basis of their own lengthy experience to expect the contrary to be the case. They would not be convinced by mere words to ignore the lessons of over two centuries of bitter experience with alien rule. And in any case, they will not take kindly to being ruled by others, whatever these others may say or do and however sweet their rule may be. The British experience in India, the beneficiary of centuries of benevolent British imperial despotism, and the resulting "ingratitude" of the Indians, should be a warning to those in Washington who believe that the benefits they believe they are extending from on high to Iraqis, Afghans, and others will be gratefully received.

This leaves the question of whether the Bush administration is either willing or able to create a functioning, sovereign, democratic state in Iraq. In fact, given the massive unpopularity among the peoples of the Middle East of most American policies in the region, the introduction of functioning democratic systems there would be likely to produce governments—like the democratic governments of western Europe, Turkey, Mexico, and elsewhere—that would differ with the United States on a variety of issues, starting with Palestine and extending to a host of others. This causes many in the Middle East to suspect that the United States is unlikely to foster real democracy in Iraq, and will try to limit Iraq's sovereignty and independence until it produces a government that does what Washington wants—shades of Hamid Karzai in Kabul today, and King Faisal in Baghdad in the 1920s. They suspect further that if a democratic government does emerge in Iraq nevertheless, it will probably produce rude surprises for the Bush administration, which will disapprove heartily of it and its actions. Similarly, Iraqi oil revenues seem likely to flow (for as long as the current administration can manage to retain sole control over Iraq) to a reconstruction process that will be managed largely for the profit of the Halliburtons and Bechtels of this world.[27] "Nation building" in Iraq as it is currently under way would thus seem to involve largely building up the balance sheets of corporations favored by the administration.

In any case, nation building, at least in the commonly accepted sense of nation building from without, is a chimera. This is because, in the first instance, nations can only build themselves: they cannot be "built" from without. Germany and Japan were nations, with sophisticated, albeit faulty, political systems, powerful state structures, a fully formed and long-standing sense of national identity, and two of the most highly developed economies in world history, long before the first American troops arrived on their soil at the end of World

War II. No "nation building" took place in either country. Even if we adopt the more modest and more accurate term *state building*, this is not precisely what happened in Japan and Germany. Instead, after these two powerful and already existing nations had been completely defeated, new, more democratic regimes were successfully installed to govern them through existing state and corporate structures that were transformed in a fairly limited fashion by the occupation. It was not nations that were "built" in Germany and Japan, but rather new, more democratic governments, within the context of modified, but preexisting, state structures.

Even the most superficial examination reveals that what happened in Germany and Japan after World War II bears no resemblance whatsoever to Iraq and Afghanistan today, or to most of the other cases to which the term *nation-building* is currently applied. Given the traditional weakness of the Afghan state and its collapse after more than two decades of war, and given the dissolution of the strong Iraqi state after the American occupation, state building from the bottom up might be required in Afghanistan, and something perhaps equally thoroughgoing but of a different nature in Iraq. But this presents the question of who would do the state building: the United States alone with no international sanction, or a state or group of states representing an international consensus and assisting the people of the countries in question. Even if one were to accept the purity of Bush administration motives, it is unlikely to have success at its stated tasks in the Iraqi and Afghan cases, since the United States seems unwilling to devote the time, patience, and resources necessary to these extremely daunting jobs, and the administration is unwilling to draw on the requisite expertise.[28] It is becoming clear, moreover, that the extremely high cost of doing these things would probably be well beyond the capability of the already strained U.S. federal budget.

It is important in any case to recognize that for all the dysfunction exhibited by the political systems of Iraq and Afghanistan in recent decades (albeit dysfunctions exacerbated by massive external intervention), both have been nations, or at least nation-states, for most of the twentieth century. For all their internal divisions, this experience of independent nationhood, however recent and however limited by external intervention, has created a certain unity and certain patterns of self-respect that outsiders ignore at their peril. Indeed, external intervention and attempts to control these countries have only intensified their nationalism. If the Charter of the United Nations and the principle of national sovereignty have any meaning, it is in any case not for Americans to dictate to Afghanis and Iraqis the form their nations should take, and if they are so arrogant as to do so, the results are likely to be far from what is desired in Washington.

This raises the question of what is to be done with what may be termed "failed states," a category into which Afghanistan falls. This category now also probably applies to Iraq. If so, Iraq is a failed state because its previous regime egregiously violated international legal and human rights norms by invading its neighbors and abusing its citizens, and because of the lawless chaos, combined with the dissolution of the state, triggered by the U.S. occupation. Other more traditional cases of failed states, like Liberia, the Congo, or Lebanon during the 1975–90 civil war, come to mind. In all of these cases, invoking the principle of national sovereignty is of extremely limited utility, since there was no longer a state to exercise sovereignty. Moreover, the instability and chaos that may radiate out from these failed states, in the form of flows of refugees, spillovers of internal conflicts, or the growth of havens for lawlessness and terrorism, mean that they are likely to constitute problems for their neighbors and perhaps the international community as a whole. One answer to the problem of failed states is simply to quarantine them and let them fester until the problem resolves itself. In a sense, that is what the international community did with Lebanon, allowing the interference and meddling of its neighbors from without and the chaos within to continue until the conflict burned itself out. Another option is for the United States or another major power to intervene more or less unilaterally, which is what the United States did in Iraq and Afghanistan in 2002 and 2003 (and, for a brief, tragically misguided moment, in Lebanon from 1982–83), and what has happened in different African states where France has repeatedly intervened.

In the Iraqi case, such unilateral intervention by the United States risks creating new and perhaps even more serious problems than the grave ones caused for the Iraqi people and for Iraq's neighbors by the atrocities of the brutal and aggressive regime of Saddam Hussein. We have seen that the United States, perceived by Iraqis and others as having ulterior motives, and failing in the initial months of occupation to establish the minimum stability and security necessary for building anything, in any case probably cannot, by itself, provide the financial resources or the military forces to do even what the Bush administration believes needs to be done. And the exclusive American control obsessively insisted upon by the civilian authorities in the Pentagon will have the inevitable effect of driving away other countries that might otherwise be willing to share the financial and military burden of jointly rebuilding Iraq. At the same time, the overbearing behavior and heavy footprint of the American military occupation have engendered both stubborn resistance against U.S. forces and savage terrorism directed mainly against innocents. Together they make the task of rebuilding the Iraqi state on a new, more democratic basis virtually impossible in the short term. For these reasons, state building and democratization in Iraq require a radically different approach than that followed thus far by the Bush administration, as is recognized virtually all over the world, except among those within and without the administration who are responsible for dragging the United States into what is rapidly becoming a quagmire in Iraq.

The United States, and the world, now faces a situation of unprecedented difficulty in Iraq. There is deep resentment among Iraqis, including those grateful for the overthrow of the Ba'th regime, at the months of chaos in Iraq since the end of the war, at the unresponsiveness of the American occupation authorities, and at the slow pace of the move toward genuine self-government. American troops increasingly risk being received as are most occupation armies, and as were the British in Iraq after World War I: with hostility and ultimately with widespread armed resistance. The paralysis of the American authorities in Baghdad, which reflects the paralysis in Washington, as the administration's factions struggle over decisions in Iraq, and the inflexible, highly ideological, and ultimately self-defeating line that has generally prevailed, have exacerbated the situation. Reliance on Pentagon-favored exiles loathed by most Iraqis, who see them as carpetbaggers, has already hurt the position of the United States in Iraq, and may lead to an even worse situation there when the inevitable backlash against their machinations sets in. This is only the tip of the iceberg, as is manifest from reporting in the non-American media on the situation on the ground in Iraq, one whose gravity has not been fully reflected in the American media—although American casualties in Iraq, and lengthy deployments of both regulars and reservists finally seem to be having an impact on American public opinion.

Any solution to this problem must recognize a few basic facts: The first is that Iraq is an artificial state, but no more so than most other states in the world today, and like them it has developed a powerful national identity and a patriotism that withstood a grueling nine-year war against its much bigger neighbor, Iran. It would be very unwise to ignore that patriotism, as is apparently being done by the Coalition Provisional Authority ("CPA stands for Condescending and Patronizing Americans," a Baghdad diplomat told a *Newsweek* reporter[29]). The second is that the Iraqi state is a creation of international agreements, and that its creation was midwifed by the world body of the day, the League of Nations, although this seems to have been long forgotten by the international community, and Iraq thus constitutes an international responsibility. The third is that Iraqis and others in the Middle East have a strong sense of history: not only do they not forget their experiences with the British occupation; they recall vividly the history of earlier occupations of Baghdad, such as that in 1258 when it was sacked by the Mongols. Bringing even a symbolic contingent of Mongolian soldiers to join the forces of the "Coalition," as the United States has done, is a perfect example of how to trample on the sensibilities of such people.

In my view, the least damaging approach to this situation at this point would be the reestablishment of an international mandate over Iraq for a strictly limited period. A new U.N. mandate may be the only viable solution if Iraq is to be rescued from the abyss in which its status as a failed state, and the thirteen-year-long conflict with the United States—from the invasion of Kuwait, through the sanctions, the invasion, and the occupation—have left the country. This means starting from the premise that Iraq as a modern state was created by an international mandate (that of the League of Nations); that on the basis of the behavior of its government toward both its people and its neighbors, the experiment that started with the first League of Nations mandate over Iraq has proven a failure; and that the international community which mandated the creation of the Iraqi state has the responsibility to step in to redo what was done wrong the first time and to help the Iraqi people rapidly reestablish their independent statehood on a democratic basis.

Such an approach, jointly decided upon in the context of the United Nations by the United States, other major powers, and Iraq's neighbors, with the express aim of establishing a stable, unified, sovereign, democratic, and nonaggressive Iraq at peace with its neighbors, would have a good chance of success in rapidly winning over an overwhelming majority of the Iraqi people and would isolate a minority that might oppose such a solution. For most of Iraq's neighbors, it would be preferable to the current situation, which promises only instability, chaos, and potential regional destabilization. It could thereby end the chapter of an increasingly hotly contested American military occupation and open a new one of an international mandate accepted by the broad majority of the Iraqi people of all religions and ethnicities.

A course of this sort would face many pitfalls: it would be difficult for the United States (and particularly for the Bush administration, with its disinclination even to listen to the views of other governments, and its international reputation as a bully[30]) to accept in effect that it was wrong all along in virtually its entire approach to Iraq. It would be difficult for the U.S. to agree on the details of how to proceed with the other major powers and Iraq's neighbors, which all have their own interests, and some of which, particularly Iraq's neighbors, are far from being paragons of democratic virtue. But for all its flaws, such a course would be immeasurably superior to the current unilateral American approach. This is doomed to failure for many reasons, perhaps the most important being that it will inevitably appear to Iraqis and their neighbors to be a futile attempt to reverse the course of history and reimpose

Western control in a part of the world that has been struggling for two centuries to resist it. By contrast, no one, except an easily isolated Iraqi lunatic fringe, could accuse the entire international community of trying to impose permanent subjugation on Iraq.

The advantages of a truly international solution are profound. Harnessing the considerable energies and skills of the Iraqi people to the rebuilding of their country would be immeasurably easier under such a scenario, as would be attracting international funds for the reconstruction of Iraq's shattered infrastructure. It would also be possible to attract badly needed international investments, in a situation where it was clear that there would be a level economic playing field, rather than a closely guarded U.S. protectorate where American corporations with connections to the Republican Party can cherry pick all the good opportunities. By contrast with the current situation, where the Bush administration is likely to continue to fail to persuade countries with large armies with combat and peacekeeping experience and developed logistical capabilities (such as France, Germany, Turkey, India, or Pakistan) to share the American military burden in Iraq, an international mandate would have the potential to attract substantial forces. Instead of joining American and British troops in a deepening quagmire of resistance, reprisals, and terrorism, these troops would be perceived as neutral peacekeepers serving to police a mandate that would have the support of the vast majority of the Iraqi people.

This may be too rosy a scenario, and bringing it about in the short run seems unlikely in any case given current realities in Washington, since it will require a wrenching change of course. But as this book has tried to show, the current course of the Bush administration in the Middle East is a doomed one. It will at best be perceived as inimical by most of the peoples of that region, and at worst will continue to create reservoirs of virulent ill-will that will harm the rest of the world, but which Americans in the Middle East—especially U.S. troops in Iraq—will suffer most from. None of this is inevitable, nor as the professional fear-mongers in Washington would have it do "they" hate us because of what we are. In the case of the overwhelming majority of Middle Easterners, their anger is caused by what misguided U.S. policies have done to them. The only way to defuse this anger is to stop doing these things, whether in Iraq, Palestine, or elsewhere in the Middle East.

Economic domination, cultural hegemony, raw power— the United States enjoys all of these things, in the Middle East and most of the rest of the world. However, though it may bestride the narrow Middle East like a colossus, it has shown again and again that it cannot affect some of the outcomes there that concern it most. If this is a lesson in anything, it is in the limitations of this raw power, and in the capacity of stubborn local realities to dissipate even the most vivid ideological projections. The Middle East is a region that clearly cannot directly resist the military power of the United States, as the rapid defeats of the Iraqi army twice in twelve years amply showed. Although Britain and France did not conquer most of the countries of the region this easily, they too eventually overwhelmed the resistance of conventional military forces, from the Mamluks to 'Urabi's troops to those of the Ottomans in Palestine and Mesopotamia and of Faisal in Damascus. However, neither power was able to dominate most parts of this region directly for long without paying an exorbitant price. This is a price—in lives, in treasure, and in reputation— that we as Americans should think very carefully about, before submitting to the siren song of those who tell us that empire is easy and cheap, and that in any case the price is worth paying.

NOTES

INTRODUCTION
The Perils of Ignoring History

1. The term *Middle East* is rather confusing: it provokes the obvious question of what this region is in the middle and east *of*. Clearly, like other such geographical terms including *Far East*, it presupposes a European perspective on the world. For more on the origin of the term, see R. Khalidi, "The 'Middle East' as a Framework for Analysis: Re-mapping a Region in the Era of Globalization," *Comparative Studies of South Asia, Africa and the Middle East* 18, no. 2 (1998): 1–8, and Roger Adelson, *London and the Invention of the Middle East* (New Haven, Conn.: Yale University Press, 1994). As used in this book, the term will refer to the region from the Atlantic to the Caucasus and central Asia that includes all the Arab countries, meaning those countries where the majority of the population speaks Arabic, as well as three non-Arab countries – Israel, Turkey, and Iran – and, occasionally, bordering countries such as Afghanistan.

CHAPTER ONE
The Legacy of the Western Encounter
with the Middle East

1. Some experts have argued that by strict criteria this war was in fact neither preemptive nor preventive: see Paul Schroeder, "Iraq: The Case against Preemptive War," *American Conservative*, October 21, 2002.
2. Harvard political scientist Steve Walt, cited by Steve Chapman, "U.S. Builds Coalition of Opponents on War," *Chicago Tribune*, February 23, 2003, sec. 2.
3. President Bush's September 17, 2002, cover letter to *The National Security Strategy of the United States of America*: www.whitehouse .gov/nsc/nss.pdf.
4. *The National Security Strategy of the United States of America*, September 2002, p. 1: www.whitehouse.gov/nsc/nss.pdf.

5. This new doctrine was foreshadowed in the strategic planning of the Defense Department at the end of the first Bush administration in the early 1990s, in the form of "Defense Planning Guidance." See David Armstrong, "Dick Cheney's Song of America: Drafting a Plan for Global Dominance," *Harper's*, October 2002, pp, 76–83. Many of the same figures that produced these plans hold top positions in George W. Bush's administration. As one observer noted: "This group kept their ideas and never lost sight of them for almost a decade when they were out of power, and when they returned to government, they added a drop of water and activated it again." Cited in Todd S. Purdum, "The Brains behind Bush's War Policy," *New York Times*, February 1, 2003, pp. A19, A21. See also Robert G. Kaiser, "Bush and Sharon Nearly Identical on Mideast Policy," *Washington Post*, February 9, 2003.

6. Michael Howard, "The Bush Doctrine: It's a Brutal World, So Act Brutally," *Sunday Times*, March 23, 2003, p. 21.

7. For details on some of the key figures in this group, inside and outside government, see Purdum, "The Brains behind Bush's War Policy"; Jason Vest, "The Men from JINSA and CSP," *Nation*, September 2, 2002; Akiva Eldar, "Perles of Wisdom for the Feithful," *Haaretz*, October 1, 2002; Tom Barry and Jim Lobe, "The Men Who Stole the Show," *Foreign Policy in Focus*, November 6, 2002; Jim Lobe, "Bush Shares Dream of Middle East Democracy," *Asia Times* (Singapore), February 27, 2003; and Robert Dreyfuss, "Tinker, Banker, NeoCon, Spy: Ahmed Chalabi's Long and Winding Road from (and to?) Baghdad," *American Prospect* 13, no. 21 (November 2002).

8. The use of gas by the Iraqi regime against its own Kurdish citizens was also widely affirmed by proponents of war and others, but the details of the most notorious such case, that of Halabja in 1988, have since been disputed. This was generally unacknowledged in the media, where Halabja became almost synonymous with the evils of the Iraqi regime, rather than reflecting what may have been a more complex, although equally lethal, reality. See Stephen C. Pelletiere's op-ed, "A War Crime or an Act of War?," *New York Times*, January 31, 2003, p. A27, which argues (on the basis of classified data to which the author was privy as the CIA's senior political analyst on Iraq during the Iran-Iraq War) that this slaughter of Kurdish civilians in March 1988 in fact involved the use of different types of gas by both Iraqi and Iranian troops in a crucial battle for control of a strategic dam in Iraqi Kurdistan, during which many innocent Kurdish civilians caught in the middle were killed by gas used by both sides. A similar version of the story, crediting American intelligence sources, was first published in the *Washington Post* two years after the event by Patrick E. Tyler:

"Both Iraq and Iran Gassed Kurds in War," U.S. Analysis Finds," May 3, 1990, p. A37.

9. Marianne Brun-Rovet, in "Americans See September 11 Link to Saddam," *Financial Times*, September 11, 2003, p. 3, noted that a "a Washington Post poll last week showed that 69 percent of Americans think Saddam Hussein was involved in the attacks," revealing little change since a CNN poll on September 2001 and a Pew Research Center poll in February 2003. She added that the Bush administration "did nothing to discourage that impression," while the president's "public speeches certainly implied that there was a link."

10. As is pointed out by Todd Purdum in "The Brains behind Bush's War Policy," the goal of "regime change" in Iraq was first enunciated by the Clinton administration in 1998. For one among a myriad of examples of the use of the term *liberation* by the neoconservative chorus preaching war on Iraq, see William Safire, "And Now: Op-Ed Diplomacy," *New York Times*, February 3, 2003, p. A29.

11. Guy Dinmore, "Hawks Set Out Bold Postwar Vision of World," *Financial Times*, March 22, 2003, p. 1. The American Enterprise Institute was perhaps the most influential of a brace of well-financed right-wing think tanks that have for years been beating the drums for the war in Iraq, and for a wider and more aggressive American role in the Middle East and many other parts of the world.

12. Ibid.

13. Richard Perle, "Thank God for the Death of the U.N.: Its Abject Failure Gave Us Only Anarchy. The World Needs Order," *Guardian*, March 21, 2003. Also cited in Ferdinand Mount, "The UN Test Nobody Dares to Mention, *Sunday Times*, March 23, 2003, p. 20.

14. Dinsmore, "Hawks."

15. This specific set of arguments in favor of "democratization" is explored further in chapter 2.

16. An *L.A. Times* poll in December 2002 found that "despite a concerted effort by the Bush administration, two-thirds of Americans believe the president failed to make the case that a war with Iraq is justified" (Maura Reynolds, "Most Unconvinced on Iraq War," *Los Angeles Times*, December 17, 2002). A *Chicago Tribune* poll a few days earlier showed similar results: the administration had "succeeded in convincing Americans that Iraq is directly linked to terrorist acts against the U.S., and at the same time failed to convince them that the nation must go to war against Saddam Hussein to protect U.S. security" (Michael Tackett, "Public Split on War, Poll Finds," *Chicago Tribune*, December 13, 2002).

17. Overwhelming majorities of from 79 to 90 percent in six major

European countries felt that the United States either should not use force in Iraq or should do so only with U.N. approval and the support of its allies, according to a poll taken by the Chicago Council on Foreign Relations/German Marshall Fund of the United States taken in the summer of 2002 (*Worldviews 2002: European Public Opinion and Foreign Policy,* Washington, D.C.: German Marshall Fund, 2002, p. 22).

18. The most striking highlight in this regard was the meeting between Donald Rumsfeld, then a presidential special envoy, and Saddam Hussein on December 20, 1983. For details, see Scott Shane, "When Hussein Was Our Ally—Iraq: Newly Revealed Documents," *Baltimore Sun,* February 27, 2003. Shane includes excerpts from recently declassified contemporary documents revealing how important the Rumsfeld mission to Baghdad of 1983, and his second visit of March 1984, were in cementing relations between the United States and Saddam Hussein's regime for the next seven years. For more graphic evidence, see the half-page color photo at the top of page 1 of the *New York Times'* "Week in Review" section of Sunday, December 8, 2002, showing a smiling Rumsfeld shaking hands with Saddam Hussein at the 1983 meeting.

19. These advisors included the head of the Defense Policy Board, Richard Perle, Undersecretary of Defense Douglas Feith, and David Wurmser, special assistant to Assistant Secretary of State John Bolton, who was later appointed Vice President Cheney's national security advisor for the Middle East. For details see Eldar, "Perles of Wisdom for the Feithful"; Jim Lobe, "Cheney's New Advisor Has Sights on Syria," *Asia Times,* October 21, 2003; and chapter 2.

20. A trenchant expression of this point came in one of Gary Trudeau's *Doonesbury* cartoon strips, where the figure of the American "viceroy" in Iraq looking out over Baghdad responds to an aide's question about when the United States will start bringing democracy to Iraq, saying: "Democracy? Ha! Think, honey! The country is 60% Shiite! A Shiite state could ally with Iran! Plus they've got all these blood scores to settle with the Sunnis who used to rule them!" This comic strip, along with Aaron MacGruder's *Boondocks,* carries more pointed critiques on policy issues than most of the mainstream news media, a sad commentary on the latter.

21. The basing of American forces in Saudi Arabia after the 1991 war (now ended), which was generally unpopular in terms of Saudi public opinion, created profound, understandable resentment against the United States, an idea that was apparently too radical for the media and the top ranks of government to grasp. A rare public expression of this under-

standing was made by Nicholas D. Kristof ("Flogging the French," *New York Times*, January 31, 2003, p. A27), who noted that "the bases radicalized many young Saudis, and persuaded Osama Bin Laden to turn his sights on the United States. What seemed a shrewd move to improve our security ended up undermining our friends and strengthening our enemies." See Patrick E. Tyler, "Saudis Plan End to U.S. Presence: Talk of Future Troop Expulsion, then Democratic Reforms," *New York Times*, February 9, 2003, pp. A1, A12.

22. This has occurred to thoughtful journalists on the spot; thus in an article entitled "Iraqi Slums Vow to Fight U.S. but It Couldn't Be Friendlier," (*New York Times*, February 1, 2003, pp. A1, A10), Ian Fisher, writing from Baghdad, noted, "This nation, where civilization stretches back thousands of years wonders why it falls to the United States to determine that their leader, whatever they think of him, must go," and cites a local observer as saying: "They are waiting to be liberated, but they are not looking at American soldiers as their liberators."

23. For an excellent account of the Islamic roots of one of the key platforms of the Ottoman reforms see Butrus Abu Manneh, "The Islamic Roots of the Gulhane Rescript," *Die Welt des Islams* 34 (1994): 173–203.

24. This was in testimony before the Committee of Imperial Defence in 1911: see R. Khalidi, *British Policy in Syria and Palestine, 1906–1914* (Oxford: St. Antony's Middle East Monographs, 1980), p. 89.

25. Charles Issawi, *An Economic History of the Middle East and North Africa* (New York: Columbia University Press, 1982).

26. Benjamin C. Fortna, *Imperial Classroom: Islam, the State and Education in the Late Ottoman Empire* (Oxford: Oxford University Press, 2002), p. 124.

27. Selcuk Somel, *The Modernization of Public Education in the Ottoman Empire* (Leiden: Brill, 2001), p. 111.

28. There is a large literature on this subject. See preeminently the seminal work of Edward Said, *Orientalism* (New York: Random House, 1978), as well as Norman Daniel, *Islam and the West: The Making of an Image* (Edinburgh: Edinburgh University Press, 1980) and Maxime Rodinson, *Europe and the Mystique of Islam* (Seattle: University of Washington Press, 1987).

29. Even some of those who knew local languages were less expert than they pretended: for all his supposed fluency, for example, T. E. Lawrence was described as follows by a fellow Englishman who spent most of his life in the Arab world: "Actually, his Arabic was rather poor stuff of a very mixed breed, and his accent was not good, though of course he spoke fluently enough" (H. St. John Philby, *Arabian Days: An Autobiography* [London: Robert Hale, 1948], p. 20). One of Lawrence's

most conscientious biographers, Suleiman Mousa, in *T. E. Lawrence: An Arab View* (Oxford: Oxford University Press, 1966), states: "Lawrence claimed that he knew twelve thousand Arabic words, but that is clear exaggeration. The fact of the matter is that his Arabic served to convey his thoughts in a limited way. All those I have spoken with or written to have unanimously agreed that as soon as Lawrence spoke one word of Arabic, it was clear to all concerned that he was a foreigner" (p. 268).

30. See Marwan Buheiry, "Colonial Scholarship and Muslim Revivalism in 1900," *Arab Studies Quarterly* 4 (1982): 1–16, for an account of how this operated in the thinking of a number of Western scholars at the turn of the twentieth century. For a sophisticated analysis of what he calls *le regard colonial* of French officials concerning the Sanusi movement in North Africa in the nineteenth and twentieth centuries, see Jean-Louis Triaud, *La légende noire de la Sanûsiyya: Une confrérie musulmane saharienne sous le regard français (1840–1930)*, 2 vols. (Paris: Editions de la Maison des Sciences de l'Homme, 1995). Triaud deftly analyzes how French official views and scholarly constructions of this important brotherhood went hand in hand, and shifted over time in keeping with the state of its relations with French colonial expansion in the Sahara.

31. Harold Temperley, *England and the Middle East, the Crimea* (London: Longman and Green, 1936), a work based largely on European diplomatic sources, notably the self-serving dispatches of the British ambassador in the Ottoman Empire, Stratford Canning, is representative of an entire genre that described reform as almost entirely the work of outsiders.

32. The best examination of how deeply grounded in indigenous trends these reforms were is Butrus Abu Manneh, "The Islamic Roots."

33. For one of the best memoirs showing how such racism was perceived, see Salama Musa, *The Education of Salama Musa*, translated by L. O. Schuman (Leiden: Brill, 1961).

34. For details, see Victor Kiernan, *The Lords of Human Kind: Black Man, Yellow Man and White Man in the Age of Empire* (New York: Columbia University Press, 1986). See also Uday Mehta, *Liberalism and Empire: A Study in Nineteenth-Century British Liberal Thought* (Chicago: University of Chicago, 1999).

35. In the words of one of the earliest and most acute critics of the French occupation of Algeria, the Marquis de la Gervaisais, writing only four years after it began, "The development of agricultural colonization will produce a fatal and detestable necessity: the expulsion and extermination of the natives." Cited in M. Buheiry, "The Conquest of Algeria and

the Apocalyptic Vision of La Gervaisais," in Marwan Buheiry, *The Formation and Perception of the Modern Arab World*, edited by Lawrence Conrad (Princeton, N.J.: Darwin, 1989), p. 41.

36. William Cleveland, *A History of the Modern Middle East* (Boulder, Colo.: Westview, 1994), p. 101.

37. For details, see Juan Cole, *Colonialism and Revolution in the Middle East: Social and Cultural Origins of Egypt's 'Urabi Movement* (Princeton, N.J.: Princeton University Press, 1993), and Alexander Schölch, *Egypt for the Egyptians! The Socio-Political Crisis in Egypt 1878–82* (London: Ithaca Press, 1981).

38. For details see Ismail Khalidi, *The Constitutional Development of Libya* (Beirut: Khayat, 1957).

39. P. J. Vatikiotis, *The History of Egypt from Muhammad Ali to Sadat*, 2d ed. (London: Weidenfeld and Nicolson, 1980).

40. The negative effects of external intervention on the prospects for the growth of democracy in the Middle East are discussed in chapter 2.

41. Briton Cooper Busch, *Britain, India and the Arabs, 1914–1921* (Berkeley: University of California Press, 1971), pp. 408–416.

42. For more details on these competing visions, see Timothy Paris, "British Middle East Policy-Making after the First World War: The Lawrentian and Wilsonian Schools," *Historical Journal* 41, no. 3 (1998): 773–93.

43. An excellent account of the revolt can be found in Michael Provence, "Plowshares into Swords: Anti-Colonial Resistance and Popular Nationalism in French Mandate Syria, 1925–26" (Ph.D. diss., University of Chicago, 2001).

44. Jamil Abun-Nasr, *A History of the Maghrib in the Islamic Period* (Cambridge: Cambridge University Press, 1987), p. 381.

45. The conflict in Palestine is dealt with in chapter 2 and is treated extensively in chapter 4.

46. Fromkin, *A War*, pp. 202–203.

47. Philip Khoury, *Syria and the French Mandate: The Politics of Arab Nationalism, 1920–1945* (Princeton, N.J.: Princeton University Press, 1987), p. 178.

48. Ibid., pp. 171, 196.

49. Wing Commander J. A. Chamier, "The Use of Air Power for Replacing Military Garrisons," *Royal United Services Institute Journal* 66 (February–November 1921): 205–212. According to Sven Lindqvist, *A History of Bombing* (New York: New Press, 2001), p. 33, the first aerial bombing of civilians was by Italy in Libya in October 1911. See pp. 37 and 42–48 for other instances of the use of air power against civilians in the Middle East between 1913 and 1924.

50. Cited in "'Shock and Awe:' Bombing Iraq for 80 Years," *CounterPunch* 10, no. 2 (January 2003): 3, 6.

51. T. E. Lawrence asserted in a letter to the *Times* that 10,000 Iraqis had been killed, although estimates differ: Charles Tripp, *A History of Iraq* (Cambridge: Cambridge University Press, 2000), p. 44, gives the number of those killed as "an estimated 6,000 Iraqis and roughly 500 British and Indian soldiers." The figure of 8,500 is given in "'Shock and Awe.'" For more on these dishonorable episodes in colonial history, see David Omissi, *Air Power and Colonial Control* (Manchester: Manchester University Press, 1990), and Tom Mockaitis, *British Counter-Insurgency, 1919–1960* (London: Macmillan, 1990).

52. Estimates of Palestinian casualties are from Walid Khalidi, *From Haven to Conquest*, rev. ed. (Washington, D.C.: Institute for Palestine Studies, 1987), appendix 4, pp. 847–49. Population figures are extrapolated from the 1931 census figures listed in Justin McCarthy, *The Population of Palestine* (New York: Columbia University Press, 1988), appendix 4, Table A4–3, p. 100.

53. In the Arab world, these historical memories are reinforced daily by live reporting on a variety of current crises presented in terms of foreign intervention, occupation, and local resistance, from Iraq to Afghanistan to Palestine, available on a half-dozen satellite channels that show graphic and powerful images that Americans are solicitously protected from seeing by American television convention and assiduous self-censorship.

54. The famous phrase warning against "entangling alliances" often ascribed to Washington in his Farewell Address in 1796 (he in fact spoke of the dangers of "complications" abroad) was actually uttered by Jefferson on leaving office in 1801: see Harold Temperley, *The Foreign Policy of Canning, 1822–1827: England, the Holy Alliance and the New World* (London: G. Bell, 1925), p. 126. In 1821 John Quincy Adams, then Monroe's secretary of state, warned that were America to go abroad "in search of monsters," as some suggested at the time, "the fundamental maxims of her policy would insensibly change from liberty to force.... She might become dictatress of the world. She would no longer be the ruler of her own spirit." Cited in Lewis H. Lapham, "Regime Change," *Harper's*, February 2003, p. 8.

55. For full details, see Temperley, *The Foreign Policy of Canning*, pp. 103ff.

56. Although espousing the principle of national self-determination, the Fourteen Points specifically touched upon the postwar disposition of Russia, Belgium, France, Italy, Austria-Hungary, Rumania, Serbia, Montenegro, and Poland, while making vague references to the wishes

of colonial populations, and of the nationalities of the non-Turkish parts of the Ottoman Empire.

57. Speaking in Parliament just before his death, Canning said of British recognition of the new South American republics, extended soon after the proclamation of the Monroe Doctrine: "I called the New World into existence to redress the balance of the Old" (Temperley, *The Foreign Policy of Canning*, p. 154).

58. See Harry N. Howard, *The King-Crane Commission: An American Inquiry in the Middle East* (Beirut: Khayat, 1963). A portion of the commission's report can be found in J. C. Hurewitz, ed., *The Middle East and North Africa in World Politics: A Documentary Record*, vol. 2 (New Haven, Conn.: Yale University Press, 1979).

59. See R. Khalidi, *British Policy in Syria and Palestine, 1906–1914* (Oxford: St. Antony's Middle East Monographs, 1980), for the background to the Anglo-French imperialist rivalry in the Middle East.

60. Ironically, the intermediary who in 1931 put the Saudi king in touch with the Americans, an initiative that led directly to the lucrative deal with Standard Oil of California two years later, was none other than Charles Crane, coauthor of the King-Crane report: H. St. John Philby, *Saudi Arabia* (London: Ernest Benn, 1955), p. 330.

61. How unprepared the United States was to play a role as a great power can be gauged from the fact that when the newly founded American intelligence service, the OSS, first assigned an officer to deal with Palestine in 1943, he found that the agency's entire archive on the subject consisted of two articles, one on the Arabs and one on the Jews: personal communication, J. C. Hurewitz, New York, September 17, 2003.

62. For some of the Arab reactions to Cold War–driven American policies, see R. Khalidi, "The Revolutionary Year of 1958 in the Arab World," in *The Revolutionary Middle East in 1958*, edited by Wm. Roger Louis (Washington, D.C.: Woodrow Wilson Press, 2002), pp. 181–208.

63. For more details, see the discussion of Middle Eastern oil in chapter 3.

64. A perfect example is Robert D. Kaplan, "Supremacy by Stealth: Ten Rules for Managing the World," *Atlantic*, July–August 2003, pp. 65–83.

CHAPTER TWO
America, the West, and
Democracy in the Middle East

1. Each of these presidential pronouncements marks a transition. For a fascinating treatment of the "American century" just completed, the American empire that is arguably succeeding it, and key moments in

the transition from one era to another—1898, the post–World War I
and World War II reshapings of the world order—see Neil Smith,
*American Empire: Roosevelt's Geographer and the Prelude to Globaliza-
tion* (Berkeley: University of California Press, 2003).

2. The actions of the Bush administration seemed likely to heighten
rather than allay this insecurity, which it exploited to pass measures
like the USA Patriot Act, some of the extensive provisions of which appear to have been prepared before the 9/11 attacks, and were rushed
through Congress so fast that many members admitted that they had
not had time to read the bill.

3. Quoted in Jim Lobe, "Bush Shares Dream of Middle East Democracy,"
Asia Times (Singapore), February 27, 2003.

4. This is not to mention the even more problematic notion of "nation
building," which is addressed in chapter 5.

5. Beyond this, doubts were raised about the sincerity of some of these
suddenly fervent apostles of democracy, since some top officeholders in
the administration had amply shown their contempt for the democratic process at home and abroad, like Elliot Abrams and Admiral
John Poindexter, both convicted of lying to Congress over the Iran-
Contra affair (the latter was forced to leave office after a furor over the
actions of the Defense Advanced Research Projects Agency [DARPA],
which he headed). Other veterans of the arms-for-hostages dealings,
and subsequent illegal funneling of profits to the Nicaraguan rebels,
with senior positions in George W. Bush's administration included
Otto Reich and John Negroponte, neither of whom was ever indicted.

6. Denizens of two of the leading right-wing think tanks, the AEI and the
Washington Institute for Near East Policy, which housed some of the
most fervent of the advocates of democratization as a war-aim in Iraq,
had in the past paid little attention to the democratization of the Arab
world in their writings, except occasionally to contrast its benighted
state with that of enlightened democratic bastions like Israel.

7. In his first public remarks a few weeks after his release, in a talk at the
University of Chicago on April 16, 2003, Ibrahim stated that such
heavy-handed and public American pressure on Egypt, as distinguished from quiet diplomacy and other forms of intercession, had
been counterproductive.

8. Jonathan C. Randal, *After Such Knowledge, What Forgiveness: My
Encounters with Kurdistan* (New York: Farrar, Straus and Giroux, 1997),
provides one of the best accounts of what Randal calls this "textbook
case of betrayal," which is how the Kurds also saw it.

9. An investigative report based on interviews with a dozen American and
British former intelligence officers and diplomats stated that Saddam

Hussein was part of a "CIA-authorized six-man squad" that failed to kill Kassem: Richard Sale, UPI, "Exclusive: Saddam Key in Early CIA Plot," April 10, 2003.

10. Roger Morris, "A Tyrant 40 Years in the Making," *New York Times*, March 14, 2003, p. A27. In addition to evidence produced during hearings held by the Congressional Select Committee on Intelligence, Morris cites the research of David Wise, author with Thomas Ross of *The Invisible Government: The CIA and U.S. Intelligence* (New York: Vintage, 1964) and other books on the CIA. The U.S. government looked favorably on coup attempts against Kassem in 1958 and 1959 according to recently released official documents, as is shown in the forthcoming book by Selim Yaqub, *Containing Arab Nationalism: The Eisenhower Doctrine and the Middle East* (Chapel Hill: University of North Carolina Press). A 1960 CIA attempt to assassinate Kassem is discussed in Thomas Powers's biography of Richard Helms, *The Man Who Kept Secrets* (New York: Knopf, 1979), pp. 128, 130. For U.S. support for the Ba'thist 1963 coup, see Andrew and Patrick Cockburn, *Out of the Ashes: The Resurrection of Saddam Hussein* (New York: Perennial, 2000). Sale, "Exclusive: Saddam," states that while the CIA had not organized the 1963 coup, it took advantage of it by providing the Ba'th with lists of communists, who were then executed.

11. Here, as elsewhere, the veteran foreign reporter Jonathan Randal, in *After Such Knowledge*, provides the most knowledgeable account. See also Susan Meisalas with Martin van Bruinessen, *Kurdistan: In the Shadow of History* (New York: Random House, 1997).

12. While that hostility is well known and amply documented, some of the reasons for it are less well understood (as is evidenced by the vapid bleating in some quarters about how "they"—whether Iranians or other Muslims—"hate our way of life"). For a perceptive analysis of these reasons, see James Bill, *The Eagle and the Lion: The Tragedy of American-Iranian Relations* (New Haven, Conn.: Yale University Press, 1988).

13. For details, see Scott Shane, "When Hussein Was Our Ally," *Baltimore Sun*, February 27, 2003, and his primary source, the treasure trove of sixty-one declassified U.S. government documents on the wooing of the Iraqi regime, in which Donald Rumsfeld played a key role, from 1980 to 1984, even as that regime was producing and using chemical weapons against Iran. These extraordinary documents are available online at the site of the National Security Archive at George Washington University: http://www.gwu.edu/fflnsarchiv/NSAEBB/NSAEBB82/index.htm.

14. National Security Archive documents 60 (satellite-derived intelli-

gence); 59 (chemical weapons); 39, 44, 55, 56 (other weapons); 57, 61 (dual-use materials for the nuclear program): http://www.gwu.edu/ fflnsarchive/NSAEBB/NSAEBB82/index.htm

15. Sale, "Exclusive: Saddam."

16. Jonathan C. Randal, *After Such Knowledge*, p. 166; the citation is from the Pike Report, in which the quote is sourced to a "high U.S. official." Asked by Randal about this cynical but typically witty remark, Kissinger admitted, "I could have said that."

17. Ilene Prusher and Ann Tyson, "Turkey Imperils U.S. War Strategy," *Christian Science Monitor*, February 23, 2003; Suzan Fraser, "Turkey: Anti-War Protests Greet U.S. General," AP, January 20, 2003.

18. These officials also described the reluctance of the Turkish government as "extortion in the name of alliance." David E. Sanger with Dexter Filkins, "U.S. Is Pessimistic Turks Will Accept Aid Deal on Iraq," *New York Times*, February 20, 2003, p. A1. Turkey's government agreed a few days thereafter to allow its territory to be used for a ground invasion of Iraq in exchange for $16 billion in grants and loans and unspecified guarantees regarding the entry of Turkish troops into Iraq along with invading U.S. forces, but the Turkish Parliament refused to ratify this agreement.

19. There are no elections, and no polling is allowed, in Saudi Arabia, and thus public opinion in that country is hard to ascertain. Nevertheless, press reports point to strong feeling among many Saudis on this point. See, e.g., John Bradley and David Rennie, "Pull-out Is Better Late than Never for Saudis," *Daily Telegraph*, April 30, 2003; as Bradley and Rennie noted, "The news that American troops will withdraw from bases in Saudi Arabia was universally welcomed in the Kingdom yesterday, although most Saudis felt their departure was 12 years overdue."

20. Dale van Natta, Jr., "Last American Combat Troops Quit Saudi Arabia," *New York Times*, September 22, 2003, p. A8.

21. The Saudi government was reported to have been planning to ask for the removal of U.S. forces even before the war in Iraq began: see Patrick E. Tyler, "Saudis Plan End to U.S. Presence: Talk of Future Troop Expulsion, then Democratic Reforms," *New York Times*, February 9, 2003, pp. A1, A12, and ibid.

22. According to Ari Berman, "Ideas the Pentagon Wishes It Never Had," *Nation*, August 23, 2003, the Pentagon's nomination of Woolsey was shot down in April by the president's senior political advisor, Karl Rove.

23. Jim Lobe, "Watch Woolsey," *Asia Times*, April 8, 2003. The hawkish Woolsey was vocal in the campaign to launch the war against Iraq, and

has long advocated that the United States wage "World War IV" (the Cold War was World War III for Woolsey) in the Middle East against Iran and Syria and other "rogue regimes."

24. Ailes is deftly profiled by Ken Auletta in the *New Yorker*, May 26, 2003.

25. For details, see e.g., Lobe, "Watch Woolsey,"; Lobe, "Bush Shares"; and Zvi Bar'el, "Can an American Woman Run Baghdad?" *Haaretz*, April 9, 2003. Most members of this group share a public relations firm, Benador Associates, discussed in a perceptive article by Jim Lobe, "Condor among the Hawks," *Asia Times*, August 15, 2003. Lobe has been the author of a number of informative articles on the neocons in *Asia Times* and elsewhere, as has Seymour Hersh in the *New Yorker*. There is good coverage of their doings as well in the leading Israeli daily, *Haaretz*.

26. The report, entitled "A Clean Break: A New Strategy for Securing the Realm," was intended to be public, and can be located at http://www .israeleconomy.org/strat1.htm.

27. Perle, nicknamed the "Prince of Darkness" by his critics (see, among other similar articles, Jim Lobe, "Perle: 'Prince of Darkness' in the Spotlight," *Asia Times*, March 25, 2003), was forced to resign in a cloud of scandal from the chairmanship as a result of an exposé by investigative reporter Seymour Hersh ("Lunch with the Chairman: Why Was Richard Perle Meeting with Adnan Khashoggi?" *New Yorker*, March 17, 2003), who reported that Perle had benefited materially from contacts available to him as a result of his (unpaid) position on the board. The impact of this revelation was compounded by a report in the *New York Times* a few days later that Perle stood to gain $735,000 from Global Crossing for similar work involving his contacts at the Defense Department.

28. For more on Bolton, see Nicholas Thomson, "John Bolton vs. the World," Salon.com, July 16, 2003: http://archive.salon.com/news/2003/ 07/16/bolton/index_np.html.

29. Reports about the ideological blinders afflicting the group advising Bush, Rumsfeld, and Cheney surfaced in the mainstream media during the second week of the invasion of Iraq when things suddenly did not seem to be going according to the neocons' optimistic plans: see Seymour Hersh, *New Yorker*, April 7, 2003; Glenn Kessler and Walter Pincus, "Advisers Split as War Unfolds: One faction Hopes Bush Nixes 'Bum Advice,'" *Washington Post*, March 31, 2003, p. A1. See also Bernard Winraub and Thom Shanker, "Rumsfeld's Design for War Criticized on the Batttlefield," and Michael Gordon, "A New Doctrine's Test," *New York Times* April 1, 2003, p. A1, which focus on how Rumsfeld and his

civilian aides imposed a war plan on the uniformed military that did not initially provide for sufficient ground forces. A media blitz by Rumsfeld, combined with progress on the battlefield, eventually blunted these criticisms. They arose anew several months later as similar criticisms were sounded regarding the Pentagon's lack of preparation and poor planning for the postwar situation in Iraq as well as the failure to find weapons of mass destruction there. See Robert Greenberger, "Postwar Difficulties Have Put Neoconservatism on the Line," *Wall Street Journal*, September 19, 2003, and Guy Dinsmore, "Cracks Starting to Show in U.S. Conservative Consensus," *Financial Times*, September 23, 2003.

30. There are numerous journalistic analyses of this report, many of them already cited, such as J. Vest, "The Men from JINSA and CSP," *Nation*, September 2, 2002; Akiva Eldar, "Perles of Wisdom for the Feithful," *Haaretz*, October 1, 2002; and Tom Barry and Jim Lobe, "The Men Who Stole the Show," *Foreign Policy in Focus*, November 6, 2002. See also: Brian Whitaker, "Playing Skittles with Saddam," *Guardian*, September 3, 2002; Robert Fisk, "The Case against War," *Counterpunch*, February 15, 2003; and Akiva Eldar, "There Is Fire even without a Smoking Gun," *Haaretz*, February 16, 2003.

31. Richard Perle, for example, stated to the BBC on October 10, 2001: "That there may be hostility in the Arab street is entirely possible. We will survive hostility in the Arab street." See also the comments on Turkey cited in note 18, and James Woolsey's cynical comments regarding elections in Iraq cited in note 23.

32. A prominent member of this group, Michael Ledeen, gave evidence of this callousness when the first reports of American military casualties in Iraq came in: "I think the level of casualties is secondary.... What we hate is not casualties, but losing." As quoted in Courtland Milloy, "War Hawks Blinded by Hardened Hearts," *Washington Post*, March 31, 2003, p. B1.

33. See in this regard, e.g., David Rhode, "Where They Hate Saddam, and Dread the U.S.," *New York Times*, March 9, 2003, sec. 4, p. 3.

34. Milloy, "War Hawks."

35. For details see Juan Cole, *Colonialism and Revolution in the Middle East: Social and Cultural Origins of Egypt's 'Urabi Movement* (Princeton, N.J.: Princeton University Press, 1993), and Alexander Schölch, *Egypt for the Egyptians! The Socio-Political Crisis in Egypt 1878–82* (London: Ithaca Press, 1981).

36. The best sources on this subject are Afaf Lutfi al-Sayyid Marsot, *Egypt's Liberal Experiment 1922–1936* (Berkeley: University of California Press,

1977), and Jacques Berque, *Egypt: Imperialism and Revolution* (London: Faber, 1972).

37. For details regarding Syria, see Khoury, *Syria and the French Mandate*; regarding Iraq, see the magisterial work of Hanna Batatu, *The Old Social Classes and the Revolutionary Movements of Iraq: A Study of Iraq's Old Landed and Commercial Classes and of Its Communists, Ba'thists and Free Officers* (Princeton, N.J.: Princeton University Press, 1978).

38. Egypt's literacy rate in 1947 was 22.8 percent according to John Waterbury, *The Egypt of Nasser and Sadat: The Political Economy of Two Regimes* (Princeton, N.J.: Princeton University Press, 1983), table 3.6, p. 44; that of Syria in 1932 was 32 percent, according to Charles Issawi, *The Fertile Crescent, 1800–1914: A Documentary Economic History* (Oxford: Oxford University Press, 1988), p. 30.

39. For more on Jordan, see R. Khalidi, "The Revolutionary Year of 1958 in the Arab World," in *The Revolutionary Middle East in 1958*, edited by Wm. Roger Louis (Washington, D.C., and London: Woodrow Wilson Press and I. B. Tauris, 2002), pp. 181–208.

40. It is worth noting that in spite of various episodes of foreign interference, in their recent history Turkey, Israel, and Iran have suffered less than most Arab countries from foreign intervention and occupation.

41. For expert accounts on the subject, see Gilles Kepel, *Jihad: The Trail of Political Islam* (London: I. B. Tauris, 2002), and François Burgat, *Face to Face with Political Islam* (New York: I. B. Tauris, 2003).

42. One example of such exaggeration is Karl Wittfogel's model of a powerful "hydraulic state" as being necessary to regulate irrigation in the great river valleys, with Egypt and Mesopotamia cited as central cases illustrating the argument: Karl Wittfogel, *Oriental Despotism: A Comparative Study of Total Power* (New Haven, Conn.: Yale University Press, 1957). For a more sophisticated analysis of non-European absolutist states see Perry Anderson, *Lineages of the Absolutist State* (London: Verso, 1979), pp. 397–549.

43. Egypt has long had a highly professional and developed judiciary that has repeatedly shown its independence by standing up to the powerful Egyptian executive branch: see Donald Reid, *Lawyers and Politics in the Arab World 1880–1960* (Minneapolis: Biblioteca Islamica, 1981). The case of the Egyptian-American professor Saad al-Din Ibrahim, who was acquitted and freed by a civilian court after a state security court had sentenced him to a lengthy prison sentence, illustrates this judicial independence.

44. This is an underappreciated tradition, which a few scholars have high-

lighted, e.g.: Edmund Burke and Ira Lapidus, eds., *Islam, Politics and Social Movements* (Berkeley: University of California Press, 1988); Edmund Burke, ed., *Struggle and Survival in the Modern Middle East* (Berkeley: University of California Press, 1993); Zachary Lockman, *Workers and Working Classes in the Middle East: Struggles, Histories, Historiographies* (Albany: State University of New York Press, 1994); and Guilan Denoeux, *Urban Unrest in the Middle East: A Comparative Study of Informal Networks in Egypt, Iran and Lebanon* (Albany: State University of New York Press, 1993).

45. In this respect it is more like France, though the Middle East has known strong statehood for far longer.

46. Some of the interesting work done on this topic can be found in Steven Heydemann, ed., *War, Institutions and Social Change in the Middle East* (Berkeley: University of California Press, 2000), and David Garnham and Mark Tessler, eds., *Democracy, War and Peace in the Middle East* (Bloomington: Indiana University Press, 1995).

47. The most sympathetic analysis of this problem in the Arab world was by George Antonious, *The Arab Awakening* (London: Hamish Hamilton, 1938). Its most caustic observer was Elie Kedourie, notably in the introduction to *Nationalism in Asia and Africa* (London: Weidenfeld and Nicolson, 1969).

48. For more on the construction of modern national identity, the concept of overlapping identities, and how they work themselves out even in the atypical case of the Palestinians, see R. Khalidi, *Palestinian Identity: The Construction of Modern National Consciousness* (New York: Columbia University Press, 1997).

49. The best analysis of this process can be found in Batatu, *The Old Social Classes*, on Iraq, and *Syria's Peasantry, the Descendants of its Lesser Rural Notables, and their Politics* (Princeton, N.J.: Princeton University Press, 1999), regarding Syria.

50. For an early analysis of the degeneration of these regimes, see R. Khalidi, "Social Transformation and Political Power in the 'Radical' Arab States," in *Nation, State and Integration in the Arab World*, vol. 3, *Beyond Coercion: The Durability of the Arab State*, edited by Adeed Dawisha and I. William Zartman (New York: Croom Helm, 1988), pp. 203–219.

51. UNDP Regional Bureau for Arab states and the Arab Fund for Economic and Social Development, "Arab Human Development Report 2002: Creating Opportunities for Future Generations," http://www.undp.org/rbas/ahdr/english.html.

52. See the National Security Archive documents cited earlier: http://www.gwu.edu/fflnsarchiv/NSAEBB/NSAEBB82/index.htm.

53. See Björn Hagelin, Pieter D. Wezeman, Siemon T. Wezeman, and Nicholas Chipperfield, "International Arms Transfers," *SIPRI Yearbook 2003: Armaments, Disarmament and International Security* (Oxford: Oxford University Press, 2003).

54. *New York Times*, April 12, 2003, p. 1.

55. See McGuire Gibson, "The Theft of Ancient Cities," *Newsday*, September 21, 2003. Gibson, a distinguished professor of Mesopotamian archaeology at the University of Chicago, visited Iraq with the UNESCO team twice after the war, and has documented both the thefts from the museum and the looting of archaeological sites.

CHAPTER THREE
The Middle East: Geostrategy and Oil

1. For a full definition of this region, see the introduction, note 1.

2. Martin Lewis and Karen Wigen's perceptive *The Myth of Continents: A Critique of Metageography* (Berkeley: University of California Press, 1997), explains the origins of the existing classification system for the continents, and details different ways of seeing this single landmass.

3. See Jared Diamond, *Guns, Germs and Steel* (New York: Norton, 1999) for one thesis as to why this was the case.

4. See, e.g., Stanford Shaw, *History of the Ottoman Empire and Modern Turkey* (Cambridge: Cambridge University Press, 1976), vol. 1, pp. 172–74, and Justin McCarthy, *The Ottoman Turks* (London: Longman, 1997), pp. 151–52. This was a gradual process, and a relative one. As McCarthy notes, "While the Middle Eastern transit trade did not quickly decline after the Portuguese discoveries, it did not increase as it always had."

5. For more on the creation of these Europe-based world empires, see Fernand Braudel, *La Méditerranée et le Monde méditerranéen à l'époque de Philippe II* (Paris: Armand Colin, 1949), and the three volumes of Immanuel Wallerstein's *The Modern World System*: 1, *Capitalist Agriculture and the Origins of the European World-Economy in the Sixteenth Century* (New York: Academic Press, 1974); 2, *Mercantilism and the Consolidation of the European World-Economy, 1600–1750* (New York: Academic Press, 1980); and 3, *The Second Era of Great Expansion of the Capitalist World-Economy, 1730–1840's* (New York: Academic Press, 1989).

6. See Alfred Thayer Mahan, *The Influence of Sea Power on History, 1660–1783* (Boston: Little Brown, 1902).

7. This process was detailed in chapter 1.

8. See R. Khalidi, *British Policy in Syria and Palestine, 1906–1914* (Oxford: St. Antony's Middle East Monographs, 1980), and chapter 2, for more on these precursors of the World War I and postwar partition agreements.

9. Bitumen from Hit and elsewhere was used extensively as "mortar" for baked bricks, for drains, and for attaching flint or obsidian blades into wooden hafts, as in prehistoric sickles dating from as early as 5500 B.C. For details, see R. J. Forbes, *Studies in Ancient Technology* (Leiden: Brill, 1965).

10. See extracts from 1871, 1914, and 1918 reports on oil prospects in Iraq and Iran in Charles Issawi, *The Fertile Crescent: A Documentary Economic History* (Oxford: Oxford University Press, 1988), pp. 402–406. According to one, oil production in 1914 at a group of wells south of Mosul amounted to the very small quantity of one thousand kilograms per day.

11. The best account of the development of the oil industry internationally is Daniel Yergin, *The Prize: The Epic Quest for Oil, Money and Power* (New York: Simon and Schuster, 1991).

12. The text of the concession is in J. C. Hurewitz, ed., *The Middle East and North Africa in World Politics: A Documentary Record*, 2d ed. (New Haven, Conn.: Yale University Press, 1975), vol. 1, pp. 482–84.

13. Mostafa Elm, *Oil, Power and Principle: Iran's Oil Nationalization and Its Aftermath* (Syracuse, N.Y.: Syracuse University Press, 1992), p. 7.

14. Winston Churchill, *The World Crisis, 1911–1918*, vol. 1 (London: New English Library, 1968), pp. 90–91.

15. For details, see chapter 1.

16. The 1901 D'Arcy concession and the provisions of the 1907 entente relating to Anglo-Russian spheres of influence in Iran were only the most recent evidence of the weakness of the Iranian state. Earlier, in 1890, a previous shah had been obliged by his treasury's straitened financial circumstances to offer a concession for the production of tobacco products to a foreigner, sparking widespread popular protests that ultimately led to the humiliating revocation of the concession. A similar desperate need for revenue had obliged the shah to grant the highly disadvantageous D'Arcy concession.

17. Stephen Longrigg, *Oil in the Middle East: Its Discovery and Development* (Oxford: Oxford University Press, 1954), p. 35.

18. For details, see chapter 1.

19. The Anglo-Persian was renamed the Anglo-Iranian Oil Company (AIOC) in 1935, and British Petroleum (BP) in 1954.

20. The best account of the fiasco of the negotiations of 1933 can be found in Elm, *Oil, Power and Principle*, pp. 31–39.

21. The company's concession was restricted to one hundred thousand square miles, but that still amounted to 15 percent of the country's area, whereas the AIOC's actual operations involved an area just over one square mile. For details, see Joe Stork, *Middle East Oil and the Energy Crisis* (New York: Monthly Review Press, 1975), p. 12.

22. The most complete account of Mossadeq's attempt to nationalize the Iranian oil industry is in Elm, *Oil, Power and Principle*.

23. This was a result of treaties made between the weak new Bolshevik regime and Turkey, Iran, and Afghanistan in early 1921 in order to secure its southern flank against British intervention against the new Soviet regime. For the texts, see Hurewitz, *The Middle East and North Africa*, vol. 2, pp. 240–48, 250–53.

24. See Yergin, *The Prize*, pp. 271–79.

25. Kermit Roosevelt, *Countercoup: The Struggle for the Control of Iran* (New York: McGraw Hill, 1979), gives the perspective of one of the key organizers of the coup. For balanced assessments, see James Bill, *The Eagle and the Lion: The Tragedy of American-Iranian Relations* (New Haven, Conn.: Yale University Press, 1988), pp. 51–97, and Mostafa Elm, *Oil, Power and Principle*.

26. Charles Issawi and Mohammed Yeganeh, *The Economics of Middle Eastern Oil* (New York: Columbia University Press, 1962), p. 122.

27. These were the provinces, or vilayets, of Basra, Baghdad, and Mosul.

28. For more on this little-known episode, see Malcolm Russell, *The First Modern Arab State: Syria under Faysal, 1918–1920* (Minneapolis: Biblioteca Islamic, 1985), and Hassan Saab, *The Arab Federalists of the Ottoman Empire* (Amsterdam: Mouton, 1958).

29. For details, see R. Khalidi, *British Policy*.

30. M. Macmillan, *Paris, 1919*, p. 382.

31. See Bruce Westrate, *The Arab Bureau: British Policy in the Middle East, 1916–1920* (University Park: Pennsylvania State University Press, 1992). Although T. E. Lawrence was the most famous of this group, he was not the most important—that distinction belonged to its chief, Gilbert Clayton, or the archaeologist David Hogarth (also a commander in the naval reserves), who first involved Lawrence in espionage. None had Lawrence's gifts for self promotion, or for writing fiction and nonfiction, all three of which blend seamlessly in *Seven Pillars of Wisdom*. Its many editions are a testament to Lawrence's writing and to the resonance of his tale with an Anglo-American reading (and movie-going) public hungry for romantic fantasies about the Arab world. See Steve Caton, *Lawrence of Arabia: A Film's Anthropology* (Berkeley: University of California Press, 1999).

32. H. V. F. Winstone, *Gertrude Bell* (London: Jonathan Cape, 1978), p. 185.

33. Kitchener's authority came from the fact that since the 1870s he had served in Palestine, the Sudan, and Egypt (as well as India and South Africa), and until 1914 he had been proconsul in Cairo; in consequence he knew Arabic and Turkish. In the mid-1870s Kitchener helped carry out the seven-volume *Survey of Western Palestine* (London: Palestine Exploration Fund, 1881–84), including a twenty-six-sheet map of the country and a list of ten thousand place names. This was a vital preliminary step in Britain's domination of the country, and another illustration of the ways in which scientific knowledge and power are related.

34. See George Packer, Letter from Baghdad, "War after the War: What Washington Doesn't See in Iraq," *New Yorker*, November 24, 2003, pp. 59–85.

35. Cited in B. Busch, *Britain, India and the Arabs*, p. 22.

36. Ibid., p. 54.

37. For more on the role of colonial armies in imperial expansion, see Victor Kiernan, "Colonial Africa and Its Armies," in *Imperialism and Its Contradictions* (London: Routledge, 1995), pp. 77–96. A brilliant novel that illuminates the role of the Indian Army in British imperial expansion is Amitav Ghosh's *Glass Palace* (New York: Random House, 2002).

38. The first book to publish the correspondence, and still a useful, albeit partisan, source, is George Antonius, *The Arab Awakening* (London: Hamish Hamilton, 1938). A. L. Tibawi's pedestrian but sound *Anglo-Arab Relations and the Question of Palestine, 1914–1921* (London: Luzac, 1977) and Elie Kedourie's tendentious but well written *In the Anglo-Arab Labyrinth: The McMahon-Husayn Correspondence and Its Interpretations 1914–1939* (Cambridge: Cambridge University Press, 1976) can both be consulted with profit for widely differing interpretations of every aspect of the topic and its historiography.

39. *Harper's*, May 2003.

40. For details, see Aaron Klieman, *Foundations of British Policy in the Arab World: The Cairo Conference of 1921* (Baltimore: Johns Hopkins University Press, 1970).

41. This understanding went through various stages, with an initial agreement in 1919, that was formalized in the San Remo Oil Agreement of April 1920: Longrigg, *Oil in the Middle East*, p. 44.

42. Stork, *Middle East Oil*, p. 16.

43. In 1928 Britain felt obliged to admit American oil companies into its cozy Iraqi oil deal, and by the Red Line Agreement of 1928, equal shares of 23.75 percent went to British, Anglo-Dutch, French, and American oil consortia, with the remaining 5 percent to Calouste Gulbenkian,

who had put the together the original TPC consortium. The text of the agreement can be found in Hurewitz, ed., *The Middle East and North Africa*, vol. 2, pp. 399–413.

44. Longrigg, *Oil in the Middle East*, p. 45.

45. The more or less romanticized portraits of this towering figure include those by his contemporary, H. St. John Philby, in *Saudi Arabia* (London: Ernest Benn, 1955), and Jacques Benoist-Méchin, *Ibn Seoud: Le loup et le leopard, ou la naissance d'un royaume* (Paris: Albin Michel, 1955).

46. On the Wahhabis see notably John Habib, *Ibn Saud's Warriors of Islam: The Ikhwan of Nejd and Their Role in the Creation of the Saudi Kingdom 1910–1930* (Leiden: Brill, 1978).

47. The text is in Hurewitz, ed., *The Middle East and North Africa*, vol. 2, pp. 57–58.

48. An excellent account of the way in which the American companies obtained their concession in the face of British opposition can be found in Yergin, *The Prize*, pp. 283–89.

49. Elm, *Oil, Power and Principle*, pp. 19–21, gives examples of how BP in effect swindled Iran for decades in this manner, cheating it of large sums that were rightly due the Iranian state even under the unequal concessions that governed production.

50. They were (to use their most common names): Exxon, Mobil, Chevron, Texaco, Gulf, Shell, and BP. See Anthony Sampson, *The Seven Sisters: The Great Oil Companies and the World They Shaped* (New York: Viking, 1975).

51. There are many examples of the extreme coziness between the oil industry and the government from the 1920s through the 1970s in Yergin, *The Prize*, e.g., the discussion on pp. 410–16 of the deal to expand ARAMCO in 1947 in such a way as to bring in three parts of the old Standard Oil empire.

52. For an explanation of how this worked, starting in the 1970s, when Saudi Arabia became "the swing producer for the entire world," see Yergin, *The Prize*, p. 594.

53. Stork, *Middle East Oil*, p. 95.

54. An account of the impact of the 1973 war and the Arab oil boycott, which coincided with negotiations that had been going on between OPEC and the oil companies, can be found in Yergin, *The Prize*, pp. 588–632.

55. There was of course a difference between nominal and real oil prices, and an even greater one between oil prices and those of gasoline: see the tables in Yergin, *The Prize*, pp. 792–93.

56. Eric Pfanner, "Iraq Is Seen as a Crucial Factor in OPEC Move to Cut Output," *New York Times*, September 26, 2003, p. W1. Pfanner reported the American-appointed Iraqi oil minister at the Vienna OPEC meeting as favoring privatization of the "downstream" parts of the Iraqi oil industry, such as refining and marketing.

57. The first step in this process was the privatization of other sectors of the economy, excluding oil: see Philip Thornton and Andrew Gumbel, "America Puts Iraq Up for Sale," *Independent*, September 22, 2003.

58. Guy Dinmore and Edward Alden, "Call for Mortgaging of Future Iraq Oil Revenues," *Financial Times*, September 26, 2003, p. 5.

59. Ibid.

CHAPTER FOUR
The United States and Palestine

1. So-called after its author, Arthur James Balfour, the British foreign secretary from 1916 to 1919. In this capacity Balfour attended the Paris Peace Conference, and the candid passages on Palestine that he included in a long confidential memo during the conference (quoted in J. C. Hurewitz, ed., *The Middle East and North Africa in World Politics* [New Haven: Yale University Press, 1979], vol. 2, p. 189) could serve as an epitaph for Britain's stewardship over Palestine. After discussing Syria, Balfour's memo states:

> The contradiction between the letter of the Covenant [of the League of Nations] and the policy of the Allies is even more flagrant in the case of the "independent nation" of Palestine than in that of the "independent nation" of Syria. For in Palestine, we do not propose even to go through the form of consulting the wishes of the present inhabitants of the country, though the American [King-Crane] Commission has been going through the form of asking what they are. The four Great Powers are committed to Zionism. And Zionism, be it right or wrong, good or bad, is rooted in age-long traditions, in present needs, in future hopes, of far greater import than the desires and prejudices of the 700,000 Arabs who now inhabit that ancient land.

Balfour continues:

> In my opinion that is right. What I have never been able to understand is how it can be harmonized with the [Balfour] declaration, the Covenant, or the instructions to the Commission of Enquiry.
>
> I do not think that Zionism will hurt the Arabs; but they

will never say they want it. Whatever be the future of Palestine it is not now an "independent nation," nor is it yet on the way to become one. Whatever deference should be paid to the views of those who live there, the Powers in their selection of a mandatory do not propose, as I understand the matter, to consult them. In short, so far as Palestine is concerned, the Powers have made no statement of fact which is not admittedly wrong, and no declaration of policy which, at least in the letter, they have not always intended to violate.

2. Over 92 percent of the population of Palestine was Arab at the end of World War I: see Justin McCarthy, *The Population of Palestine: Population Statistics of the Late Ottoman Period and the Mandate* (New York: Columbia University Press, 1990), Table 1.4D, 10, and 23-24, which shows that according to the best contemporary figures available in 1914–15, Palestine had a Jewish population of under fifty-seven thousand in a total population of well over seven hundred thousand.

3. This is the burden of the argument that Edward Said's *Orientalism* (New York: Vintage, 1978) develops, in particular with regard to the greatest colonial powers in the Middle East and the Islamic world, Britain and France.

4. See the revelation in this regard of J. C. Hurewitz, charged with setting up a bureau on Palestine in the OSS, predecessor of the CIA, cited in chapter 1, n. 61.

5. The familiarity of this narrative perhaps explains the incalculable impact on American public opinion of the 1958 Leon Uris novel *Exodus,* and even more the 1960 film adaptation, both of which reprised such familiar images of brave, white, European pioneers confronting swarthy, dangerous natives.

6. Peter Novick argues in *The Holocaust in American Life* (Boston: Houghton Mifflin, 1999) that American Jewish attitudes toward Zionism were profoundly changed in response to the Holocaust. American Zionists were only able to make credible claims that there was majority support among the American Jewish community for their position after an American Jewish conference they organized in Pittsburgh in January 1943: Richard Stevens, *American Zionism and U.S. Foreign Policy 1942–1947* (New York: Pageant Press, 1962).

7. Margaret Macmillan, *Paris 1919: Six Months That Changed the World* (New York: Random House, 2002), pp. 422–23.

8. Harry N. Howard, *An American Inquiry in the Middle East: The King-Crane Commission* (Beirut: Khayat's, 1963).

9. Fred Lawson, "The Truman Administration and the Palestinians," in *U.S. Policy on Palestine: From Wilson to Clinton,* edited by Michael

Suleiman (Normal, Ill.: Association of Arab-American University Graduates, 1995), pp. 59–80. See also John Snetsinger, *Truman, the Jewish Vote and the Creation of Israel* (Stanford, Calif.: Hoover Institution Press, 1974), and Kathleen Christison, *Perceptions of Palestine: Their Influence on U.S. Middle East Policy* (Berkeley: University of California Press, 1999).

10. See Tom Segev, *One Palestine, Complete: Jews and Arabs under the Palestine Mandate* (New York: Metropolitan Books, 2000) and Sahar Huneidi, *A Broken Trust: Herbert Samuel, Zionism and the Palestinians* (London: I. B. Tauris, 2001); both authors explore how central the British were to the success of Zionism. See also Ken Stein, *The Land Question in Palestine, 1917–1939* (Chapel Hill: University of North Carolina Press, 1984); Stein shows how the nucleus of a Jewish state was already in place by 1939.

11. For details, see Lawson, "The Truman Administration," and Snetsinger, *Truman*.

12. According to the U.N. partition plan, although the Jewish population was only 31 percent of the total (McCarthy, *Population of Palestine*, p. 36), they were to get 56 percent of the country, less than 7 percent of which they owned at the time (Khalidi, *Haven to Conquest*, appendix 1, p. 843). Israel ended up controlling a total of 78 percent of mandatory Palestine by the time the 1948 war with the Arab states was over.

13. Quoted in William A. Eddy, *F. D. R. Meets Ibn Sa'ud* (New York: American Friends of the Middle East, 1954), p. 37.

14. According to a poll of six thousand Europeans in six countries funded by the German Marshall Fund of the United States and the Chicago Council on Foreign Relations, United States policy on the Arab-Israeli conflict was seen as "poor" or "fair" by 74 percent of respondents, the second highest such negative figure recorded for a specific issue area: *Worldview 2002: European Public Opinion and Foreign Policy* (Washington, D.C.: German Marshall Fund of the United States, 2003), p. 24.

15. Among the most striking examples are the cases of Mahmud Salah in Chicago and Dr. Sami al-'Arian in Florida, who are accused of supporting Hamas and Islamic Jihad, respectively. The former's assets were frozen by the U.S. Treasury on the basis of his conviction by an Israeli court grounded in a confession he claimed was obtained through the use of torture. The latter is currently being prosecuted by the federal government for terrorism, and has been fired by the University of South Florida, although he has tenure and has been convicted of nothing thus far.

16. The Israeli human rights group B'Tselem lists 2,265 Palestinians and 795 Israelis killed from September 29, 2000 to September 17, 2003, the overwhelming majority on both sides being civilians (www.btselem.org). The Palestine Red Crescent Society's figures for the same period were 2,471 Palestinians killed and 23,582 wounded (www.palestinercs.org). The Israeli military's figures for September 30, 2000 to September 30, 2003 were 865 Israelis killed and 5,887 wounded; the military also indicated that the great majority of both were civilians (www.idf.il). Many more on both sides died in succeeding months.

17. Ibn Sa'ud's foreign policy advisor, Hafiz Wahba, confided to former Yemoni prime minister Dr. 'Abd al-Karim al-Iryani that there was never any Saudi follow-up to the meeting between the King and Roosevelt: author interview with Dr. 'Abd al-Karim al-Iryani, Sanaa, Yemen, June 22, 2003. For a sense of how little impact Saudi concerns had on U.S. policy-makers, see Steven Spiegel, *The Other Arab-Israeli Conflict: Making America's Middle East Policy, from Truman to Reagan* (Chicago: University of Chicago Press, 1985), pp. 47–49.

18. The best account of the attack is contained in the report of Danish major general Vagn Bennike, chief of staff of the U.N. Truce Supervision Organization, to the 631st meeting of the Security Council on October 29, 1954. See also the similar account by Israeli journalist Uzi Benziman, *Sharon: An Israeli Caesar* (New York: Adama, 1985), pp. 51–54.

19. Abraham Ben-Zvi, *Decade of Transition: Eisenhower, Kennedy and the Origins of the American-Israeli Alliance* (New York: Columbia University Press, 1998), correctly locates the shift in U.S. policy during the early 1960s.

20. In his memoirs, *My Home, My Land: A Narrative of the Palestinian Struggle* (New York: Times Books, 1981), p. 24, Abu Iyyad, one of the founders of Fateh, describes how fellow Fateh founder Abu Jihad was arrested by the Egyptian authorities after a raid against Israel in 1954. Abu Jihad's own corroborative account and further details can be found in Alan Hart, *Arafat: Terrorist or Peacemaker* (London: Sidgwick and Jackson, 1984), pp. 98–103. For details of how Jordan combated attempts to attack Israel, see John Bagot Glubb, *Soldier with the Arabs* (London: Hodder and Stoughton, 1957). See also Benny Morris, *Israel's Border Wars, 1949 1956* (Oxford: Oxford University Press, 1993).

21. The United States, which had voted for the original General Assembly resolution calling for the refugees to be allowed to return to their homes or receive compensation, GA 194 of December 11, 1948, continued to support this position until 1992 with votes in the General

Assembly. Thereafter it joined Israel in abstaining on the annual resolution reiterating the provisions of GA 194.

22. For details see Ilan Pappe, *The Arab-Israeli Conflict 1947–1951* (London:
I. B. Tauris, 1994), pp. 195–273; Avi Shlaim, *The Iron Wall: Israel and the
Arab World* (New York: Norton, 2001); and Itamar Rabinovich,
The Road Not Taken: Early Arab Israeli Negotiations (Oxford: Oxford
University Press, 1991). See also the review by Reuven Pedatzur in
Haaretz, June 6, 2003, of a new book by Israeli author Motti Golani,
Milhamot lo Korot Mei'atzman (Wars Don't Just Happen), which
Pedatzur indicates makes the same argument very forcefully.

23 The United States also quietly gave Germany permission to transfer
American M-48 tanks to Israel. See George Ball and Douglas Ball, *The
Passionate Attachment: America's Involvement with Israel 1947 to the
Present* (New York: Norton, 1992), p. 324, note 7, and Douglas Little,
American Orientalism: the United States and the Middle East since 1945
(Chapel Hill: University of North Carolina Press, 2002), p. 98.

24. A good account of how this happened is David Hirst, *The Gun and the
Olive Branch: The Roots of Violence in the Middle East*, 2d ed. (New
York: Thunder's Mouth Press, 2003). It remains superior to the over-
praised Michael Oren, *Six Days of War: June 1967 and the Making of the
Modern Middle East* (Oxford: Oxford University Press, 2002). See also
the memoirs of Mahmud Riyad, Egyptian foreign minister in the run-
up to the 1967 war: *Mudhakirrat Mahmud Riyad, 1948–1978* (in Arabic)
(Beirut: al-Mu'assassa al-'Arabiyya lil-Dirasat wal-Nashr, 1981) pp.
29–76. There are a number of memoirs by other participants, such
as those of Amin Huwaydi, Nasser's national security advisor, and
Muhammad Hassanayn Heikal, Nasser's close confidant, which
confirm how the Egyptian regime was dragged unwillingly into the
1967 confrontation, although it had over sixty thousand troops and
much of its air force bogged down in a losing war in Yemen.

25. The PLO was founded in 1964 by the Arab states largely as a means of
keeping control of burgeoning Palestinian nationalism, but was taken
over by independent Palestinian groups, led by Fateh, in 1968. See
Helena Cobban, *The Palestinian Liberation Organization* (Cambridge:
Cambridge University Press, 1984), and William Quandt, Fuad Jabber,
and Ann Lesch, *The Politics of Palestinian Nationalism* (Berkeley:
University of California Press, 1973).

26. This is shown by Alvin Rubinstein, *Red Star over Egypt, the Soviet-
Egyptian Influence Relationship* (Princeton, N.J.: Princeton University
Press, 1977), a book that its hawkish author states was originally in-
tended to show that the Soviet Union manipulated its Arab clients.

27. See Oles Smolansky, *The Soviet Union and the Arab East under*

Khrushchev (Lewisburg, Pa.: Bucknell University Press, 1974), and Karen Dawisha, *Soviet Foreign Policy towards Egypt* (New York: St. Martin's, 1979); both highlight the rifts with the Soviets, as does Mohamad Heikal, *The Sphinx and the Commissar: The Rise and Fall of Soviet Influence in the Middle East* (London: Collins, 1978).

28. Lawrence Whetten, *The Canal War: Four-Power Conflict in the Middle East* (Cambridge, Mass.: MIT Press, 1974).

29. On the war of attrition, see Yaacov Bar-Siman-Tov, *The Egyptian-Israel War of Attrition, 1969–1970: A Case-Study of Limited Local War* (New York: Columbia University Press, 1980), and Whetten, *The Canal War.*

30. According to Robert Pranger, a deputy assistant secretary of defense at the time, in *American Policy for Peace in the Middle East, 1969– 1971: Problems of Principle, Maneuver and Time* (Washington, D.C.: American Enterprise Institute, 1971), this was in part the intention of the Rogers Plan.

31. Likud grew out of parties rooted in the underground Irgun and Stern Gang headed by Menachem Begin and Yitzhak Shamir. Their intellectual forebear was Vladimir Jabotinsky, founder of the radical Revisionist wing of Zionism, which opposed Chaim Weizmann, David Ben-Gurion, and the Labor Party establishment that dominated the Zionist movement and Israeli politics until 1977.

32. For more details see Rashid Khalidi, *Under Siege: PLO Decisionmaking during the 1982 War* (New York: Columbia University Press, 1986), and Ze'ev Schiff and Ehud Yaari, *Israel's Lebanon War* (New York: Simon and Schuster, 1984).

33. The only comparable gathering to the 1991 Madrid Peace Conference was the 1939 St. James Conference, where the best the British were able to do was to bring the Arab parties together, while they met separately with the leaders of the Jewish Agency. During the 1949 armistice negotiations, military representatives of each Arab country sat separately with Israeli military officers. The 1973 Geneva conference convened by Henry Kissinger included only Egypt, Jordan, and Israel, in addition to the U.S. and the USSR, and met for only a few hours.

34. These ground rules were laid down in the American-Soviet Letter of Invitation to the Madrid conference, dated October 18, 1991, and in the Letter of Assurance from the United States to the Palestinians, issued at the same time. For the texts of both, see *Journal of Palestine Studies* xxi, no. 2 (winter 1992): 120–21 and 118–19.

35. Ibid.

36. "Looking Back, Looking Forward: An Interview with Haydar 'Abd al-Shafi," *Journal of Palestine Studies* 32, no. 1 (Autumn 2002): 28–35.

37. In a completely different context, see Daniel Barenboim's comments

about tempo in Daniel Barenboim and Edward Said, *Parallels and Paradoxes: Explorations in Music and Society* (New York: Pantheon, 2002), pp. 74–75, where he suggests that a given content requires a certain tempo. Clearly, accords that might have produced a result if implemented rapidly were dead letters when dragged out over more than seven years.

38. Perhaps the most farcical example of this bias occurred when the representatives of the United States, with much fanfare, consented to depart from their role as honest brokers and on May 12, 1993, provided a bridging proposal for an "Israeli-Palestinian Joint Statement," which in the end proved to be less forthcoming than the last propositions made to the Palestinians by the Israelis themselves on May 6, 1993, entitled "Non-Paper, Informal Draft for Consideration: *Agreed Statement of Principles.*" (Original documents from the Palestinian-Israeli negotiations in possession of the author.) Another example was the manifest irritation of two American officials when members of the Palestinian delegation informed them during a meeting on June 18, 1993, that Israeli negotiators had already informally acceded in secret negotiations to the introduction of PLO forces to the occupied territories, something they had steadfastly maintained throughout the talks (and throughout their careers) that Israel could and would never accept. (Original documents from the Palestinian-Israeli negotiations in possession of the author.)

39. The text can be found in *Journal of Palestine Studies* 23, no. 1 (Autumn 1993): 115–21.

40. The best account of this fiasco is in Hussein Agha and Robert Malley, "Camp David: The Tragedy of Errors," *New York Review of Books*, August 9, 2001, www.nybooks.com/articles/14380.

41. This myth is debunked in Agha and Malley, "Camp David." For details of various proposed territorial solutions, see the excellent maps produced by the Foundation for Middle East Peace, and available at their website: http://www.fmep.org/maps/.

42. The maps of the Foundation for Middle East Peace, at http://www.fmep.org/maps/, show how close the two sides were.

43. Regular, professional polling by the Nablus-based Palestine Center for Research and Studies (PCRS) and the Jerusalem Media and Communications Center (JMCC), starting in the early 1990s, has for the first time made it possible to track fluctuations in Palestinian public opinion over time. As late as 1997, Arafat retained the support of more than 73 percent of those polled, according to PCRS's twenty-ninth survey, carried out from September 18–20, 1997. The JMCC

poll in April 2003 showed Arafat and his Fateh faction were "trusted" by only 23.6 percent of those polled, the lowest figure ever: for all their poll results since 1993, see: http://www.jmcc.org/publicpoll/results .html.

44. Sharon had reportedly been escorted onto the third most holy site in Islam by one thousand Israeli security personnel, and was accompanied by the leaders of the Temple Mount Faithful, a group seeking to destroy the mosques on the site, the Haram al-Sharif, and replace them with a new temple.

45. Details on casualties on both sides can be found at the B'Tselem website, with tabulation of Palestinian casualties at the Palestine Red Crescent site, and of Israeli casualties at the Israeli army site, all three cited in note 16 above.

46. See the concise but detailed account of this evolution by the Israeli scholar Tanya Reinhart, *Israel/Palestine: How to End the War of 1948* (New York: Seven Stories Press, 2002), starting on p. 95.

47. Reports on this topic include: Arieh O'Sullivan, "Civil Administration: We Didn't Practice Retaking PA Areas," *Jerusalem Post*, June 25, 1997; "Report: Army Simulated Re-entering Palestinian Cities," Associated Press Worldstream, July 18, 1997; and Akiva Eldar, "Letters to Mutually Disappointed Camp Leaders," *Haaretz*, November 26, 2002, and "They Just Can't Hear Other," *Haaretz*, March 11, 2003. See also the description of the evolution of Israeli military planning for this operation, dubbed "Field of Thorns," in Reinhart, *Israel/Palestine*, pp. 133–38.

48. For details on suicide bombings see Robert Pape, "The Strategic Logic of Suicide Bombing," *American Political Science Review*, 97, 3, August 2003, p. 360, where the author gives a table listing all such bombings to December 2001. See also Reinhart, *Israel/Palestine*, pp. 95 ff. for details.

49. The Israeli group B'Tselem (for both Palestinians and Israelis), the Palestinian Red Crescent Society (for Palestinians), and the Israeli military (for Israelis), have provided running tabulations of casualties and breakdowns of whether the victims are civilians or military personnel that are generally consistent with one another. See the websites and breakdowns of the figures cited in note 16 above.

50. It would be worthy doing a study of the images printed and broadcast in the U.S. of the suicide attacks as opposed to the scenes of attacks on Palestinian towns and villages.

51. The idea that the neocons and Likud are joined at the hip is reinforced by a revealing piece of intellectual affinity: University of Chicago professor Leo Strauss, the revered mentor of Paul Wolfowitz, his deputy in the Pentagon Avram Shulsky, and many other neocon leading lights,

was a great admirer of Vladimir Jabotinsky, founder of the extreme ul-
tranationalist Revisionist branch of Zionism from which Likud has
grown. Strauss talks about being a follower of Jabotinsky, with whom
he met several times, in an autobiographical interview in: Leo Strauss,
*Jewish Philosophy and the Crisis of Modernity: Essays and Lectures
in Modern Jewish Thought*, edited by Kenneth Green (Albany: State
University of New York Press, 1997), p. 319.

52. This harsh assessment of the Sharon government's approach was
    echoed by the surprising remarks of hard-line army chief of staff
    Yaalon, reported in the *New York Times*, October 30, 2003, and by the
    even more scathing critique offered by the last four heads of Israel's
    General Security Services, the Shin Bet, to *Yediot Ahronot*, November
    14, 2003.

53. Interview with Ari Shavit in *Haaretz Magazine*, August 30, 2002.
    Quoted in Arnaud de Borchegrave, "Road Map or Road Rage?"
    Washington Times, May 28, 2003.

CHAPTER FIVE
Raising the Ghosts of Empire

1. The comparison between the two empires is the subject of a fascinating volume edited by Patrick O'Brien and Armand Clesse: *Two He-
   gemonies: Britain 1846–1914 and the United States 1941–2001* (Aldershot,
   U.K.: Ashgagte, 2002). See also the review of the book by Niall
   Ferguson in "Hegemony or Empire," *Foreign Affairs* 82, no. 5 (Septem-
   ber/October 2003): 154–61, which in itself constitutes a significant contribution to this debate, albeit one discreetly favorable to the idea of
   America openly acknowledging its imperial mission.

2. Robert Kagan and William Kristol, "The Present Danger," *National
   Interest* (spring 2000): 58.

3. In *The Tragedy of Great Power Politics* (New York: Norton, 2001); *The
   Paradox of American Power: Why the World's Only Superpower Can't Go
   It Alone* (New York: Oxford University Press, 2002); *American Empire:
   Roosevelt's Geographer and the Prelude to Globalization* (Berkeley:
   University of California Press, 2003); and *Rogue Nation: American Uni-
   lateralism and the Failure of Good Intentions* (New York: Basic Books,
   2003).

4. *L'Empire du chaos: Les Républiques face à la domination américaine dans
   l'après-guerre froide* (Paris: La Découverte, 2002); *L'Europe, l'amerique,
   la guerre: Réflections sur la mediation européene* (Paris: La Découverte,
   2003); and *After the Empire: The Breakdown of the American Order*

(New York: Columbia University Press, 2004). For an original, long-term perspective on the status of the American empire, see Immanuel Wallerstein, "The Eagle Has Crash Landed," *Foreign Policy* (July/August 2002): 60–68, which is based on Terence Hopkins and Immanuel Wallerstein, eds., *The Age of Transition: Trajectory of the World-System, 1945–2025* (London: Zed Books, 1996). See also the brilliant article by Régis Debray, "The Indispensable Nation," *Harpers*, January 2004, pp. 15–18.

5. President Bush said as much in speeches in June and November 2002: see Michael Ignatieff, "The Burden," *New York Times Magazine*, January 5, 2003.

6. This has been signaled by articles in influential publications like Michael Ignatieff's "The Burden" and Robert D. Kaplan, "Supremacy by Stealth," *Atlantic,* July/August 2003, pp. 66–83. The trend is reinforced by well-publicized books whitewashing the British imperial past and calling for an unashamed approach to American empire, like Niall Ferguson's *Empire: The Rise and Demise of the British World Order and the Lessons for Global Power* (New York: Basic Books, 2002) and Max Boot, *The Savage Wars of Peace: Small Wars and the Rise of American Power* (New York: Basic Books, 2002).

7. Ferguson, "Hegemony or Empire," p. 160.

8. David Calleo, cited in Ferguson, "Hegemony or Empire."

9. Jean-Pierre Stroobants, "Un ex-agent de la CIA dénonce les égarements de l'agence de renseignement américaine," *Le Monde*, June 29–30, 2003, p. 5. (My translation.)

10. This resulted in what Kwiatkowski called " 'groupthink', a technical term defined as 'reasoning or decision-making by a group, often characterized by uncritical acceptance of conformity to prevailing points of view.' " Jim Lobe, citing an article for Knight-Ridder by Kwiatkowski, "Insider Fires a Broadside at Rumsfeld's Office," *Asia Times* (Singapore), August 6, 2003.

11. For a devastating assessment of the damage done to U.S. interests in the Arab world by these attacks, see David Ignatius, "Tongue-Tied in the Arab World," *Washington Post*, July 11, 2003.

12. The first salvo was fired in Robert D. Kaplan's, *The Arabists: The Romance of an American Elite* (New York: Free Press, 1993). Thereafter came Martin Kramer's *Ivory Towers on Sand: The Failure of Middle Eastern Studies in America* (Washington, D.C.: Washington Institute For Near East Policy, 2001). Kramer is a key figure in the campaign against academic experts on the Middle East, abetted by Daniel Pipes, head of the Middle East Forum, which sponsors a website,

Campuswatch, urging students to spy on their professors and calling a number of Middle East specialists unpatriotic, un-American, and biased, some because of their ethnic origins. This multipronged campaign includes the ubiquitous appearances of such individuals on TV, columns in Rupert Murdoch–owned organs like the *New York Post* and Conrad Black–owned papers like the *New York Sun,* and attacks by Stanley Kurtz, of the Hoover Institution, on Middle East programs funded by the U.S. Department of Education, in his testimony before the House Subcommittee on Select Education on June 19, 2003, and in articles in the *National Review.*

13. This was Graham Fuller, a veteran Middle East analyst then serving as vice chair of the National Intelligence Council and National Intelligence Officer for the Middle East, who in 1984 was made the scapegoat for an abortive overture to Iran that North and his colleagues chose to carry out with a cake and Bible.

14. Among those who died in April 1983 in the first of three bombings of the U.S. Embassy in Beirut was the CIA's top Middle East analyst, Robert Ames, one of Fuller's predecessors. For details of this policy disaster see the books by experienced former senior American diplomats George Ball and Richard B. Parker, respectively, *Error and Betrayal in Lebanon: An Analysis of Israel's Invasion of Lebanon and the Implications for U.S.-Israeli Relations* (Washington, D.C.: Foundation for Middle East Peace, 1984) and *The Politics of Miscalculation in the Middle East* (Bloomington: Indiana University Press, 1993); see also Jonathan Randal's book *Going All the Way: Christian Warlords, Israeli Adventurers and the War in Lebanon,* rev. ed. (New York: Vintage, 1984).

15. A recent example is the almost wholly unsubstantiated claim implicit in the title of Laurie Mylroie, *Bush vs. the Beltway: How the CIA and the State Department Tried to Stop the War on Terror* (New York: Regan, 2003). Also notable were former House Speaker Newt Gingrich's attacks on the State Department: see, e.g., Barbara Slavin, "Gingrich Takes Swipe at State Department," *USA Today,* April 23, 2003. Another example of this abuse was the scorn directed against army chief of staff general Eric Shinseki and other senior uniformed army officers who questioned the neocons' dangerous illusions about Iraq: Eric Schmitt, "Washington Squabbling over Who Says What War Would Cost," *International Herald Tribune,* March 1, 2003.

16. See editorial, "Was the Intelligence Cooked?" *New York Times,* June 8, 2003, Week in Review sec., p. 12, and Jean-Pierre Stroobants, "Un exagent de la CIA," p. 5.

17. See in this regard the hard-hitting article by John Barry and Evan Thomas, "The Unbuilding of Iraq," *Newsweek,* October 6, 2003, that

describes how the Pentagon cut sixteen of twenty State Department officials from "a team of experts to rebuild Iraq" who were removed because they "were deemed to be Arabist apologists, or squishy about the United Nations, or in some way politically incorrect to the right-wing ideologues in the White House or the neocons in the Office of the Secretary of Defense."

18. The many books by Philby on Arabia and pre-Islamic history are still valuable references: see, e.g., *The Background of Islam: Being a Sketch of Arabian History in Pre-Islamic Times* (Alexandria: Whitehead Morris, 1947), *The Heart of Arabia: A Record of Travel and Exploration* (London: Constable, 1922), and *Arabia of the Wahhabis* (London: Constable, 1928). Bell's *Amurath to Amurath* (London: Macmillan, 1924), one of over a dozen works she produced, is a travel and ethnographic classic, while Lawrence's *Seven Pillars of Wisdom* is a classic of another sort, as discussed in note 31 of chapter 3.

19. The results of Kitchener's pioneering surveying work in Palestine are cited in note 33, chapter 3. Curzon wrote two influential books as a result of his own travels in the region: *Russia in Central Asia in 1889, and the Anglo-Russian Question* (London: Longmans, 1889) and *Persia and the Persian Question* (London: Longmans, 1892). Churchill's descriptions of his own experiences as an officer and a journalist in the Sudan, India, and elsewhere were published numerous times, notably in *The River War: An Account of the Reconquest of the Sudan* (London: Macmillan, 1899).

20. Elie Kedourie's most notable attack on the spinelessness of British officials who did not give the Arabs the harsh treatment he believed they deserved can be found in *The Chatham House Version* (London: Weidenfeld & Nicolson, 1974). Since Kedourie's death in 1992, the torch of urbane, condescending contempt for Arabs, Muslims, and Middle Easterners has passed to Bernard Lewis, who has held it high since then. This school includes Martin Kramer, Barry Rubin, and Daniel Pipes, who combine scornful derision for Middle Eastern political movements with a striking lack of sympathy for most of the peoples of the region. Needless to say, they have found ready audiences in the Washington of the early twenty-first century.

21. Mark Lynch, "Taking Arabs Seriously," *Foreign Affairs* 82, no. 5 (September/October 2003): 81–94, analyzes what he calls the administration's "crude, tone-deaf style" in dealing with the Arabs, and its "misguided assumptions about the Arab world."

22. A genteel example of this disdainful attitude was apparent at a conference held at Columbia University in 1986 when Martin Kramer argued that Arab newspapers were unreliable sources, implying that it was bet-

ter to rely on foreign ones. See R. Khalidi, L. Anderson, M. Muslih, and R. Simon, eds., *The Origins of Arab Nationalism* (New York: Columbia University Press, 1991), p. ix.

23. An excellent analysis of the differences between the direct and indirect forms of British imperial control in the Middle East, what he calls the "Lawrentian" and the "Wilsonian" schools (named for T. E. Lawrence and Arnold Wilson, respectively), can be found in Tomothy Paris, "British Middle East Policy-making after the First World War: The Lawrentian and Wilsonian Schools," *Historical Journal* 41, no. 3 (1998): 773–93.

24. A typical example was Whitehall's insisting on sticking to a policy of direct rule in Iraq long after its bankruptcy was clear. The scathing articles of T. E. Lawrence in the *Times* in 1920 helped turn opinion in London against this approach. Lawrence did not mince words: "The people of England have been led in Mesopotamia into a trap from which it will be hard to escape with dignity and honour. They have been tricked into it by a steady withholding of information. . . . Our unfortunate troops, Indian and British, under hard conditions of climate and supply, are policing an immense area, paying dearly every day in lives for the willfully wrong policy of the civil administration in Baghdad." See Charles Glover, "Lawrence's 1920 Report Eerily Topical," *Financial Times*, June 30, 2003, p. 3. Although the parallels drawn by Glover (and other European, Indian, and Arab commentators) between Britain in Iraq in 1920 and the United States in Iraq in 2003 seem obvious, they are rarely stressed in the U.S. media.

25. The similarities between the exaggerations and deceptions of the Bush administration and the Blair government over Iraq have been noted by some journalists: see, e.g., James Harding and Deborah McGregor, "Flawed Intelligence, Media Smears, a Criminal Inquiry: The 'Wilson Affair' Casts a Shadow over the White House," *Financial Times*, October 2, 2003. Harding and McGregor draw parallels between the David Kay and Joseph Wilson scandals.

26. Some observers and officials on the spot are aware of this contradiction: David Rhode, in "U.S. Said to Plan Bigger Afghan Effort, Stepping Up Aid," *New York Times*, August 25, 2003, p. A3, writing from Kabul, notes that "Afghan and Western officials are acutely aware of the need to avoid the appearance of being a colonial power, particularly in a country with a long history of humbling foreign occupiers. . . . Afghan officials say they would welcome more aid, but must retain control of their ministries. American officials pledged that they would and that the new advisors would not resemble the 'shadow ministers' that the

Soviet Union installed when it occupied the country in the 1980's. But aid officials say an increase in American-paid foreign advisors working in government ministries could stoke Afghan nationalism."

27. See Neela Banerjee, "Rivals Say Halliburton Dominates Iraq Oil Work," *New York Times,* August 8, 2003, pp. C1, 5. She wrote: "Working in Iraq has helped turn around Halliburton's financial performance, its second quarter results showed. The company made a profit of $26 million, in contrast to a loss of $498 million in the quarter a year earlier. The company stated that 9 percent, or $324 million, of its second-quarter revenue of $3.6 billion came for its work in Iraq." See also Michael Dobbs, "Halliburton's Deals Greater Than Thought," *Washington Post,* August 28, 2003. Dobbs notes: "Halliburton, the company formerly headed by Vice President Cheney, has won contracts worth more than $1.7 billion under Operation Iraqi Freedom and stands to make hundreds of millions more dollars under a no-bid contract awarded by the U.S. Army Corps of Engineers, according to newly available documents. The size and scope of the government contracts awarded to Halliburton in connection with the war in Iraq are significantly greater than was previously disclosed."

28. An individual who worked in Baghdad in late 2003 and asked not to be identified noted that the Pentagon officials in charge of Iraq had rejected many regional experts with Arabic-language expertise to fill posts in Iraq by the State Department: personal communication with author, September 28, 2003.

29. John Barry and Evan Thomas, "The Unbuilding of Iraq."

30. Adam Gopnik, "Paris Journal: The Anti-Anti-Americans," *New Yorker,* September 2003 pp. 30–36, points out that even outspoken French supporters of the United States such as Bernard Henry Levy and Andre Glucksmann, who are critics of those in French intellectual life whom they consider to be anti-American, have great difficulty defending the Bush administration.

ACKNOWLEDGMENTS

There are many people without whose support and assistance I could not have written this book, or written it in the way that it was written. First, chronologically and in other ways, comes Bill Ayers. He persuaded me a little over a year ago that I should write this book, and he put me in touch with my editor, Helene Atwan, who has done all that I imagined a good editor could do and more. Bill was particularly generous in letting me use his family's dining room table to do some of the writing for the project. Helene was most helpful in many ways, not least of them in prodding me when I needed it, and especially at restraining me when my indignation, or my infatuation with my own rhetoric, threatened to get the better of me. Besides Helene, only one person read the entirety of the manuscript, my good friend and colleague Jim Chandler. His sensitive and skilled reading, which to my surprise produced many penetrating comments nearly identical to those of Helene, helped me see the book through the eye of a nonspecialist, and like that of Helene, strengthened it greatly. Chapter 4 also benefited from the careful reading of my colleague Nadia Abu El Haj, who sharpened and clarified its argument. Rena Barakat helped me with some of the research, tracking down sources and collecting material.

Others helped in different ways. My wife, Mona, my children, Lamya, Dima, and Ismail, and my brother, Raja, all gave me encouragement from the different parts of the globe in which they were located, and kept pushing me to finish it so that it could play a part in the vital debate about the Middle

East taking place in the United States. Lamya also read parts of the manuscript and corrected several errors, while Mona and Raja provided me with a number of useful articles and other sources. Bernardine Dohrn continually encouraged me to keep working on the book when I was traveling and at home, Becky Chandler was an inspiration and a support when I was at home in Chicago, and my colleagues in Chicago, Susan Gzesh, Evalyn Tennant, and Vera Beard, all helped out in various ways, some of them moral and some material.

I also benefited greatly from the feedback from receptive audiences at the University of Iowa Law School, the Chicago Council on Foreign Relations, the City University of New York Graduate Center, the School of Oriental and African Studies at the University of London, the Yemeni Research and Studies Institute in Sanaa, and the Ibrahim Abu Lughod Institute of International Studies at Bir Zeit University, where I presented early drafts of parts of this book as lectures. Needless to say, none of those mentioned above bears any responsibility for the faults of this work.

I should mention finally my friend Edward Said, who constantly encouraged me in the writing of this book at a time when his courageous battle with disease was coming to its inevitable end. It is a source of deep regret to me that he could not directly contribute his insight to it, and that he was not able to see it published. I dedicate it respectfully to his memory.

INDEX